PENGUIN BOOKS
MOVING PARTS

NINA SHENGOLD edited *The Actor's Book of Contemporary Stage Monologues* and coedited *The Actor's Book of Scenes from New Plays* for Penguin Books. She received the ABC Playwright Award and the L.A. Weekly Award for her play *Homesteaders,* produced by Capital Rep, the Long Wharf, and other regional theaters from Atlanta to Toronto. Her one-acts *Finger Food* and *Women and Shoes,* commissioned by the Actors Theatre of Louisville, have been seen at the Ark Theatre and Manhattan Punchline. Ms. Shengold's translation of Soviet playwright Alexander Galin's *Tonight or Never* was recently produced by Fordham University. She was an executive story editor for the ABC series "Hothouse," has written TV scripts for all three networks, and adapted Jane Smiley's novella *Good Will* for American Playhouse. Ms. Shengold attended Wesleyan University. She lives and gardens in Krumville, New York.

ERIC LANE is co-editor with Nina Shengold of *Moving Parts: Monologues from Contemporary Plays* and *The Actor's Book of Scenes from New Plays.* He is Artistic Director of Orange Thoughts, a not-for-profit theater company in New York City. His writing has been performed at LaMama, St. Mark's Church, Nikolais/Louis ChoreoSpace, the Ethnic Folk Arts Center, and the Nat Horne Theatre. Mr. Lane has acted in several off-off Broadway productions and is author of *Crunchy Apples,* a children's musical performed at Symphony Space. His plays include "Dancing on Checkers' Grave," "The Heart of a Child," "Glass Stirring," "So Slow It Whirls," "Blue Christmas," and "Jersey Bounce." For his television work on *Ryan's Hope,* he received a Writer's Guild Award. Mr. Lane is an honors graduate of Brown University.

MOVING
PARTS

*Monologues from
Contemporary Plays*

EDITED BY

NINA SHENGOLD
&
ERIC LANE

PENGUIN BOOKS

To the memory of Marc Helman, Charles Ludlam, Robert Chesley, B. Rodney Marriott, Dennis McIntyre, Alan Bowne, Eddie Stone, Ethyl Eichelberger, and too many others who should still be with us

PENGUIN BOOKS
Published by the Penguin Group
Penguin Books USA Inc.,
375 Hudson Street, New York, New York 10014, U.S.A.
Penguin Books Ltd, 27 Wrights Lane, London W8 5TZ, England
Penguin Books Australia Ltd, Ringwood, Victoria, Australia
Penguin Books Canada Ltd, 10 Alcorn Avenue,
Toronto, Ontario, Canada M4V 3B2
Penguin Books (N.Z.) Ltd, 182–190 Wairau Road, Auckland 10, New Zealand

Penguin Books Ltd, Registered Offices: Harmondsworth, Middlesex, England

First published in Penguin Books 1992

11 13 15 17 19 20 18 16 14 12 10

LIBRARY OF CONGRESS CATALOGING IN PUBLICATION DATA
Monologues for everyone/edited by Nina Shengold and Eric Lane.
p. cm.
Includes bibliographical references and index.
ISBN 0 14 01.3992 3
1. Monologues. 2. Acting. I. Shengold, Nina. II. Lane, Eric.
PN4305.M6M598 1992
808.82′45—dc20 91–19283
Printed in the United States of America
Set in Caledonia
Designed by Robert Bull Design

EDITORS' PREFACE

In putting together this book, we read hundreds of plays by an exhilarating range of contemporary playwrights. (This is probably the first anthology to contain monologues by the president of Czechoslovakia, Václav Havel, and a recent candidate for the presidency of Peru, Marios Vargas Llosa.) We made a conscious effort to choose recent plays that are not as well-known as they should be and to represent a wide variety of minority artists. Above all, we looked for monologues that stand on their own as good theater, giving actors a well-defined character, a story to tell, and a range of behaviors and feelings.

The book is designed for easy browsing. The monologues are grouped by sex and age, and an index by subject (Asian Plays, Black Plays, British Plays, etc.) will help minority actors and those seeking accent work to locate appropriate material. However, we strongly encourage actors to search throughout the book for monologues that speak to them, regardless of category. More and more theaters are taking a sane and enlightened approach to nontraditional casting in this multi-ethnic society. And a casting director friend swears the best audition he ever saw was two actresses playing the brothers in *True West*.

We hope this book will introduce actors and readers to playwrights and plays. (Think of us as a dating service.) We have provided brief introductions for each monologue, but we urge actors who want to perform these pieces to *read the whole play*. Our synopses are no substitute for the playwright's wealth of detail about the character who is

speaking. Also, playwrights who write monologues tend to
write *lots* of monologues: the one we chose for this book
may not be the one you choose to perform. We have included the publisher's name with each selection for your
convenience. We have also included premiere information
as a way of honoring the theaters that launched these exciting new plays.

A number of the monologues in this book were ex-
cerpted from solo performances, which have proliferated
in unprecedented numbers in the budget-conscious nineties. In recent New York seasons, "downtown" performers
Eric Bogosian, Spalding Gray, Sandra Bernhard, John
O'Keefe, Karen Finley, Wallace Shawn, and the late Ethyl
Eichelberger have performed their own work off-Broad-
way. Uptown, Broadway stars Robert Morse, Cleavon Little, Julie Harris, Pauline Collins, and Lily Tomlin appeared
in the one-character plays *Tru, Shirley Valentine, All God's
Dangers, Lucifer's Child,* and *The Search for Signs of Intelligent Life in the Universe.* One could theorize about a
decade of isolation and loneliness. Or one could point the
finger at producers cowed by rising costs and a sorely threatened National Endowment for the Arts.

A peculiar corollary to the solo phenomenon seems to
be that as cast sizes shrink, playwrights' names expand. The
nineties appear to be the decade of the three-name playwright. This book alone includes pieces by David Henry
Hwang, Jonathan Marc Sherman, Jon Robin Baitz, Maria
Irene Fornes, Philip Kan Gotanda, Mario Vargas Llosa,
John Ford Noonan, José Ignacio Cabrujas, Cindy Lou
Johnson, and John Patrick Shanley. It's as if the marquee
is the only place we still have enough room to express
ourselves.

This is a difficult time to do theater. Writers, directors,
and actors are leaving in droves for more lucrative film and
TV work. Ticket costs are exorbitant, audiences and critics
impatient. Institutional theaters are threatened with cen-
sorship by the New Right. Our community has been rav-

aged by AIDS. The usual pundits are sounding the usual death knell for theater. But nothing compares to the power and immediacy of actors and audience in the same room. A character in Jane Wagner's *The Search for Signs of Intelligent Life in the Universe* describes this interaction as "the goose bump experience . . . to see a group of strangers sitting together in the dark, laughing and crying about the same things." We hope that these monologues bring you a flurry of goose bumps.

Nina Shengold
Eric Lane
December 1990

ACKNOWLEDGMENTS

Grateful thanks to everyone who helped us with this book, especially Alan Amtzis, Elizabeth Benedict, Stephen Elliott, Louis and Edith Fisher, Michael Goodwin, Wiley Hausam, Gary Jennings, Nancy-Elizabeth Kammer, Lisa Kaufman, Richard Krawetz, Jeffrey Lane, Rick Leed, Susan Marcus, Masterpiece Supper, Helen Merrill, Michael Millman, Susan Moldow, Ken Mueller, New Dramatists, Sarah Noll, Ron Nyswaner, Orange Thoughts, Pan Asian Rep., River Arts, Laura Ross, Sasha and Masha, Eleanore Speert, Scott Stohler, Jeffrey Sweet, Shelley Wyant, the Lane family, the Shengold family, and, most of all, the playwrights who let us borrow their words.

CONTENTS

Women
Teens–20s

Women
30s–40s

Women
50s and Older

Men
Teens–20s

Men
30s–40s

Men
50s and Older

Charles
Monologues for Men Playing Women

WOMEN
TEENS—20s

•

American Dreams
Studs Terkel

Adapted for the stage by Peter Frisch

Premiere: Victory Gardens Theatre, Chicago, Illinois, 1985
Publisher: Dramatists Play Service, Inc.
Setting: Bare stage, an interview space

In this theatrical adaptation of Studs Terkel's oral history, an ensemble of six actors plays a range of real-life Americans speaking about their dreams. The play is divided into sections called "Fantasies," "Nightmares," "Hallucinations," "Sweet Dreams," "Broken Reveries," and "Visions." This piece is from "Hallucinations." The speaker, Emma Knight, is described by the playwright as "a non-believer, savvy, with an easy warmth and intimacy she shares with her audience."

EMMA KNIGHT

It's mostly what's known as t and a, tits and ass. No talent. For many girls who enter the contest, it's part of the American Dream. It was never mine. I had come to a model agency one cold day, and an agent came out and said, "I want you to enter a beauty contest." I said, "No, uh-uh, never, never, never. I'll lose, how humiliating."

I filled out the application blank: Hobbies, measurements, blah, blah, blah. I got a letter: "Congratulations. You have been accepted as an entrant into the Miss Illinois-Universe contest." Now what do I do? I'm stuck. So I called up the lady who was running it. Terribly sorry, I can't do this. I don't have the money. She calls back a couple of days later: "We found you a sponsor, it's a lumber company."

I went as a lumberjack: blue jeans, hiking boots, a flannel shirt, a pair of suspenders, and carrying an axe. You come out and do your pirouettes. I'm thinking, this will soon be over; I don't have a prayer. They called my name. I was the winner. Emma Knight, Miss Illinois. All I could do was laugh. I'm twenty-two, standing up there in a borrowed evening gown, thinking: "What am I doing here? This is like Tom Sawyer becomes an altar boy."

I was considered old for a beauty queen, which is a little horrifying when you're twenty-two. That's very much part of the beauty queen syndrome: the young, untouched, unthinking human being. I had to go to this room and sign the Miss Illinois-Universe contract right away. Miss Universe, Incorporated, is the full name of the company. It's owned by Kaiser-Roth Incorporated, which was bought out by Gulf & Western. Big business.

I'm sitting there with my glass of champagne and I'm reading over this contract. "Oh, you don't have to read it." I never sign anything that I don't read. They're all waiting to take pictures, and I'm sitting there reading this long document. The phone rang. The guy was from a Chicago paper and said, "Tell me, is it Miss or Ms.?" I said: "It's Ms." He said, "You're kidding?" I said, "No, I'm not." I thought, I was a feminist before I was a beauty queen, why should I stop now?

I won the Miss U.S.A. pageant. I started to laugh. They tell me I'm the only beauty queen in history that didn't cry when she won. It was on network television. I said, "You're kidding?" Bob Barker, the host, said, "No, I'm not kidding." In the press releases, they call it the great American Dream. There she is, Miss America, your ideal. Well, not my ideal, kid.

From the day I won Miss U.S.A. to the day I left for Universe, almost two months later, I got a day and a half off. Parades, shopping centers, and things. Snip ribbons.

Public speaking. They said, "You want a ghost writer?" I said, "Hell no, I know how to talk." I wrote my own speeches.

One of the big execs from General Motors asked me to do a speech in Washington, D.C., on the consumer and the energy crisis. So I stood up and said, "The reason we have an energy crisis is because we are, industrially and personally, pigs. And unless we wake up to what we're doing to our air and our water, we'll have a dearth, not just a crisis." They weren't real pleased.

When it came out in a newspaper interview that I said Nixon should resign, that he was a crook, oh dear, the fur flew. They got very upset. I got an invitation to the White House. I figured they're either gonna take me down to the basement and beat me up with a rubber hose or they're gonna offer me a cabinet post. I was dying to bring a tape recorder but thought if you mention the word "Sony" in the Nixon White House—cardiac arrest. When one of 'em got me in his office and talked about all the journalists and television people being liberals, I brought up blacklisting, Agnew, Pentagon Papers. He changed the subject.

That final evening. They call over the PA: "Time for the old queen's walk." I'm now twenty-three and I'm an old queen. And they have this idiot farewell speech playing over the airwaves as the old queen takes the walk. And you're sitting on the throne for about thirty seconds, then you come down and they announce the name of the new one and you put the crown on her head. And then you're out.

I've seen photographers shove the girl who has just given her reign up thirty seconds before, shove her physically. It is very difficult for girls who are terrified of this ending. All of a sudden

(Snaps fingers.)

you're out. Several times during my year as what's-her-face I had seen the movie *The Sting*. There's a gesture the characters use which means the con is on:

(She demonstrates.)

In my lasting fleeting moments as Miss U.S.A., as they were playing that silly farewell speech and I walked down the aisle and stood by the throne, I looked right into the camera:

(Repeats gesture.)

The next day, the pageant people spent all their time telling people that I hadn't done it. I spent the time telling them that, of course, I had. I simply meant, "the con is on."

Black Friday?
Audrey Butler

Premiere: Actors' Theatre Lab, Toronto, Ontario, Canada, 1990
Publisher: Women's Press (in *Radical Perversions: Two Dyke Plays*)
Setting: In and around a living room in Cape Breton, Canada

Spike is an outspoken black lesbian in her early twenties, "the twenty-first century's first dyke philosopher." A "bike dyke," she and her lover, Terry, ride her motorcycle from Toronto to Cape Breton to visit Terry's mother, grandmother, and ex-boyfriend. Over the course of the play, Terry comes out of the closet. Here Spike describes her own coming out.

NOTE: The playwright notes in her introduction that while the original production cast Spike as black and the other characters as white, this is by no means carved in stone.

SPIKE
My girlfriend and I were in the bathtub fooling around havin' a ball—
everybody was out working, we made sure of that.
I'm fourteen, she's fifteen.
We're up to our ass in Mr. Bubbles.

Our hands are all over each other.
We're getting so carried away,
we don't know what to touch next or how.
Then, the door flies open—
my sister—
who's in my girlfriend's class—

I've never heard anyone scream that loud before
or since—except you, Aunt Effie.

Well, she didn't waste any time
telling our mother
or the whole school for that matter.

Biggest favor my sister ever did for me.

Brilliant Traces
Cindy Lou Johnson

Premiere: Circle Repertory Company, NYC, 1989
Publisher: Dramatists Play Service, Inc.
Setting: A starkly furnished barn in Alaska

Rosannah Deluce is described by the playwright as being "in her twenties. She is filled with rage and has good manners." Several weeks ago, Rosannah fled her own wedding and drove blindly across the country, stopping only for gas and candy bars till her car died in a snowstorm in the middle of nowhere, Alaska. Still wearing her wedding dress, she bangs on the door of the nearest building—the home of an enigmatic young recluse named Henry Harry—and passes out.

Henry Harry takes diligent care of her till she recovers. But as Rosannah begins to reveal her emotional scars—the "brilliant traces" of the title—and to probe into his, he turns a cold shoulder. Eventually, Rosannah will learn that he holds himself responsible for the death of his baby daughter and is afraid to let himself feel anything, for fear that his love will turn into pain again. This is her response.

ROSANNAH

Did you ever think that one time, a long time ago, when you were a little child, you were visited by extraterrestrials? They say that when you are visited by an extraterrestrial— after the visit, the extraterrestrial puts this spell on you so you cannot remember the encounter at all, and you wake up only with this sad kind of longing for something, but you don't know what. And you carry that sad longing with you all the rest of your life. And they say that if, by chance, you get hypnotized, then you reveal the encounter, under hypnosis, and when you wake up, you remember it, and then, it is no longer a sad longing, but a real thing, which you know about, and even if people think you're crazy, talking all the time about your extraterrestrial encounter, that's ok, because in your heart you know what it was that had been locked up for so long and you are greatly relieved.

(*Beat.*)

I have often wondered what it would feel like to be greatly relieved.

(*She rises and approaches* HENRY HARRY
*standing closer, but still unable to touch
him.*)

I am not a very healthy person as I have said. I am, at this point in my life, relying on the long shot. I have really truly reached a point where I almost have expectations that an extraterrestrial will come to me. That I will see him and feel connected to him—right away, and he will say, Yes! It was me! It was me who touched you. And I won't care if he is very small or if he is milky white. I won't care at all, if I just know he is the one.

(*Beat.*)

If I just know he is the one.

Catholic School Girls

Casey Kurtti

Premiere: Douglas Fairbanks Theatre, NYC, 1982
Publisher: Samuel French, Inc.
Setting: St. George's School, suburb in New York State, 1962–1970

Catholic School Girls follows four girlfriends through eight years of Catholic school. (The same four actresses also play the Sisters who teach them.) Wanda is the "good girl," the daughter of a Polish butcher. Colleen is precocious, free-thinking, and usually in trouble with the nuns. Maria Theresa is a poor student with a violent father. Elizabeth is at odds with her family and has filled up her loneliness with an invisible girlfriend named Mr. Gunderson. As she gets older, she begins to question the Church. All four girls have monologues in between the play's scenes.

————— 1 —————

COLLEEN

I used to go out with this guy, Ricky. I liked him a lot for a while. We hung around Cross County Shopping Center on Saturdays. We used to get red pistachio nuts and then we'd wait till our hands got all red and sweaty. Then we'd go upstairs on the escalator to the Wedding Shop and smear all the white dresses with our hands. It looked like The Bride of Frankenstein, I swear. One time we went to the movies on a Friday night. Me and Ricky saw *Born Free*. It was okay for a while but then toward the end it got bad. The girl lion gets killed and it's really sad. I started to cry even, but I didn't let that Ricky see. I hate to let a boy see me cry. The day we broke up, Ricky and me were sitting in the back of his father's car in the garage. He gave me his ID bracelet and then he tried to put his hand somewhere. I ran right out of that car but I kept the bracelet just for spite. I told my mother about it. Me and my mother are just like this.

(Holds two fingers together.)

She told me I did the right thing. Then she started giving me a speech about sex stuff. She told me about the change and how it was part of becoming a woman. She told me when I got it, it would be such a happy day that we would go out to lunch and have a party all day long. Just me and her. Ha. I don't want to be a woman. I like myself the way I am. My chest is growing, and I think there is hair coming out of, you know, down there. Well anyway, Sister told everyone to finish up with their desks and to pack up. I felt something. I tried to close my legs so it would stop. I held my stomach in, real hard, but it kept leaking. I didn't know the whole thing was so messy. I didn't want to move. I took my sweater off and I wrapped it around me. I knew what it was. After Monica put the wastebasket back, Sister Mary Germaine told me to take my seat. But even before I started to move, she asked me about my sweater. She thought I was trying to show off with sex or something, I guess. She said, "Take that sweater off, it's seventy degrees in this classroom." "My stomach hurts, it makes me feel better." "I'll ask you one more time, take if off." The boys began to come into the classroom, she didn't care, she let them. I couldn't look at her. She hit me. I put my hands to my face and she ripped the sweater off, digging her nails into my side. I just stood there against the blackboard. Everyone was looking at me. Then she made an announcement to the class, that in all her years of teaching, she had never come across someone with such a lack of concern for their personal hygiene. She said these things right in front of the boys. I thought I was going to die. A couple of drops of blood got on the floor. She made one of the boys go down to the janitor's closet and get a mop. The nurse came in and took me out of class. I never want to go back there again. She is trying to make me feel guilty. I do feel guilty.

I am a jerk. I wish I was dead, and never had to see you
or anybody else again. I wish I had never become a woman.
I'm no good at it. Is that what you wanted to hear, Sister?
All right, I'm no good at it.

———— 2 ————

ELIZABETH
(To God, as if she is in church.)

Hey, come on out, I want to talk to you. It's me, Elizabeth.
You can hide behind any statue in this place, but you better
listen to me. I don't know if you know this but after my
grandmother moved in with us, everything was different.
We used to sit in my room, after school. She'd ask me
questions about all sorts of things. Then she'd listen to my
answers real close because she said I was an important
person. Some nights, after we went to bed, I would hear
her talking to my grandfather in the dark. If I made any
noise she'd stop. Because it was private. One night I saw
that she was crying. I made some noise and she stopped.
Then she asked me if I remembered my grandfather. I did,
she liked that. We fell asleep on her bed like sisters. Sunday
mornings were kind of strange. Nobody would give up
eating bacon and some smells made her sick. My father
would tell her if the grease bothered her so much, to take
her eggs and go into the bedroom and wait until breakfast
was over. I helped her stuff towels into the cracks under
the door, but the smell got in anyway. Then my father
would make me come back to the table and eat with the
rest of the family. I'd go, but I wouldn't eat that bacon.
Sometimes, if she was feeling a little better, we'd take short
walks. After we had rested, she'd tell me stories about my
mother and bring along pictures that I had never seen. I
didn't know why my mother was so sad and neither did my
grandmother. One day, my father came home from work
and told me that my grandmother would have to move back

to the Bronx. He said it was just not working out. She needed more care and besides she was making the family crazy. I told him that she wasn't making me crazy. I told him she let me be near her. He didn't understand that. And now I see that you didn't either. You took her and I don't think that's fair. You're supposed to do the right thing, all the time. I don't believe that anymore. You just like to punish people, you like to interrupt their lives. You didn't let me finish. She doesn't know what I think, and I was almost ready to tell her. Why don't you take my mother next time? Oh, you like to take little kids, don't you? Grab one of my brothers next, they're all baptized. Why don't you take my whole stinking family, in one shot, then you won't waste any time. That would be some joke. But I want to tell you something. It's a personal message, I'm delivering it, myself. Don't you ever lay your hands on me, cause if I ever see you, you can strike me dead . . . try . . . I will spit all over your face, whatever it looks like. Because you and everyone else in this world are one big pack of liars. And I really think I hate you. Something else: You don't exist.

The Colored Museum
George C. Wolfe

Premiere: Crossroads Theatre Company, New Brunswick, New Jersey, 1986
Publisher: *American Theatre* magazine
Setting: A stylized museum

An ensemble of two men and three women portray a gallery of living "exhibits" in what the playwright describes as "a museum where the myths and madness of black/ Negro/colored Americans are stored." The following exhibit is called "Permutations."

(Lights up on NORMAL JEAN REYNOLDS. *She
is very southern/country and very young.
She wears a simple faded print dress and
her hair, slightly mussed, is in plaits. Between her legs is a very large white egg.)*

NORMAL

My mama used to say, God made the exceptional, then
God made the special, and when God got bored, he made
me. Course she don't say too much of nuthin no more, not
since I lay me this egg.

Ya see it all got started when I had me sexual relations
with the garbage man. Ooowee did he smell.

Not, not bad. No! He smelled of all the good things
folks never shoulda thrown away. His sweat was like can-
taloupe juice. His neck was like a ripe-red strawberry. And
the water that fell from his eyes was like a deep, dark, juicy-
juicy grape. I tell ya, it was like fuckin a fruit salad, only I
didn't spit out the seeds. I kept them here, deep inside.
And three days later, my belly commence to swell, real big
like.

Well my mama locked me off in some dark room, refusin
to let me see light of day 'cause "What would the neighbors
think." At first I cried a lot, but then I grew used to livin
my days in the dark, and my nights in the dark. . . .

(She hums.)

And then it wasn't but a week or so later, my mama off at
church, that I got this hurtin feelin down here. Worse than
anything I'd ever known. And then I started bleedin, real
bad. I mean there was blood everywhere. And the pain
had me howlin like a near-dead dog. I tell ya, I was yellin
so loud. I couldn't even hear myself. Nooooooooo! Noooooo!
Carrying on something like that.

And I guess it was just too much for the body to take,
'cause the next thing I remember . . . is me coming to and
there's this big white egg layin 'tween my legs. First I
thought somebody musta put it there as some kind of joke.

But then I noticed that all round this egg were thin lines
of blood that I could trace to back between my legs.

(Laughing.)

Well, when my mama come home from church she just
about died. "Normal Jean, what's that thing 'tween your
legs? Normal Jean you answer me girl!" It's not a thing
Mama. It's an egg. And I laid it.

She tried separatin me from it, but I wasn't havin it. I
stayed in that dark room, huggin, holdin onto it.

(She hums.)

And then I heard it. It wasn't anything that coulda been
heard round the world, or even in the next room. It was
kinda like layin back in the bathtub, ya know, the water
just coverin your ears . . . and if you lay real still and listen
real close, you can hear the sound of your heart movin the
water. You ever done that? Well that's what it sounded
like. A heart movin water. And it was happenin inside
here.

Why I'm the only person I know who ever lay themselves an egg before so that makes me special. You hear
that Mama? I'm special and so's my egg! And special things
supposed to be treated like they matter. That's why every
night I count to it, so it knows nuthin never really ends.
And I sing it every song I know so that when it comes out,
it's full of all kinds of feelings. And I tell it secrets and laugh
with it and . . .

*(She suddenly stops, puts her ear to the egg
and listens intently.)*

Oh! I don't believe it! I thought I heard . . . yes!

(Excited.)

Can you hear it? Instead of one heart, there's two. Two
little hearts just pattering away.

Boom-boom-boom. Boom-boom-boom. Talkin to each
other like old friends. Racin toward the beginnin of their
lives.

(Listening.)

Oh no now there's three . . . four . . . five, six, more

hearts than I can count. And they're all alive, beati[n]
life inside my egg.

*(We begin to hear light drumming, the
heartbeats inside Normal's egg.)*

Any day now, this egg is gonna crack open and what's
gonna come out a be the likes of which nobody has ever
seen. My babies! And their skin is gonna turn all kinds of
shades in the sun and their hair a be growin every whichaway. And it won't matter and they won't care 'cause they
know they are so rare and so special 'cause it's not every day
a bunch of babies break outta a white egg and start to live.

And nobody better not try and hurt my babies 'cause
if they do, they gonna have to deal with me.

Yes any day now, this shell's gonna crack and my babies
are gonna fly. Fly! Fly!

*(She laughs at the thought, but then stops
and says the word as if it's the most natural
thing in the world.)*

Fly.

Darleen Dances

Betsy Robinson

Premiere: Ensemble Studio Theatre, NYC, Octoberfest, 1986
Publisher: —
Setting: Not specified

Darleen Rosengarten, in her late twenties, early thirties, *not* an all-American "pretty girl," is dancing her heart
out. The first scene of this one-act play is printed here in
its entirety.

DARLEEN
(Ponying.)
I been doin this for 6 hours, 22 minutes, and 17 seconds.

(Fancy Dance.)

Not the fancy stuff. I just do that to goose myself whenever I start feeling bored or like I'm gunna pass out or throw up or somethin—takes my mind off the time. Of which I got a lot more to go yet if I'm gunna get in the book.

(Stroll.)

Raymond, my boyfriend, he thinks I'm crazy. "Darleen, baby, you're crazy. I mean, what's so hot about gettin in a beer book?"

(Resume pony.)

That's how smart he is; he thinks anything with the word *Guinness* in it gotta be about beer. I mean, why even bother trying to explain to a person with that intellectual mentality?

He left about a hour ago.

The thing is, is I got no ovaries.

That's a lie.

(Freeze for half a beat. Pony.)

I got em, but they don't work so good, and they hurt me a lot, so this doctor, he's gunna take em out on Friday, and I figured if I started saying right now that I got none, maybe it'd help me get used to the idea, you know?

Anyway, the point is, I'm a cashier at Blimpies which don't exactly make me a household name, and now I'm never gunna have a kid, so I figured if I got my name in the book, maybe somebody a hundred or a thousand or so years from now—maybe they'd know I was here!

(Throw up arms . . . no response.)

(Swim.)

You see, if I get my name in the book, it'd be like there'd be this little piece of me that, after I get old and decrepit and eventually dead, this little piece'd go on. Cause people'd read the book and they'd know who Darleen Rosengarten was: "Oh, Darleen Rosengarten—she's the Blimpies cashier with no ovaries who set the record for

(Jerk.)

nonstop, free-style rock 'n' roll dancing to no music!"

(Pony turn.)

I woulda had music but my stereo's broke and somebody ripped off my walkman.

(Tap dances. Pause.)

. . . I was named after the Mouseketeer . . . Darlene Gillespie! Actually I did it myself when I was a kid. My real name is something too boring to even tell you. But it didn't really make any difference—changing my name— seeing as *she* was the Mouseketeer. I woulda been one, but we lived in Secaucus, New Jersey, and they didn't send no talent scouts there. So I got a lot of wasted time to make up for. I mean if I'da known *then* that I wasn't gunna have any ovaries, I'da started earlier on this book thing, ya know.

(Fast dance.)

Sometimes I think if I dance real fast it'll make the time go quicker. But that's just a whadeyacallit—a illusion, I know. Never changes anything. Just wears me out.

(Checks time.)

6 hours, 24 minutes, and 38 seconds.

Raymond, Raymond, he says I should slow down and be happy just to be alive. He says alive with no ovaries is better'n dead with a full set. He says I shouldn't get so depressed cause what with all this transplantin that's going on maybe I could get a new set. That after all, they're puttin monkey parts in babies now, so you never know . . . Can you imagine?

I said, "Raymond, this is not a science fiction, this is my life, and that's all I need is a set of monkey ovaries poppin out little monkey eggs every month. No thank you," I said. "I'd rather dance!"

(Monkey. Pony.)

I really like to dance. Maybe not for 6 and a half hours, but a hour or so here and there makes me feel really—, I don't know. It's like good sex, if you'll pardon my French.

It's like feeling all of you—alla your parts—of which I won't have after next Friday—but it's like God.

I mean I'm not real religious or anything, but when I dance I feel like God's going all through me—up and down, in and out, and I feel whole!

So the thing is, if I can *do* this—if I can dance so long and so hard that I get in the book, even if all they write is that some girl with no ovaries set the record, and even if they leave out the God part, which they probably will, I just got this feeling like—I don't know. Like even though I was never a Mouseketeer, and even *if* Raymond thinks I'm crazy, and even if nobody a hundred or a thousand or so years from now ever reads the damn book, at least *I*'ll know. I'll know somethin's in there. And then maybe—. Maybe—. Maybe then Friday won't seem so bad.

(*Ponies hard.*)

the dreamer examines his pillow

John Patrick Shanley

Premiere: Double Image Theatre, NYC, 1986
Publisher: Dramatists Play Service, Inc.
Setting: Two New York City apartments

Donna had a passionate, burnout affair with a young man named Tommy. Since they split up, he's been living in a filthy basement, painting deranged self-portraits, drinking beer, and talking to his refrigerator. Donna finds out he's also been sleeping with her sixteen-year-old sister, Mona. Furious, she tracks Tommy down and blisters him with abuse. But she can't stay away from him. Overwhelmed by the strength of her feelings, she goes to the Heights to ask her father some questions.

Dad is a tough-talking painter with a lot of primal wisdom about men and women. Initially reluctant ("Oh no no no no no no. It's my daughter come to make me a parent."), he agrees to give Donna advice. But he insists that she tell him the deepest truth of her feelings: "It's way down. An it's dark. An it's as old as the motherfuckin stars. If you want somethin from me, or if you wanna tell me somethin, that's where we're gonna haveta be." After a long pause, Donna responds.

DONNA

Alright.

(A long pause.)

Tommy an me . . . When he loves me. In bed. When he puts his arms around me, and I can feel his skin, his heart beating, his breath, and I smell him, it's like Africa. It's like, I get scared because all of my guts shake . . . Sometimes I press my hands against myself because I think things are coming loose inside. He just touches me, starts to barely touch me, and I'm so frightened because it's so much, it's so hot, it's so close to losing my mind. It's beyond pleasure. It's . . . He takes me over. Like there's a storm, I get caught in this storm with electricity and rain and noise and I'm blind I'm blind. I'm seeing things, but just wild, wild shapes flying by like white flyin rain and black shapes. I feel I feel this this rising thing like a yell a flame. My hair I can feel my hair like slowly going up on its toes on my skull my skull. Everything goes up through me from my belly and legs and feet to my head and all these tears come out but it can't get out that way, so it goes down against my throat swells an through down to where it can get out GET OUT GET OUT. But it doesn't go out, so I, I EXPAND. Like to an ocean. To hold the size of it. An then it's maybe something you could speak of as pleasure, since then somehow I can hold it. I'm this ocean with a thousand moons and comets reflecting in me. And then I come back. Slowly. Slowly. From such a long way. And such a different size. And I'm wet. My body my hair. The bed is just soaked, torn up and soaked. There ain't a muscle left in me. I'm all eyes. My eyes are the size of like two black pools of water in the middle of an endless night. And Tommy's there. And he did it to me. He took me completely. I wasn't me anymore. I was just a blast a light out in the stars. What could be better than that? What could be better? It's like gettin to die, an get past death, to get to the universe, an then come back. In the world where we talk and fight and he fucks me over, it all just seems so unimportant after that. I don't understand how he can do that for me an then turn around an be such a, well, smaller. It is a small world this world, in comparison to where we go in bed. And I guess we gotta be smaller in it.

The Harvesting
John Bishop

Premiere: Circle Repertory Theatre, NYC, 1984
Publisher: Dramatists Play Service, Inc.
Setting: Mansfield, Ohio, July 1–4, 1976

A series of three shooting murders shakes a small Ohio town. The gunman, Tommy Heisler, is a mercenary out for vengeance on the father who abused him and "accidentally" killed his baby brother. (The other murder victims were Tommy's mother and her lover.) Tommy crashes at the home of a loyal Vietnam buddy, Gary Majors. In the middle of their heated conversation, Gary's "old lady" Louise comes home from work.

Louise Cline is "in her twenties, black, sexy, bright, but a bit tough in manner." She didn't expect to come home to find Gary's white buddy planning to sleep on her couch.

LOUISE

Christ, what a rotten night. Husband and wife come in
plastered. Hubby collapses in the salad bar. I mean *in* the
fuckin' thing. Slides to the floor with ice up his nose and
Russian dressing in his eyebrows. Wife comes over to
help . . . slips on a scallion, honest to God, and WHOP!
In she goes. Only she is up to her elbows in condiments.
Then plop! She's on the floor dripping garbanzo beans . . .
dress up around her garter belt, screamin' she's gonna' sue
the joint. Dave is gone, Harry is gone. Who's next in line?
La hostess . . . me. I gotta get these two assholes off the
floor, and meanwhile one of the busboys is pretending to
help her up but is really grabbin' handfuls of bare thigh,
and she catches on and bats him. Then the husband gets
heroic and takes a swing at the cat and here's me in the
middle, and the waiters all just standin' around in their
leather aprons and blonde hair, twitterin' like a bunch of
doves on a telephone pole. Jesus.

[TOMMY

So'd you get them out?]

LOUISE

Got them to a table. Dinner on the house. Talked 'em out
of suing us.

[GARY

A born leader, Louise.]

LOUISE

That's not all. On the way out, her old man pats me on the
ass, you ready? I was so goddamn mad I chased 'em into
the parking lot. I called that son of a bitch everything I
could think of. Wifey comes over and swings at me with
her purse. I take the bitch's bag . . . open it up . . . whirl
it around my head.

(Laughs.)

I trashed that girl's life all over the goddamn parking lot.

The Heart of a Child
Eric Lane

Premiere: Orange Thoughts Theater Company, NYC, 1991
Publisher: Orange Thoughts
Setting: A small town somewhere along the railroad tracks be-
tween Warm Springs, Georgia, and Washington, D.C.,
April, 1945

Mary Alice is pretty, sweet, spirited, and around
twenty. She begins the play very much still a girl. By the
play's end, she has matured into a young woman.

She is married to Jimmy, a pilot stationed in the South
Pacific during World War II. Her husband is killed in the
war. Carrying their newborn baby, she visits the graves of
her husband and her father-in-law, John. He has also died
recently, and she loved him very much.

MARY ALICE

I named him Isaac. Everybody thinking I'm gonna name
him Jimmy John, but I called him Isaac so that his time
come, the Lord'll reach down and spare my son.
  (To John, her father-in-law.)
I remember how you be talking how when one soul
dies, a child's born for him to enter. Well, that's nonsense.
A soul goes to heaven or hell. But not in my child.
  (To Jimmy, her husband.)
They give me your dog tags. And your medals. Some
you didn't even tell me. Radio mechanic.
  (Smiles.)
I would've liked to've seen that. And for your missions.
They give me them and I keep them, but they don't mean
nothing to me without you. I know I ain't supposed to say
that but it's true.

I miss you so much. I know you been away and maybe
I thought I'd be used to it, but that was different 'cause I
always knew you were coming back. I love you so much.
I love you both. You like his name, don't you?

(Sings name.)

I-saac. I-saac. He's got your eyes. And his own soul.

(Whispers.)

Isaac.

Icarus's Mother
Sam Shepard

Premiere: Caffe Cino, NYC, 1965
Publisher: Bantam Books (in *The Unseen Hand and Other Plays*)
Setting: Picnic spot near a beach

Five young picnickers—Jill, Bill, Howard, Pat, and Frank—lie on their backs, belching and watching the sky. An airplane is making vapor trails that may or may not be skywriting. The group is waiting for dark, when there will be fireworks. Frank wanders off by himself, then Pat and Jill go for a walk on the beach, leaving Howard and Bill to make smoke signals over the campfire. Pat and Jill return barefoot, both laughing hysterically.

JILL

Do you know—do you know what this idiot did? Do you know what she did! She—we're walking up the beach, see—we're walking along like this.

(She walks very slowly with her head down.)

Very slowly and dejected and sad. So suddenly she stops. We both stop and she says, guess what? And I said, what? She says I really do—I really do have to pee after all.

(They both break up.)

So I said all right. I'm very serious with her, see. I say all right, Patsy dear, if you have to you have to. So then she said I have to pee so bad I can't even wait. I have to go right now. Right this very minute. So we're in the middle of the beach with nothing around but sand. No bushes or nothing. So she whips down her pants and crouches right there in the middle of the beach very seriously. And I'm standing there looking around. Sort of standing guard. And do you know what happens?

(They crack up.)

All of a sudden I have to pee too. I mean really bad like she has to. So I whip my pants down and crouch down right beside her. There we are sitting side by side on the beach together.

(She crouches down in the position.)

Like a couple of desert nomads or something. So. You know how it is when you have to pee so bad that you can't pee at all?

(BILL and HOWARD nod their heads.)

Well that's what happened. Neither one of us could get anything out and we were straining and groaning and along comes our friend in the jet plane. Except this time he's very low. Right above our heads. Zoom! So there we were. We couldn't stand up because then he'd really see us. And we couldn't run because there was nowhere to run to. So we just sat and pretended we were playing with shells or something. But he kept it up. He kept flying back and forth right above our heads. So do you know what this nut does?

(HOWARD and BILL shake their heads.)

She starts waving to him and throwing kisses. Then he really went nuts. He started doing flips and slides with that jet like you've never seen before.

(She stands with her arms outstretched like a plane.)

He went way up and then dropped like a seagull or something. We thought he was going to crash even. Then I started waving and the guy went insane. He flew that thing upside down and backwards and every way you could imagine. And we were cracking up all over the place. We started rolling in the sand and showing him our legs. Then we did some of those nasty dances like they do in the bars. Then we both went nuts or something and we took off our pants

and ran right into the water yelling and screaming and
waving at his plane.

Kennedy's Children
Robert Patrick

Premiere: John Golden Theatre, NYC, 1975
Publisher: Samuel French, Inc.
Setting: A bar on New York's Lower East Side

Kennedy's Children is a play composed entirely of monologues. One rainy night in February 1974, five lonely
people come to the same bar to drink by themselves:
Wanda, a woman obsessed with J.F.K. and his assassination; Mark, a Vietnam vet with a tenuous grasp on reality;
Sparger, a queeny off-off-off-Broadway actor; Rona, an an-
tiwar activist whose dreams have gone sour; and Carla.
Carla is a disillusioned model who dreamed of becoming
the next Marilyn Monroe. She has just taken seventy-four
sleeping pills and come to the bar "to wash them down."

CARLA

I wanted to be a sex goddess. And you can laugh all you
want to. The joke is on me, whether you laugh or not. I
wanted to be one—one of *them*. They used to laugh at
Marilyn when she said she didn't want to be a sex-goddess,
she wanted to be a human being. And now they laugh at
me when I say, "I don't want to be a human being; I want
to be a sex-goddess." That shows you right there that something has changed, doesn't it? Rita, Ava, Lana, Marlene,
Marilyn—I wanted to *be* one of them. I remember the
morning my friend came in and told us all that Marilyn had
died. And all the boys were stunned, rigid, literally, as they
realized what had left us. I mean, if the world couldn't
support Marilyn Monroe, then wasn't something desper-

ately wrong? And we spent the rest of the goddamned sixties finding out what it was. We were all living together, me and these three gay boys that adopted me when I ran away, in this loft on East Fifth Street, before it became dropout heaven—before anyone even said "dropout"—way back when "commune" was still a verb? We were all—old-movie buffs, sex-mad—you know, the *early* sixties. And then my friend, this sweet little queen, he came in and he passed out tranquilizers to everyone, and told us all to sit down, and we thought he was just going to tell us there was a Mae West double feature on somewhere—and he said—he said—he said—"Marilyn Monroe died last night"—and all the boys were stunned—but I—I felt something sudden and cold in my solar plexus, and I knew then what I wanted to do with my life. I wanted to be the next one. I wanted to be the next one to stand radiant and perfected before the race of man, to shed the luminosity of my beloved countenance over the struggles and aspirations of my pitiful subjects. I wanted to *give* meaning to my own time, to be the unattainable luring love that drives men on, the angel of light, the golden flower, the best of the universe made womankind, the living sacrifice, the end! *Shit!*

Lily Dale
Horton Foote

Premiere: Samuel Beckett Theatre, NYC, 1986
Publisher: Dramatists Play Service, Inc.
Setting: Pete Davenport's home in Houston, Texas, 1909

A young man named Horace Robedaux boards a train from Harrison, Texas, to Houston with money his mother has sent him. Horace is visiting his mother and teenage sister, Lily Dale, while his stepfather, Pete Davenport, is away on business. Pete dotes on Lily Dale, whom he raised as his own, but has no use for Horace, who grew up with relatives after his parents' separation and his father's death from alcoholism. The visit is cut short by Pete's early return, but Horace boards the wrong streetcar and misses the last train to Harrison. Penniless, he walks all the way back to his stepfather's home and promptly collapses. He has malaria. Feverish and too weak to stand, Horace is confined to the couch in the living room for three weeks while family tensions rage around him.

Lily Dale is "eighteen years old, emotional, strong-willed, self-involved. A feminine, Southern belle. Plays the piano with enormous confidence and little talent." Her boyfriend, Will, wants to marry her and Pete doesn't like him. Her mother thinks Lily Dale is too young to get married. When Will gains their trust, Lily Dale herself starts to have second thoughts. She is panicked by the idea of sex and the pain of childbirth. And she is sick of the friction between Pete and Horace.

Horace is obsessed with the family past and wants to find out all he can about his real father, while Lily Dale is fiercely loyal to Pete: "Mama didn't love our papa. She loves Mr. Davenport because he doesn't drink and neglect her; he's been good to her and to me. So don't you ever let me hear you say a word against him again. Because if you do, I'll tell him exactly what you said, and he'll never let you in this house again to upset me and Mama. Never! Never! Never! Never! Never!" Horace declares that he's leaving this minute, gets out of bed, and falls. Lily Dale comforts him.

LILY DALE

Oh, Brother. Brother! I'm sorry! Oh, dear Brother! I'm so sorry! I didn't mean a word of those terrible things I said. Not a one. I don't know what gets into me. I have a terrible disposition, Brother, a terrible disposition. It's the Robedaux coming out in me. Forgive me, please, please forgive me.

(She and Horace are crying.)

I loved Papa. Believe me, I did. Just as much as you did. I loved him, but it hurts me so to talk about him, Brother. And it scares me, too. You don't know how it scares me. I wake sometimes in the night, and I think I can hear Papa coughing and struggling to breathe like he used to . . . and I didn't mean that about you leaving, Brother. I'm glad you're here and I want you to stay until you're all well and strong again. Because you're the only brother I have and sometimes at night, I see you dead and in your coffin and I cry in my dreams like my heart will break. I am really crying because my crying wakes me up and I say to myself, "Brother is alive and not dead at all, that's just a dream," but still I feel so miserable, I just lie there sobbing, like my heart will break. And sometimes Mama hears me and comes in and says, "Why are you crying, Lily Dale?" And I say, "Because I dreamt again that Brother was dead and had gone to heaven and left us."

(She holds him tighter.)

You're all the family I have, Brother, you and Mama. And we must never leave each other. Promise me you'll never leave me and promise me you'll forgive me. Promise me, promise me . . .

Living at Home
Anthony Giardina

Premiere: Playwrights Horizons, NYC, 1978
Publisher: Dramatists Play Service, Inc.
Setting: The kitchen of the Bogle family house in Watertown, Massachusetts, November, 1963

John is the younger son of a bowling alley manager, Eddie Bogle. He has dropped out of college and come home to live with his father, teenage sister, and dying mother. His aggressive, unquestioning older brother, David, is going to medical school and dating a Brandeis senior named Alice. John has a job in the family bowling alley but seems to spend most of his time in the kitchen, brooding over a paperback copy of *Long Day's Journey into Night* and watching TV coverage of John F. Kennedy's assassination and funeral.

John's father thinks he is "lost." David thinks a nice girl would solve all his problems and arranges a date with Alice's kid sister, Mary. The four go out to a movie, and when they return, David brings Alice upstairs, leaving Mary with John. He is caustic and defensive, asking, "What do you think of me? I mean, am I all right? Would you classify me as all right?"

They start drinking scotch and getting to know one another. John asks Mary about the night of her senior prom, unwittingly hitting a nerve. She says, "I was always trying to be different. So I wore my hair down— everyone else wore theirs up—and wore my sister's two-year-old dress." Her date's name was Gordon. John probes further and finds out that after the prom Gordon, Mary, and six of their friends drove up to his family's cabin in New Hampshire and went for a moonlight swim.

MARY

I remember the way it felt treading water. Everybody else was on shore, having a good time, like somebody had told them they had to have the classic raucous good time or they were never going to be able to make it over the hump, you know, the loss of high school, the next step. I didn't care. I just wanted to get away from them and have a good time all by myself. I just wanted to swim.

(*Beat. She sips.*)

[JOHN

Yes.

MARY

Oh, the rest is boring.

JOHN

Do I look bored to you, Mary? Do I? Now, come on. There you were, the little water sprite in your "neat, black bathing suit."

MARY

Yes.

JOHN

Getting away. From it all
                    (*Beat.*)
I'm with you, Mary.

MARY
                    (*Beat. She looks at him.*)]
I guess I must have gotten pretty far out, because I couldn't hear anything anymore. Only Gordon's voice calling me from somewhere. Then a splash and a steady rippling of water, and then Gordon's face was beside me in the water, and I had to laugh, he suddenly looked so stupid, just this maze of yellow hair and two eyes and a nose and a mouth full of teeth, all of it wet, and there was all of a sudden no more of a person there than I might have felt in a fish or a seal that had swum up beside me. Just some happy animal that I had nothing whatsoever to do with.
                    (*Beat.*)
And the next thing was—out in the middle of this lake was a small island. I'd never really noticed it when we'd been to the lake before, but suddenly here it was, right in front of us—and I remember thinking, Now what is this doing here? Because it was obvious that the happy animal and I would have to somehow deal with it's being there. We couldn't just swim around it.
                    (*Beat.*)
So we stood up. That is, *he* stood up. I sat there on the edge of the sand, letting the water run up my suit and down it because I *loved* the way it felt. And here we were on this tiny little Eden, and I knew exactly what the happy

animal was thinking, if he was thinking anything at all—it was like God or somebody had put this island here for us tonight—and then of course I was being kissed all over, but not really *there* at all, somewhere else, and my beautiful new black bathing suit was being taken off me and thrown aside. My one clear action, the one thing I, my real self, remembers doing, was breaking apart to retrieve the suit. But by that time it was too late. It had gotten washed away. So I sat there, waiting for it to come back. All of a sudden I was obsessed by what I had been when I bought it, different, I mean I suddenly felt so different from the girl who had gone into Filene's on the damn trolley to buy herself a bathing suit. I liked *her* so much, and I hated myself just then.

(Beat.)

The last thing I remember was Gordon—he was Gordon now, he'd regained something of a personality—asking me what the matter was. I wanted to swim. I said that. Maybe it was just in my head but I remember saying that—I just wanted to swim.

Lovers
Brian Friel

Publisher: Farrar, Straus & Giroux, Inc.
Setting: A hill overlooking Ballymore, Northern Ireland

Lovers is a play in two sections, titled "Winners" and "Losers." In "Winners," a boy and girl plan their future together while narrators on both sides of the stage make it clear that both will have drowned by the end of the day. The title is only partly ironic: it's already clear that these young lovers are seriously mismatched and would never again be as happy as they are today.

Margaret Mary Enright is an Irish schoolgirl, "seventeen, bubbling with life, inclined to be extreme in her enthusiasms. Although she is not really very beautiful, her vivacity gives her a distinct attraction. Whatever she likes, she loves; whatever she dislikes, she hates—momentarily. She is either very elated or very depressed, but no emotion is ever permanent." Mag is pregnant. In three weeks she is going to marry her boyfriend, Joe, an earnest and studious boy half a year her senior. The two have climbed a hill this Saturday morning with the stated intent of studying for final exams, though Mag is distracted by anything and everything else that crosses her mind.

MAG

I'll tell you a tip.

(Pause.)

Joe.

(Pause.)

D'you want to know a clever trick I have, Joe? In all exams the smart thing to do is to write down everything you know—no matter what the question is. Les oiseaux qui en sont dehors désespèrent d'y entrer; et d'un pareil soin en sortir, ceux qui sont au-dedans; if the moving line is at right angles to the plane figure, the prism is a right prism; in 1586 Sir Philip Sidney met his death at Zutphen from a wound in the nether regions of his body; the volume of a cone is $\frac{1}{3}\pi$ dh multiplied by—my God, and that's the one thing I know! Shakespeare, the Bard of Avon, besides writing thirty-four extant plays, was married to a woman eight years his senior, and was the father of twins. Like Papa. As flies to wanton boys are we to the gods; they kill us for their sport. Sister Pascal says that you always know Protestants by their yellow faces and Catholics by their dirty fingernails.

(She rises, moves away from JOE, *who is lost in his books, and stands at the edge of the hilltop. She looks down over the town.)*

Nuns are screams—if you don't take them seriously . . . I don't know what things I take seriously . . . Never books or school or things like that . . . Maybe God sometimes, when I'm in trouble . . . and Papa . . . and being a good wife to you . . . It's so quiet, with the whole world before me . . . Joe.

(She turns to face him.)

Joe, you'll have to talk a lot more to me, Joe. I don't care if it's not sensible talk; it's just that—you know—I feel lonely at times . . . Of course I'll have Joan; she'll visit us; Phil and herself. And you'll like her better when you get to know her. All that's wrong with her is that she's not mature yet; and she can be cruel at times . . .

After we're married we'll have lots of laughs together, Joe, won't we? We'll laugh a lot, won't we?

(She begins to cry inaudibly.)

Joe, I'm nervous; I'm frightened, Joe; I'm terrified . . .

The Mighty Gents
Richard Wesley

Premiere: Ambassador Theatre, NYC, 1978
Publisher: Dramatists Play Service, Inc.
Setting: Newark, New Jersey, 1978

In the 1960s, the Mighty Gents were the toughest black teen gang in Newark. Now the former street warriors are pushing thirty. Aimless, bored, and out of work, the men hang around on street corners, reminiscing about their glory days. Rita is twenty-eight years old and desperately wants a baby. She and her husband, Frankie, have been trying unsuccessfully for ten years, and their marriage is permeated with sadness. She tells the audience how it was in the old days.

RITA

I used to be a street-warrior's woman—a "deb." We never
called ourselves "girls." "Girls" went to high school but
didn't know nothin' and thought love was like what you
read in the magazines and saw in the movies. "Girls"
screwed with their clothes on in the back seats of cars, and
in the hallways of tenements with their drawers stuffed in
their boyfriends' hip pockets while they stood pinned to
crumbling walls holding their skirts up . . . yea . . . Char-
lene, Cynthia, Donna, Martha, and me, well, we were
women. We belonged to the Mighty Gents, who didn't
screw us. They "made love" to us. We was wise enough to
know the difference and made sure our men understood
what was happenin'. They loved us in their clubhouse on
real beds, and let us carry their weapons for them, and
took us places, and showed us more things than most of
"the girls" could even imagine in their wildest dreams. The
Mighty Gents told us we were their queens. We were
special, then, and every day was filled with sunshine and
light. We wasn't children no more. Just sixteen. Wasn't
children no more. Childhood was a drag. Only people I
ever saw enjoy bein' kids was those little rich kids on TV
with their shining blue eyes and blonde hair, runnin' round
sayin' stuff like, "Jeepers" and "Golly" all day. Well, our
life was different. You know? I mean . . . uh . . . different . . . well, you know what I mean. I mean, we understood early that the rules was on Monday you was born,
and on Tuesday you was grown up. That's just the way it
was . . . "Jeepers" . . . Ain't that nothin'?

*(She falls silent and takes a swig from the
can of beer.)*

Hey, the excitement never seemed to end, though. There
was the moonlight bus rides to Bear Mountain on hot summer nights. . . . And the parties at Tiny's house on Bergen
Street. One 20-watt red-tinted light bulb in the basement
and nothin' but slow records playin' an' everybody clutchin'

each other and doin' the Grind. Alla us teenagers holdin' onto each other, clutchin' and clutchin', tryin' to get to somethin' we all knew we didn't feel in the real world, but, still, tryin' to get it from each other. Somehow, hopin' that . . . hey . . . that's okay, forget it. Then, there were the fights. Yea, the fights . . . everybody fought. Men *and* women. Me and my women . . . well, we was the baddest debs in the city. Fifteen hair-pullers, and we didn't lose nary one. That's right . . . nary one. The Zombies' debs were the toughest. I still see some of them around. We good friends now. All that stuff is past. Know what I mean? . . . But, The Mighty Gents and their fight against the Zombies' men . . . well, that's another story . . . one I don't like to think about. . . . I found out a lot about a lotta things after that fight.

(She falls silent again.)

. . . Like the night I carried Frankie to the hospital with that knife stickin' outa his chest . . . only time I ever really prayed and meant it . . . yea . . . it . . . was . . . all . . . so . . . much . . . *fun.* That's right. We were somebody, then. We debs . . . we women . . . now . . .

Night Luster
Laura Harrington

Premiere: New Dramatists, NYC
Publisher: New American Library (in *100 Monologues: An Audition Sourcebook From New Dramatists*)
Setting: Urban streets and a call girl's apartment

Roma is an aspiring singer and songwriter who keeps getting involved with abusive men but never loses hope. Here she talks to her best friend, Mink, a call girl, about her self-image and dreams of success.

ROMA

I don't think people see me. I get this feeling sometimes like I'm invisible or something. I can be standing there in a room and I'm talking and everything, and it's like my words aren't getting anywhere and I look down at myself and *jesus*, sometimes my body isn't getting anywhere either. It's like I'm standing behind a one-way mirror and I can see the guys and I can hear the guys, but they can't see me and they can't hear me. And I start to wonder if maybe I'm ugly or something, like maybe I'm some alien species from another planet and I don't speak the language and I look totally weird. But I don't know this, you see, because on this other planet I had this really nice mother who told me I was beautiful and that I had a voice to die for because she loved me so much, not because it was true. And I arrive here on earth and I'm so filled with her love and her belief in me that I walk around like I'm beautiful and I sing like I have a voice to die for. And because I'm so *convinced* and so strange and so *deluded,* people *pretend* to listen to me . . . because they're being polite or something—or maybe they're afraid of me. And at first I don't notice because I sing with my eyes closed. But then one day I open my eyes and I find out I'm living in this world where nobody sees me and nobody hears me.

(Beat.)

I'm just lookin' for that one guy who's gonna hear *me*, see *me* . . . really take a chance. I mean, I hear *them*. I'm listening so hard I hear promises when somebody's just sayin' hello.

Jesus, if anybody ever heard what I've got locked up inside of me . . . I'd be a *star*.

Quilters

Molly Newman and Barbara Damashek

Premiere: The Denver Center Theatre Company, Denver, Colorado, 1984
Publisher: Dramatists Play Service, Inc.
Setting: The American frontier

Quilters is a musical homage to America's pioneer women. An elderly woman named Sarah McKendree Bonham is piecing together a "legacy quilt" for her daughters, in which each block represents a piece of her story. Seven actresses play a variety of characters from Sarah's personal history and the larger history of women on the frontier. This monologue is part of Block Fifteen, "Crosses and Losses."

CASSIE

My husband and I married back in Virginia and he wanted to go out west as soon as he could. He got a job laying track for the first railroad into New Mexico. When that job was done he got put to work inspecting twenty miles of track. He walked it. He could do it in a day easy if there wasn't any repair work. I was home caring for the stock and the kids and I wanted to make something nice for him so I started on a quilt that took me two years to finish. I was always hidin' it before he came in . . . sometimes runnin' when he hit the door . . . or stashin' it in the craziest places . . . like one time in the stove. When it was done, I called in Elizabeth, my oldest to give it to him. He took it and studied it and studied it—I was just thinkin' maybe somethin' was wrong with it, when he rushed over to me and wrapped the quilt around me, swung me off my feet and sashayed me all around the kitchen. Both of us laughin' to beat the band. He was some man all right. Next spring, I had wrapped up my work for the day and was piecin' up some scraps to cover the baby that was due in the summer. I had just lit the lamp when we heard a lot of horses comin' up the road and ridin' hard. My heart stopped and I reached way down to get my breath and ran out to the porch. There was five men from the railroad. They were sweatin' and talkin' over one another's words. There was this big bushel basket on the ground in front o' them. Jim Rice thought maybe he fell and hit his head on the tracks. Slim Henson thought maybe the heat had got him. None of 'em could figure out why he didn't hear the train. We never did get a clear reason, but they had to bring him home to us in that bushel basket. They tell me I didn't cry or say a word. I just sat down on the porch kinda in a little ball and started rockin' back and forth—rockin' and starin', rockin' and starin'. Course I don't remember much now . . . hardly anything in fact. Just what they tell me. I stayed in the back room . . . never came out. I guess it musta been my momma came in and set a piecin' bag in front of me, a needle, a spool of thread, a pair of scissors. I didn't know what those things were for. But one morning, my hands reached out . . . my hands remembered . . . they grabbed the top piece and sewed it to the next piece and the next— didn't matter what it looked like. I never laid a cuttin' edge to any of 'em. Four months later I had a whole quilt and the baby was born; and my eyes came clear again.

Sarita
Maria Irene Fornes

Premiere: INTAR, NYC, 1984
Publisher: Performing Arts Journal Publications (in *Maria Irene Fornes: Plays*)
Setting: South Bronx and other New York locations, 1939–1947

Sarita is a spirited young woman from the South Bronx. She is thirteen years old at the start of the play. Her best friend, Yeye, is reading her cards to find out if Sarita's boyfriend, Julio, loves her and if he is cheating on her. In the next scene, Julio has left and Sarita is fourteen and pregnant. Refusing to marry the old man of her mother's choice, she continues her anguished affair with the unfaithful Julio.

After three years of heartbreak, Sarita writes him a suicide note and heads for the top of the Empire State Building. An American soldier named Mark prevents her from jumping and falls in love with her. They are married, but Sarita cannot leave Julio alone. Here she prays in front of an altar in her mother's living room. She is nineteen years old.

SARITA

If one has one love in one's lifetime, only one, and one has been true to that love, does one go straight to heaven?—for being true?

(*Short pause.*)

I hope so. Because here it's hell.

(*Short pause.*)

I just want to know if you know about this?

(*Short pause.*)

Is this your idea?—Or is the devil doing it?

(*Short pause.*)

Give me a sign.

(*Short pause.*)

Say something.

(*Short pause.*)

Go on.

(*Short pause.*)

Do something.

(*She palms her hand as if there were a small person in it. She lowers her voice.*)

Good Lord, child, somebody made a mistake. I put you in for an easy life. You're my favorite kid. Don't worry about a thing, honey. I'll take care of things.

(*Using her own voice.*)

Oh, God! Thank you God.—God. I am serious. I cannot breathe. I'm burning. I'm turned inside myself. Do you know what I'm saying?—I feel my life's leaving me. I feel I'm dying. God, I want to love Mark and no one else.

The Search for Signs of Intelligent Life in the Universe

Jane Wagner

Premiere: Plymouth Theatre, NYC, 1985
Publisher: Harper & Row
Setting: Bare stage

The Search for Signs of Intelligent Life in the Universe is a free-ranging one-woman show created for Lily Tomlin. What seem at first to be individual character sketches criss-cross and blend into a composite portrait of modern life. This is the first appearance of a fifteen-year-old punk performance artist named Agnus Angst.

AGNUS ANGST

Hello, Charlotte, listen, it is *vital* I stay
over at your house tonight!
Don't ask me to explain.
You've got to make your mom let me stay over!
Can't you force her to say yes?

Look, my parents think you're a bad influence on *me,*
    too.

Just for that, you can't run the equipment at my gig tonight.

You are out of my life, Charlotte;

you are *her*story. You are the "crumb de la crumb." Drop off my

tapes at the Un-Club, or I'll sue you for all you're worth.
It is vital, Charlotte!

Don't you eyeball me, you *speck!* Can't you see I am
    USING this
PHONE!! And don't you *touch* that cage.
That's my parakeet in there.

Hello?
Look, it's vital I talk to the radio shrink. My name's Agnus.
I'm fifteen. My *parents* locked me out of the house today.
I want to find out if that is *legal.* I'm in the
ladies' room, House of Pancakes. I can't wait long.

Hello? Is this Dr. Kassorla, the psychologist? Look, Doctor,
for years I've been going home after school, nobody
would be there—

I'd take my key
from around my neck and
let myself in.
But today I go home,
I put my key in the door . . .

THEY CHANGED THE LOCKS ON ME!

Yeah, maybe it *was* something I did. I didn't say I was
    innocent.

Whatever I do is wrong, anyway. Like, last night, my step-
    mom,
she accuses me of leaving dirty fingerprints on the *cheese*.
Even getting an innocent piece of cheese becomes a crim-
    inal act.
But the problem goes deeper: My real mother's not around
much right now. She's in Europe, Germany or someplace,
doing her art thing. She's a performance artist. Like me.

There was this big custody beef, see, 'cause
my real mother's a lesbian. So the *court* gave me to my
    dad.
He's a gene-splicer, a bio-businessman at this research lab
    of
*mis*applied science. Where he's working on some new bio-
    form
he thinks he'll be able to patent.
He doesn't get that *I* am a new bio-form.

I AM USING THIS PHONE!! You IHOP speck!

So today I go by my dad's lab, to get some money for some
    gear
for my act.
and I see this like glob of bio-plasm
quivering there in this petri dish.
I don't know why I did it.
Maybe it was sibling rivalry.
But I leaned over
and I spit into it.
And of course, my dad had a MAD SCIENTIST ALERT!
    He says I've
ruined years of research.
The truth is he loves that *bio-form* more than *me*.

Yeah, I thought of calling the hot line for runaways,
    but I'm
worried maybe they don't take
throwaways like me. I have other family, my grandparents,
but we have nothing in common, except that we are all
carbon-based life forms.

What?
A commercial?
I can't believe you're brushing me off.
To sell some product

that probably killed some poor *lab rat.*
You've been about as helpful as an acid FLASHBACK!

Serious Bizness
Jennifer Allen, David Babcock, Winnie Holzman, and Don Perman

Premiere: O'Neals' Cabaret Theatre, NYC, 1983
Publisher: Samuel French, Inc.
Setting: Cabaret stage

Serious Bizness is an evening of blackout sketches and songs for two men and two women. The following sketch is called "Maid of Honor."

> (NEALLA *enters wearing a flowery headpiece
> and carrying a hand corsage. She sits and
> primps in an imaginary mirror as she speaks
> to imaginary girls on either side of her. She
> speaks with a heavy New York accent.*)

NEALLA

Well, *that* ceremony's over . . . thank you, God. Now if we're smart we'll hurry up and hit that dance floor, 'cause in ten minutes it'll be sardine city. Believe me, I know. Any idea how many times I've been a maid of honor? Nine. That's not counting the six times I was a regular bridesmaid, plus—before my divorce came through? I was a *matron* of honor *twice.* So . . . oh, can I have a hit off that number, please? Thanks.
> (*She takes a drag off an imaginary joint.*)

Christ, I hate these dresses. I hate peach. As a color, as a flavor, as a . . . *concept.* I mean, peach makes you look like a slut, it's a slut *look.* But you can't tell Sharon anything. Fr'instance she says to me—"I want a white gown." What am I gonna say? "Sharon, you've been divorced, you *shouldn't* wear white"? Maybe it's not my place to say, but if it was me, I wouldn't wear white to my second marriage. Don't ask me why. Don't! Don't ask me why! I just wouldn't. The second time around you wear off-white, you wear cream, you wear bisque, you wear off-bisque. White you wear once in your life. Once. If you're lucky.

But you can't tell Sharon that. Did you see the cake? Did you *see* the cake she's got out there? Did you see what kind of cake it is? Carrot. A carrot wedding cake. I mean—carrot cake is like . . . for a snack, at most it's a brunch food. It's a *casual* cake, it's not for a formal wedding.

I mean, I have been a little concerned about Sharon, quite frankly. Do you know what she said to me, not two weeks ago? We were in Altmans, looking. And she's trying on *this*, trying on *that*, but . . . *half-hearted*, ya know? Finally, I say "Sharon, let's go" and she turns to me, and out of the clear blue sky she says—this is Sharon—"which d'ya think would get you more depressed, losing a limb, or losing your entire family in a boating accident?" I mean, this is from a woman who is getting married in two weeks and has not even purchased a *gown*.

But look, maybe it will all work out for the best. That's what Sharon's aunt Arlene says. Do you know her aunt Arlene? A doll. An angel. And a very, very *ill* woman.

(*MUSICAL CUE: James Bond theme.*)

Oh, there's the band. We'd better get going. Yeah, they're gonna start off with Sharon and Murray's favorite song— "The Love Theme from *Octopussy*." Could ya die?

Sideshow
Miguel Piñero

Publisher: Arte Público Press (in *Outrageous*)
Setting: The inner city

Sideshow concerns the street world of drug dealers, addicts, pimps, prostitutes, hustlers, and con men. Sugar is a fiteen- to eighteen-year-old Puerto Rican prostitute with an abusive pimp. Her dope is wearing off, and she has started to crash.

(SUGAR *is lying on the bed. Her jones is coming down. She is in pain, she searches around for her dope. Finding nothing, she falls back on the bed.*)

SUGAR

Mama-Mama-Mama, can you hear me, Mama?
It's me, Mama, it's your baby, Mama.
Papa done hit me again, Mama.
He was drunk, Mama. I know he ain't my Papa, Mama,
but every time you're sleeping he comes into the room,
he comes and sits on my bed and feels on my leg, Mama.
Mama, he scares me when he's like that,
breathing all hard and fast and hot, spit falling on me,
him shaking and groaning like an animal.
I know, Mama . . . the landlord . . . the food . . .
Mama, where are you?
I didn't mean for you to die like you did
but you told me you'd be around
when I needed you.
Mama, where have you been?
Mama, where have you been?
Mama, where have you been?
Mama, I need you.
I love you.
I need you now, Mama. I need you now.

I needed you then.
And you tell me to wait 'til tomorrow,
tomorrow is here, Mama.
It's here and it's now yesterday, Mama.
Mama, where have you been?
Shit, Mama, I'm getting sick.
Mama, me, your baby, I needs me a fix.
Mama, I'm a junkie, Mama,
A HOPE TO DIE DOPE FIEND.
Mama, please, it beginning to hurt.
My legs, Mama, they hurt like hell.
Mama, someone is crushing them to nothing,
into powder, Mama,
into powder, Mama, white powder, Mama,
like the one I needs,
like I needed you, Mama,
like when I laid in the bed crying
from fear of the many papas
that came into my room.
Like I needed you, Mama. I needed to put
   my head between
the hollow of your breast, Mama,
like the johns need to put their heads between the hollow
of my breasts, Mama, and call me Mama.
Mama, they call me trickie now 'cause I've turned more
   tricks in one night
than you turn in a lifetime.
                    (Screams.)
Mama, it getting worse.
The monkey is traveling down my back,
calling to my mind to feed my veins.
Mama, please help me, Mama. I'm tired of turning tricks,
committing crimes. I wanna kick, I wanna fix.
I want you to need me.
Mama, I can do it with your help,
with your care, your love.
Mama, love me like you mean it Mama.

The pain open the door.
Help me, Mama, please help me, please, please, Mama,
I-I-I . . .
SHIT, YOU IS DEAD.

spell #7
Ntozake Shange

Premiere: New York Shakespeare Festival, NYC, 1979
Publisher: New American Library (in *Nine Plays by Black Women*)
Setting: A theater bar where black performers congregate

Subtitled "geechee jibara quik magic trance manual for technologically stressed third world people," *spell #7* is a series of poetic and choreographic solos for and about black performers. The play opens with a giant representation of a black-face minstrel show mask and contains interludes of dancing "that identify every period of afro-american entertainment." Its characters are actors, magicians, singers, and dancers who hang out in an afterhours bar where the bartender is a poet and the barmaid, Lily, an unemployed actress. After another performer's solo, "the lights change to focus on Lily and she begins to say what's really on her mind. the rest of the company is not aware of Lily's private thoughts."

LILY
(Illustrating her words with movement.)
i'm gonna simply brush my hair. rapunzel pull yr tresses back into the tower. & lady godiva give up horseback riding. i'm gonna alter my social & professional life dramatically. i will brush 100 strokes in the morning/ 100 strokes midday & 100 strokes before retiring. i will have a very busy schedule. between the local trains & the express/ i'm gonna

brush. i brush between telephone calls. at the disco i'm gonna brush on the slow songs/ i dont slow dance with strangers. i'ma brush my hair before making love & after. i'll brush my hair in taxis. while windowshopping. when i have visitors over the kitchen table/ i'ma brush. i brush my hair while thinking abt anything. mostly i think abt how it will be when i get my full heada hair. like lifting my head in the morning will become a chore. i'll try to turn my cheek & my hair will weigh me down

(LILY *falls to the floor.* BETTINA *helps lift her to her knees, then begins to dance & mime as* LILY *speaks.*)

i dream of chaka khan/ chocolate from graham central station with all seven wigs/ & medusa. i brush & brush. i use olive oil hair food/ & posner's vitamin E. but mostly i brush & brush. i may lose contact with most of my friends. i cd lose my job/ but i'm on unemployment & brush while waiting on line for my check. i'm sure i get good recommendations from my social worker: such a fastidious woman/ that lily/ always brushing her hair. nothing in my dreams suggests that hair brushing/ per se/ has anything to do with my particular heada hair. a therapist might say that the head fulla hair has to do with something else/ like: a symbol of lily's unconscious desires. but i have no therapist

(*she takes imaginary pen from* BETTINA, *who was pretending to be a therapist, & sits down at table across from her.*)

& my dreams mean things to me/ like if you dreamed abt tobias/ then something has happened to tobias/ or he is gonna show up. if you dream abt yr grandma who's dead/ then you must be doing something she doesnt like/ or she wdnta gone to all the trouble to leave heaven like that. if you dream something red/ you shd stop. if you dream something green/ you shd keep doing it. if a blue person appears in yr dreams/ then that person is yr true friend

& that's how i see my dreams. & this head full hair i have in my dreams is lavender & nappy as a 3-yr-old's in a apple tree. i can fry an egg & see the white of the egg spreadin in the grease like my hair is gonna spread in the air/ but i'm not egg-yolk yellow/ i am brown & the egg white isnt white at all/ it is my actual hair/ & it wd go on & on forever/ irregular like a rasta-man's hair. irregular/ gargantuan & lavender. nestled on blue satin pillows/ pillows like the sky. & so i fry my eggs. i buy daisies dyed lavender & laced lavender tablemats & lavender nail polish. though i never admit it/ i really do believe in magic/ & can do strange things when something comes over me. soon everything around me will be lavender/ fluffy & consuming. i will know not a moment of bitterness/ through all the wrist aching & tennis elbow from brushing/ i'll smile. no regrets/ "je ne regrette rien" i'll sing like edith piaf. when my friends want me to go see tina turner or pacheco/ i'll croon "sorry/ i have to brush my hair."

i'll find ambrosia, my hair'll grow pomegranates & soil/ rich as round the aswan/ i wake in my bed to bananas/ avocados/ collard greens/ the tramps' latest disco hit/ fresh croissant/ pouilly fuissé/ ishmael reed's essays/ charlotte carter's stories/ all stream from my hair.

& with the bricks that plop from where a 9-year-old's top braid wd be/ i will brush myself a house with running water & a bidet. i'll have a closet full of clean bed linen & the lil girl from the castro convertible commercial will come & open the bed repeatedly & stay on as a helper to brush my hair. lily is the only person i know whose every word leaves a purple haze on the tip of yr tongue. when this happens i says clouds are forming/ & i has to close the windows. violet rain is hard to remove from blue satin pillows

Tenement Lover: no palm trees/ in new york city

Jessica Hagedorn

Premiere: The Kitchen & The Basement Workshop, NYC, 1981
Publisher: TCG (in *Between Worlds: Contemporary Asian-American Plays*)
Setting: New York City and the Philippines

Tenement Lover is a full-length performance piece combining music, poetry, theater, slides, and recorded voice. In this monologue, a twenty-four-year-old Filipina woman sits munching banana chips out of a bag, totally transfixed by the television.

I like New York okay. I like my apartment okay. It's no house, but it's a nice place, *di ba?* We had a house when I was growing up in the Philippines . . . it was made of bamboo with a thatched roof, really I'm not kidding, and we had to walk a long way to take a bath. You should have seen the first place Tito and I had here in New York. Terrible *talaga*. Rats and cockroaches all over, even though I kept cleaning and cleaning. I went to sleep with a mop and broom right next to me, it was terrible but nothing helped. No one ever fixed anything that broke. The walls were falling, the ceiling was cracked. Am I in America? I kept asking my husband.

(Pause.)

I like New York okay. I like my new apartment okay. It's not a house, but it's a nice place. We had a house when I was growing up back home, but it was made of bamboo with a thatched roof, and we had to walk a long way to take a bath. . . . I'm so happy with my new apartment now I don't care if we're broke—I just stay home and watch TV, is okay, I don't care if I never go out. *I watch all the programs!*

(Pause.)

We didn't have a telvision in the Philippines.

(Pause.)

And my family was afraid when I left them to marry Tito. *What are you afraid of?* I asked them. *I'm going to America!*

(Pause.)

Tito was a marine . . . stationed at the base near where we lived.

(Pause.)

We didn't know what a Puerto Rican was—it was funny when my family met him. *Ano bu iyan?* MENUDO? But Tito's American, I told them—something close to being Spanish, not dark at all. *I'm dark.* But Tito doesn't mind, he calls me beautiful.

(Pause.)

Tito liked being in the marines. He says it's too hard in the outside world. But now with two kids, he can't go back in the marines—they keep telling him he's got too many dependents . . .

(Pause.)

I'm twenty-four years old, and I'm glad we're off welfare. You should have seen our first apartment. Rats, roaches, the walls falling in. Are we in America? I asked my husband.

(Pause.)

Once I worked as a clerk to help out with the family income. It made Tito so crazy! The only job he can get is as a security guard. We don't have a bank account because it isn't worth it—we keep taking out as soon as we put in.

(Pause.)

Tito hated me working, especially when he hadn't started his guard job and he had to stay home with the kids. "It's not right," he kept saying, "I don't feel like a man." I lost my job anyway, so it all worked out. I guess.

(Pause.)

Tito's a good man—he doesn't drink or get high. He doesn't look at other women. One time I got angry with him. Only once.

(Pause.)

We went to visit his friends in Brooklyn and I was feeling homesick. His friend's wife spoke Tagalog and asked me how come we never go dancing like they did. I got angry and asked Tito when we got home how come we never did that, dancing I mean—I love dancing, don't you? All Tito had to say was we better not see those people anymore because I was getting too jealous.

(Pause.)

They were his only friends.

(Pause.)

It's nice to have friends, but if they give you trouble I'd just as soon stay home . . .

(Pause.)

We have two television sets, one in color. Tito watches sports games, but I like talk shows. Actually, I'll watch anything. So do the kids—we watch TV all day and all night, sometimes.

(Pause.)

One of my real worries is that I'll never see my family back home again . . . and my parents will die and all this time will pass and I'll never have the money to go back . . . and this wavy black line, this black line that's been appearing on the bottom half of the screen of our color set . . . I can't call the repairman, we don't have any money. I just pretend the black line isn't there. Every day the black line gets worse, sometimes the pictures on the screen turn orange or pink, I think I'm going blind but no one else seems to notice . . . Look, I tell my husband, it's going *bad*. It's on the *blink* . . . What are we going to do?

(Pause.)

Is okay, Tito tells me. Go watch the little set. I can't—I hate black-and-white TV—I keep telling Tito he should know this about me, I've told him many times, the same thing over and over again . . .

(Pause.)

"Black-and-white's more realistic," he tells me, "you'll get used to it."

The Vietnamization of New Jersey
Christopher Durang

Premiere: Yale Repertory Theatre, New Haven, Connecticut, 1977
Publisher: Dramatists Play Service, Inc.
Setting: An American Home. Piscataway, New Jersey, 1967–1976

In this savage parody of 1950s family sitcoms (and David Rabe's influential Vietnam play "Sticks and Bones"), the mother is named Ozzie Ann, the father Harry, and the younger son Et. There's also a black maid named Hazel, played by a man. As the play begins, older son David is fighting in Vietnam, sending his family strange postcards in French. When David comes home, he is blind—and so is his Vietnamese wife, Liat. Or so it seems.

Throughout her first scenes Liat speaks in heavily accented pidgin English ("Allo. I go to American Aramy School. My teachuhs best fucking stick men in the whole Vietnamese bush.") But soon she lets slip an unaccented sentence about growing up in Schenectady. In fact, she is neither Vietnamese nor blind, and her original name was Maureen. When she was five, her family went to Thailand on vacation. Their plane crashed over Vietnam. Her parents were murdered, and she went to work in a child brothel, later becoming a go-go dancer by day and a terrorist by night. When she met blind and guilt-obsessed David, she decided to pose as a blind Vietnamese girl to get him to marry her and bring her back to America. Liat is obsessed with *The King and I*.

LIAT

I remember the day President Kennedy was killed. I was a go-go dancer in Vietnam at the time and I was killing Diem supporters in the evening. And I was go-going away when I heard the news Kennedy was shot, and I thought,

"Oh God, life is awful." I wish life were like *The King and I*. You know President Kennedy's favorite musical was *Camelot* and mine is *The King and I*. Well, I presumed *Camelot* must really be terrific, I mean he was the president and he went to Harvard and everything. But then I saw it. I mean, no wonder we got involved in Vietnam if that was his judgment. *Camelot* isn't very good at all, the book is very weak, and it's about this king whose wife commits adultery with Robert Goulet. I mean, do you think Jacqueline really did things like that? And they say *he* slept with Marilyn Monroe. I mean, no wonder things are a mess.

(*Cries.*)

I want to be in *The King and I*. I don't like this house any more. Nothing's worked out the way I wanted.

(*Cries.*)

Women of Manhattan
John Patrick Shanley

Premiere: Manhattan Theatre Club, NYC, 1986
Publisher: Dramatists Play Service, Inc.
Setting: Manhattan

Three women meet for a dinner celebrating their friendship. Rhonda Louise, the hostess, is "twenty-eight, hails from the Deep South, speaks and moves in a very deliberate way, and is slender and slow to react. Her frizzy dark brown hair frames a delicate, sensitive face. She is, by nature, always a trifle weary and a trifle solemn, or very weary and very solemn." Her two closest friends are Billie, a dramatic beauty, and Judy, a Yankee cynic.

Though it's a "girls' night," the three have decided to get decked out in their sexiest clothes. The topic inevitably turns to men. Rhonda Louise theorizes, "It's cause we're dressed for men. These clothes evolved outta a situation where observations were made about which kinda garments are effective to wear to attract the male of the species." Billie is married, Judy is chronically single, and Rhonda Louise has just kicked out her boyfriend, Jerry. Jerry's red sneakers are sitting in the middle of the floor, and Judy asks Rhonda Louise why she doesn't get rid of them. Rhonda Louise says, "I know what you think this is, but it's not. I don't keep the sneakers because I love him."

RHONDA

I guess my big mistake was I revealed myself to him. That's where I really went wrong. You know, that thing that most people can't do? That thing that's supposed to be like the hardest thing to get to with another person? It took me time, but I struggled and strove and succeeded at last in revealing my innermost, my most personal soul to him.

[BILLIE

And what is that?

RHONDA

Never you mind.

JUDY

And what did he do?

RHONDA

Nothing. Zip. Nothing.] He just sat there with a coke in his hand like he was watching television, waiting for the next thing. Like that was a nice stop on the way to WHAT I CAN'T IMAGINE! The whole thing with him was such a let-down. But why am I surprised? You know? I mean, here I was congratulating myself on being able to show myself, show my naked self to a man. But what's the achievement? I chose to show myself to a wall. Right? That's why I was able to do it. He was a wall and I was really alone, showing myself to nobody at all. How much courage does that take? Even when I got it together to throw him out, and I made this speech at him and got all pink in the face and noble as shit. He just said alright and left. What did I delude myself into thinking was going on between us

if that's how he could take it ending? "Alright. Just lemme
get my tools together, Rhonda Louise, and I'll get on to
the next thing." You know how in that one school a thought
you're the only thing real in the world, and everything else
is just a dream? All these people and things, the stars in
the sky, are just sparks and smoke from your own lonely
fire in a big, big night. I always thought what a lotta intellectual nonsense that was until Jerry. I mean, to tell you
the naked truth, I'm not even sure there was a Jerry. It
seems impossible to me that there was. Sometimes I think
I just got overheated, worked myself into a passion and fell
in love with that wall right there. It must've been! It
must've been that wall and me, crazy, loving it cause I
needed to love. And not a human man. I couldn't have
poured everything out to a really truly human man, and
him just stand there, and take it, and give nothing back.
It's not possible. But when I get too far gone in that direction of thinking—and alone here some nights I do—at
those times it does me good to look and see these sneakers
there sitting on the floor. His sneakers. He was here. It
happened.

WOMEN:
30s—40s

•

All She Cares About Is
the Yankees
John Ford Noonan

Premiere: American Kaleidoscope Inc., NYC
Publisher: Samuel French, Inc.
Setting: 299 W. 12th St., Apt. #15J, New York City

Maureen "Spanky" Oberfeld is a passionate Yankee fan and a severe agoraphobic. She lives in a studio apartment full of baseball dolls and "shelves and shelves of neatly arranged and carefully labeled notebooks: 'LETTERS TO MYSELF' . . . 'NOTEBOOK 13' . . . 'NOTEBOOK 17' . . . 'A DREAD A DAY' . . . 'GREAT SENTENCES,' etc." Spanky has not left her room in forty-three days, since her boyfriend Jeffrey turned her down. She lives on Chinese-food deliveries and communicates with the outside world by telephone and tape-recorded letters. Jeffrey has just telephoned Spanky and agreed to come see her the following day—on the condition that she fulfill her promise to make a tape for her father.

MAUREEN "SPANKY" OBERFELD
(Crosses to recorder, inserts clear tape,
presses PLAY button, attempts letter to
Father.)
Dear Dad: My window faces West across the Hudson. I know when I'm looking out, I face toward home and you. I'm looking now. Can you feel my eyes?

*(Suddenly singing chorus of Bob Dylan's
"Idiot Wind," repeating several times.
Laughing.)*

That's Bob Dylan. He was from right up the road in Hibbing. You never liked him much.

(Forced good cheer.)

Gee, Dad, how have you been? . . . I'm sorry I haven't written in over two months, but I've been so busy. I hardly get to bed and . . . and CLANG, CLANG, CLANG goes my alarm clock. Time to face another exciting New York day. For me everything's been so great, I don't know where to start . . . Where do I start? . . . I'm still as popular with the boys as I was back in Chisolm. Just listen!

*(SPANKY suddenly bangs on table to simulate
loud knocking.)*

Another one trying to knock down the door! All joking aside, I've got a great new job doing . . . actually they're still deciding exactly—

(Long silence.)

Dad, the reason I haven't written in over two-plus months is that I haven't been able to leave my room. You ask why? Well, one day I just couldn't get to the door. It's been forty-three days, Dad. I don't want you to worry. Fifty-six days is my limit. If I'm still stuck here after that long, I've got a real clear plan for what happens next.

*(Suddenly singing opening line of Buffy St.
Marie song, "Until It's Time for You to
Go.")*

"YOU'RE NOT A DREAM, YOU'RE NOT AN ANGEL, YOU'RE A MAN."

(Laughing, closing eyes.)

Now there's one you mostly liked . . . Every time I close my eyes and send my mind back to Chisolm, all I see is you rocking on the porch. Every June we'd pull it down

from the loft out in the barn and lug it up on the porch.
The winter would've made the squeak even worse so I'd
squeeze some "3-in-1" on all the joints. You'd try it first
and then I'd sit on your lap. I'd purr, "Dada, the squeak's
still there." You'd laugh and say back, "Gives us something
everyday to get our talking started." God, did we go on
and on. Remember when I was eleven what you told me
about sentences: ". . . that all the great sentences that still
hadn't been used were floating just above our heads and
that if we kept reaching up as hard as we could, we'd sooner
or later grab the one we needed." Dada, your little baby
still believes in sentences. Lots of times I half quote you
and pretend it's me.

(Laughing.)

You're the only one I can't be angry at. That's about the
one clear thing of the last forty-three days. Every day I get
more angry. Every day I add more names to the list. Dad,
I've got this list I spend most of my mornings on. It's called
THE OBERFELD REVENGE LIST. It's based on my carefully computed quotient of "Oberfeld Hate and Rage."
There are five columns I put the people in. Column One
is "worth murdering." Column Two is "worth maiming."
Three is worth causing a "crippling injury." Four is "worth
causing serious but temporary damage." Five is "worth
ruining their week." Many people move from column to
column according to how I feel from day to day. Mom's
never moved. She's always been "worth murdering." Right
now I'm angrier at her than when she was here. At least
once a day I want to rip off her arm and beat her head in
with it. So much for lists.

(Forced good cheer.)

Anyway, here's my plan at the end of fifty-six days. I'm
coming home to Chisolm. Dada, I'm heading West to be
with you. I don't know how I'll get that knob turned but I
will. Somehow I'll get down to the lobby and out the door.
Hail a cab out to JFK. In the air. Land in Minneapolis and

hop on that bus north. Once I get on that bus north, watch
out. You and I are going to spend hours and hours rocking
away and going over just about everything. I think that's
what you have to do sometimes: go all the way back to
where the trouble started and see where it was you veered
off. Dada, your baby started veering off the day I left you
and mom at the Minneapolis Airport. The person I was
faded pretty fast only not a lot came to take her place. New
York City's great if you've got a vicious reason for being
here . . . but if you're just sorta here looking for what it is
you might like to try, *WATCH OUT!!* I've got a real good
friend named Brian who makes all my dolls and he describes
my problem as follows . . .

("Doing" Brian's voice.)

"Kid, you're an 80-watt bulb and New York's a thousand-
watt socket. Every time you plug in, you blow out!" Dada,
that's all I am: 39 years of sorta looking for what it is I might
like to try. Was what I lacked already in my eyes when I
came out of mom? Or maybe was it something like a fog
that came over me at 12 or 15? Once I'm settled a few days
into Chisolm, it's something we can go over! I'd really like
to know when you started to worry? Was I ever tested for
anything and found lacking? Was there ever some game
even at three or four that I truly loved to play? Would you
call me a child with a clear sense of life? A look of purpose?
Did I ever possess any deep drives? If so, when did they
leave me? As a baby was I fun to play with? Did I smile a
lot? Did I already . . . Was I even then . . . Were . . .

(Can't go on, takes breath, does go on.)

Going back even farther, was I a baby you and mom
wanted? Planned for? Hugged each other over late into the
night? Did you ever once make a list of a few things you
dreamed I might become? How many times did you wish
I never was? How often did I pull crap that made you want
to kill me? Were you ever truly proud of anything I did?
When I led the girls' basketball team to the county title,

were you ecstatic? Embarrassed? Jealous? All three? Did you enjoy watching me move around the court? To your eye was my jumpshot a thing of rare beauty? What about my ass? Did my buns make you wonder? Did my tits make you gasp? Was it you or mom who went with me to confront Coach Johnson because I always refused a bra under my uniform? I kept explaining I couldn't get full extension on my jumper wearing one but Johnson kept insisting I was out to tease guys? Tease guys?!! All I had on my mind was going to the hoop. I remember I was crying after. Did you hug me? Did you want to and couldn't? I know these are the kind of questions you hate to hear, but when you're stuck like I am, it's often . . . sometimes I . . . I have another close friend named Jeffrey who says I'm so mad at you I don't even know it. He says the sentence is so scarey I can't even put it in the air . . . "DADDY, I AM VERY . . . AT YOU!" He says your silence has stuffed me up so bad I have twenty years of vomit to get up. He says . . . he says . . .

(Can't go on. Takes breath, does go on.)

One thing I'd like you to do the minute you get this letter is write back back real quick and tell me how Alicia Carmody's doing. I got a letter from her last Christmas about moving back to Chisolm and how she loved finding everything so much the same. She said what she had run away from was what she really wanted all along . . . Anyway, she mentioned in her last paragraph about seeing you out back of the Hubert Humphrey Junior High doing jumps with Rusty. Dada, can Rusty still jump like he used to? Do you still clean his stall all by yourself? Does riding bring you a peace that is like nothing else? Does living in Chisolm make you feel like you have a place where you belong? I sometimes think I've never had a place in my life where I truly belong and feel at home. Talking to you like this and I'm already half way there . . . I'm watching you read this sitting on the john. Remember how the mail used to come

and how you'd go read it on the john, locking the door
behind. Are you crying? Do I hear some sobs? . . . To say
goodbye I'll sing you your favorite.

> (SPANKY *sings a couple of lines from "Tea*
> *for Two." Can't remember next lines of*
> *verse. Repeats opening two but again no*
> *more.*)

Love, Dada, . . . from your only child and favorite daughter.

> (SPANKY *presses STOP button, removes*
> *tape, lays it gently on table. Silence.*)

Aunt Dan and Lemon
Wallace Shawn

Premiere: New York Shakespeare Festival, NYC, 1985
Publisher: Dramatists Play Service, Inc.
Setting: Lemon's London apartment and various flashbacks

Lemon is an invalid who never goes out and subsists
on vegetable juices, bread, and memories. The most important person in her life was her parents' best friend, an
iconoclastic young American who taught at Oxford and
called herself Dan. "Aunt" Dan used to tell young Lemon
bedtime stories about her bohemian friends, her sex life,
and her bizarre political views (she worships Henry Kis-
singer). She has just gone straight from a story about a
married lover with whom she spent three consecutive days
in bed to the following self-revelation.

AUNT DAN
Now Lemon, I have to tell you something very important
about myself. And there aren't many things I'm sure of
about myself, but this is something I can honestly say with
absolute confidence, and it's something that I think is very

important. It is that I *never*—no matter how annoyed or angry I may be—I *never, ever shout at a waiter*. And as a matter of fact, I never shout at a porter or a clerk in a bank or anybody else who is in a weaker position in society than me. Now this is very, very important. I will never even use a *tone of voice* with a person like that which I wouldn't use with you or your father or anyone else. You see, there are a lot of people today who will simply *shout* if they're angry at a waiter, but if they happen to be angry at some powerful person like their boss or a government official, well then they'll *very respectfully disagree*. Now to me that's a terrible thing, a horrible thing. First of all, because I think it's cowardly. But mainly because it shows that these people don't recognize the value and importance of all those different jobs in society! They think a waiter is less *important* than a president. They look down on waiters! They don't admire what they do! They don't even notice whether someone is a good waiter or a bad waiter! They act as if we could sort of all afford to have no respect for waiters now, or secretaries, or maids, or building superintendents, because somehow we've reached a point where we can really just *do without* these people. Well, maybe there's some kind of a fantasy in these people's minds that we're already living in some society of the future in which these incredible robots are going to be doing all the work, and every actual citizen will be some kind of concert pianist or a sculptor or a president or something. But I mean, where are all these robots, actually? Have you ever seen one? Have they even been invented? Maybe they *will* be. But they're not here *now*. The way things are *now*, everybody just can't *be* a president. I mean—I mean, if there's no one around to cook the president's lunch, he's going to have to cook it himself. Do you know what I'm saying? But if no one has put any food in his kitchen, he's going to have to go out and buy it himself. And if no one is waiting in the shop to sell it, he's going to have to go out into the countryside and *grow* it himself, and, you know, that's going to be a full-

time job. I mean, he's going to have to resign as president
in order to grow that food. It's as simple as that. If every
shop clerk or maid or farmer were to quit their job today
and try to be a painter or a nuclear physicist, then within
about two weeks *everyone* in society, even people who used
to *be* painters or nuclear physicists, would be out in the
woods foraging for berries and roots. Society would completely break down. Because regular work is not one tiny
fraction less necessary today than it ever was. And yet we're
in this crazy situation that people have gotten it into their
heads that regular work is somehow unimportant—it's
somehow worth nothing. So now almost everyone who isn't
at *least* a Minister of Foreign Affairs feels that there's something wrong with what they do—they feel ashamed of it.
Not only do they feel that what they do has no value—they
feel actually *humiliated* to be doing it, as if each one of
them had been singled out for some kind of unfair, de-
grading punishment. Each one feels, I shouldn't be a la-
borer, I shouldn't be a clerk, I shouldn't be a minor official!
I'm better than that! And the next thing is, they're saying,
"Well, I'll show them all—I won't work, I'll do nothing,
or I'll do *almost* nothing, and I'll do it badly." So what's
going to happen? We're going to start seeing these embittered typists typing up their documents incorrectly—and
then passing them on to these embittered contractors, who
will misinterpret them to these huge armies of embittered
carpenters and embittered mechanics, and a year later or
two years later, we're going to start seeing these ten-story
buildings in every city collapsing to the ground, because
each one of them is missing some crucial screw in some
crucial girder. Buildings will collapse. Planes will come
crashing out of the sky. Babies will be poisoned by bad
baby food. How can it happen any other way?

Bad Habits
Terrence McNally

Premiere: Astor Place Theatre, NYC, 1974
Publisher: Dramatists Play Service, Inc.
Setting: Two institutions, Ravenswood and Dunelawn

Harry Scupp is a patient at an unconventional mental hospital called Ravenswood. His attractive wife, Dolly, grudgingly comes for a visit. Before seeing her husband, she speaks to his doctor, Jason Pepper, M.D. Dr. Pepper is a pop-psychology pundit who uses a wheelchair and has a porous platinum plate in his skull. He tells Dolly, "Your absence has made Harry's rehabilitation somewhat more difficult, you understand. I prefer to treat couples who are having difficulties *as* couples." Dolly responds that there's nothing wrong with *her*. Dr. Pepper points out that she and her husband have been trying to kill each other since Labor Day Weekend, 1963. (Dolly's foot is still in a cast from their last run-in.) She defends herself.

DOLLY

Our wedding night was terrific. From then on, it's been down hill all the way. His hobby is tropical fish. I hate tropical fish, Doctor.

[DR. PEPPER

You hate tropical fish?

DOLLY]

Not all tropical fish. Harry's tropical fish. There's something about them. Maybe it's the fact he talks to them. Or the names he gives them. Eric, Tony, Pinky. There's one round, mean-looking one he calls Dolly. When they die he buries them in the backyard. We're the only house in Larchmont with a tropical fish cemetery in the backyard. I know this sounds crazy, Doctor, but I hate those fish. I resent them in my living room and I resent them under my lawn. I'm a mature, sensible, and, I think, rather intelligent woman and I hate those fish. How do you hate a tropical fish?

(She stands.)

You know something else I hate? Stereo equipment. Harry's got woofers, weefers, tweeters, baffles, pre-amps. He puts gloves on when he plays those records. White gloves like your friend.

(She indicates Otto.)

Don't get me started, Doctor. There's so many things about Harry I hate. I hate his black Volvo station wagon with the snow tires on in August. He worries about early winters. He worries about everything. We're the only people in Larchmont with drought insurance.

(She is pacing.)

I know it's none of my business, but I hate the way he dresses. I hate his big, baggy boxer shorts. The only shoes he'll wear are those big clumpy cordovans. Even on the beach. But my favorite outfit is his "Genius At Work" barbecue apron he wears over the pink Bermuda shorts and black, knee-high Supphose. Oh, I'm married to a snappy dresser, Doctor! And try taking a trip with him. He reads road signs. Every road sign. Out loud. "Soft shoulders, Dolly." "Slippery when wet, Dolly." "Deer crossing, Dolly." "Kiwanis Club meeting at noon, Wednesday, Dolly." Who gives a good goddamn? He's not even a member of the Kiwanis Club! Who'd want him? A man who puts on an apron after a bridge party and vacuums up isn't exactly a load of laughs. Neither is a man who takes you to Arizona for your anniversary. You know what's in Arizona? The London Bridge! Don't get me wrong, Doctor. I love my husband. I just can't stand him.

Boy on the Straight-Back Chair
Ronald Tavel

Premiere: American Place Theatre, NYC, 1969
Publisher: Performing Arts Journal Publications (in *Wordplays*)
Setting: A small town in the Utah desert

A guitar-playing balladeer and two middle-aged women named Stella and Della narrate this tale of a "nice quiet town" whose misfit native son, Toby Short, turns into a serial killer. Stella's daughter Mary, a thrill-seeking high-school girl with a hard facade and a beehive hairdo, is Toby's first victim. Toby invites her to "party" and bashes her skull with a rock while his sidekick holds her immobile. This monologue follows the murder.

STELLA
Quiet town. Real quiet town. Been real quiet since Mary run away . . .
> (ROMEO *drags the body behind* TOBY'S *chair and we can hear the evil sound of shoveling.*)

Sometimes, now and again, I think of my little girl, my little girl who run away . . . wonder where she is, Mary, where are you, little girl, late at night, middle of the night. Mary, Mary?—Is that you? Is that you, Mary? Keep thinkin' I hear Mary comin' up the front steps, keep thinkin' keep thinkin' . . . guess I jist think too much these days, think too much at night, but, ah, the night is lonely since my little girl run away. I had such plans for her. You shoulda seen the graduation dress I had picked out for my little girl, pretty thing it was, with flower . . . with a bright little flower emblem, you know the kind, a flower paisley design, a green center with a thin red border running around in a . . . in a . . . yes . . . You know the kind . . . had nice buttons, simple buttons, sham pearl they was I think . . . in a . . . I used to love pearl when I was a kid . . . always dreamt of having a graduation dress with pearl buttons when I was a kid . . . Course, we couldn't afford real pearl buttons for Mary, wouldn't have been practical anyhow, you know how kids are, always pullin' a button, gettin' it caught in somethin' and then before ya know it, pop, and it's lost, gone, gone forever, lost, jist like that . . . nothin' easier, nothin' easier than losin' a button on a dress, pearl button or what have ya . . . pearl buttons get lost easy as plain ones, sure they do, ask anyone, anyone knows that, why any fool knows that . . . Quiet town, real quiet around here. Don't hear a sound. Not a sound. Nary a sound. Hard to hear. Hard to hear things around here, hard to hear a sound. Course, I'd be complainin' if there *was* noise, somebody'd be complainin' if there was noise, still, ya know, it's not bad to hear a, a little sound once and again, now and then, keeps, gets lonely . . . sorta lonely without even a little, little . . . little? . . . small? . . . my baby . . . hmmmmmmmmm . . . Mary? That you, Mary?

Cold Air
Virgilio Piñera

Translated and adapted by Maria Irene Fornes

Premiere: INTAR Hispanic American Theatre, NYC, 1985
Publisher: TCG Plays in Process/Broadway Play Publishing
Setting: The Romaguera family home in Havana, Cuba, 1940–
1954

Angel and Ana Romaguera have four adult children. Enrique is a civil servant who resents his parents' poverty and begrudges them money, Luis lives in New York, and Oscar is a poet who refuses to work at anything but his writing. The burden of keeping the family alive falls on the middle child and only daughter, Luz Marina. Luz Marina works as a seamstress, making clothes for more fortunate neighbors on a sewing machine in the living room. She is obsessed with money and what it could buy if she had any. A strident, melodramatic woman, Luz Marina fights bitterly with Enrique but dotes on Oscar, saving pesos to help him publish a book of his poems. She is a fatalist and often talks about killing herself to end her life's misery.

When the play begins, Luz Marina is thirty years old and thinks of herself as an old maid. By act three, she is forty-four, still dirt-poor and deeply enmeshed with her family, but married. Oscar, who's been away, says to his sister, "He seems like a nice man. How did you trap him?" She replies, "Out of desperation."

Luz Marina

One day . . . as usual . . . I was desperate, very nervous . . . unpaid bills . . . worries. Papa came in to tell us that he had met Don Benigno in the street, that he hadn't seen him for a long time and that he had invited him for dinner. So Mama started to worry about how to borrow twenty cents so we could buy eggs to feed Don Benigno because we didn't have anything to put on the table. I went crazy and I started screaming out the window.—I really went crazy. And then I ran out the door screaming "I can't take it anymore. I can't take it anymore. I'm going to go to bed with the first man I see. I'm going to bed with the first man I see." I got on a bus and I sat in the back and I started to cry and the conductor said "Did your daddy die, honey?" and he sat next to me. And that was that. We fell in love.

Fen

Caryl Churchill

Premiere: Joint Stock Theatre Group, Essex, England, 1983
Publisher: Methuen
Setting: Farming village in the Fens of England

The Fens are an agricultural region boasting "the most expensive earth in England." Once under water like Holland, they were drained in the 1600s to provide an ideal, black-earth farmland. Today, the farms are owned by international conglomerates, and the villagers who work them are as poor as the land is rich. In a series of pungent, brief scenes, *Fen* explores the working-class life of one such village.

Nell is forty, an authority-baiting fieldworker who lives by herself. Her unmarried status and habit of talking to herself has led local children to dub her a witch and a "morphrodite . . . A man and a woman both at once." Here she is sorting onions with co-workers Shirley, Alice, and Angela. The other women are bickering, and Nell, who is known for her stories, tells this one about her grandfather.

NELL

He used to swear this really happened. When he was ten his mother died in childbirth, and his father soon got a woman in he said was a housekeeper, but she slept with him from the first night. My grandfather hated her and she hated him, and she'd send him to bed without any tea, and his father always took her side. So after a few months of this, early one morning when his father had gone to work but she wasn't up yet, he took some bread and some cold tea and he run off. He walked all day and it got real dark and he was frit as hell. There was no houses on the road, just an old green drove sometimes going off towards the coast, so he thought he'd have to sleep by the road. Then he sees a little light shining so he set off down the drove that led to it and he comes to an old stone house. So he knocks on the door and the woman comes, and she'd a candlestick in one hand and a big old copper stick in the other. But when she sees it's only a boy she says come in and she makes him sit by the fire and gives him a bowl of hot milk with some fat bacon in it and a hunk of brown bread. Then she says, "Me and my husband are going out but you can sleep by the fire. But you must stay here in the kitchen," she says, "whatever you do, you mustn't go through that door," and she points to the door at the back of the kitchen. Then her husband came and said the pony trap was ready and he didn't look too pleased to see the boy but he didn't say nothing and off they went for their night out. So he sat by the fire and sat by the fire, and he thought I'll just take a look through that door. So he turned the handle but it was locked. And he saw a key lay on the dresser and he tried it and slowly opened the door, and then he wished he hadn't. There was a candle in the window which was the light he'd seen, and a long table, and on the table was a coffin with the lid off, and inside the coffin there was a body. And he was just going to shut the door and hurry back by the fire when the body in the coffin sat up and opened its eyes, and said, "Who are you, boy?" Oh he were petrified. But the body said, "Don't be afraid. I'm not dead." He said, "Where have they gone?" meaning the woman and the husband. When he heard they were out he got out of the coffin and come in the kitchen and made some cocoa. Then he told my grandfather his missus had been having an affair with the chap from the next small-holding, and she was trying to get rid of him by putting rat poison in his food, and he'd fed it to some pigeons and they'd died. So what he'd done, he'd pretended to die, and she'd told the doctor he'd had a heart attack, and he'd been put in the coffin. And before that he'd sold the farm without telling the wife and had the money safe in the bank under another name. So he give my grandfather a screwdriver and said when the couple came home and screwed down the coffin, after they was in bed he was to unscrew it again.

So he went back by the fire and pretended to be asleep, and he heard them screw up the coffin and laughing about how they'd got the old man's farm and kissing, and later he got the old fellow out and he were real glad because he said he wanted a pee so bad he could almost taste it. Then he got a large two tined pitchfork and a pickaxe handle and he said, "Come on, it's time to go." My grandfather thought they were going to leave, but the old fellow crept upstairs, and gave the boy the candle and the pickaxe handle to carry, and he crept up and opened the door of the bedroom. There was the couple lying close together, completely naked and fast asleep. Then suddenly he raised the pitchfork and brung it down as hard as he could directly over their bare stomachs, so they were sort of stitched together. They screamed and screamed and he grabbed the pickaxe handle off of my grandfather and clubbed them on their heads till they lay still. Then he gets the man and takes him downstairs and puts him in the coffin and screws it up. He says, "They'll bury him tomorrow and think it's me, and when they find her dead they'll know she was out drinking with her fellow and they'll think he killed her and done a bunk, so the police won't be looking for me," he said, "they'll be looking for him. And I'm going to start a new life in London or Australia, and if you talk about it I'll find you and slit your throat from ear to ear." And he never did till he was so old he knew the old man must be dead, and even then he waited a good few years more, and I was the first person he ever told. The old fellow gave my grandfather a gold sovereign and told him to walk west and look for a job on a farm over that way, so he walked five days and slept five nights in barns, and got a job on a farm near Doncaster.

Frankie and Johnny in the Clair de Lune

Terrence McNally

Premiere: Manhattan Theatre Club, NYC, 1987
Publisher: Dramatists Play Service, Inc.
Setting: A walk-up tenement apartment in New York's West 50s

Frankie, a seasoned New York waitress, has brought home Johnny, the new short-order cook at the restaurant where she works. They have just had sensational sex, and Johnny is scaring the hell out of her by declaring his no-holds-barred romantic intentions. The playwright describes Frankie as follows: "Striking but not conventional good looks. She has a sense of humor and a fairly tough exterior. She is also frightened and can be very hard to reach."

Eventually, Johnny wears down her resistance and they begin to make love again. Unfortunately, he has what he says is his first bout with impotence. Frankie seems almost relieved, and she asks him to make her a Western omelet. But Johnny is too upset to cook. He says, "It's male menopause. I've been dreading this." Frankie replies, "'You know what I think it was? The moonlight. You were standing in it. It was bathing your body."

NOTE: The playwright requests that when performing this as a monologue, the actress should say Johnny's line, "It's supposed to make them romantic." Johnny's next line, "What do you mean, 'remember'?" should be omitted.

FRANKIE

I've always been very suspicious of what moonlight does to people.

JOHNNY

It's supposed to make them romantic.

FRANKIE

Or turn you into a werewolf. That's what I was raised on. My grandmother was always coming into my bedroom to make sure the blinds were down. She was convinced sleep-

ing in the moonlight would turn you into the wolfman. I
thought if I slept in the moonlight I'd wake up a beautiful
fairy princess, so I kept falling asleep with the blinds open
and she kept coming in and closing them. She always denied
it was her. "Wasn't me, precious. Must have been your
Guardian Angel." Remember them?

[JOHNNY
What do you mean, "remember"?
FRANKIE]

One night I decided to stay awake and catch her in the act.
It seemed like forever. When you're that age, you don't
have anything to stay awake *about*. So you're failing ge-
ography, so what? Finally my grandmother came into the
room. She had to lean across my bed to close the blinds.
Her bosom was so close to my face. She smelled so nice.
I pretended I was still sleeping and took the deepest breath
of her I could. In that one moment, I think I knew what
it was like to be loved. Really loved. I was so safe, so
protected! That's better than being pretty. I'll never forget
it. The next thing I knew it was morning and I still didn't
look like Audrey Hepburn. Now when I lie in bed with the
blinds up and the moonlight spilling in, I'm not thinking I
want to be somebody else. I just want my Nana back.

A Girl's Guide to Chaos
Cynthia Heimel

Premiere: American Place Theatre, NYC, 1986
Publisher: Simon & Schuster
Setting: Downtown New York

A *Girl's Guide to Chaos* follows three female friends
through "the great boyfriend crunch" of New York in the
eighties. Cynthia has been dating an outrageously handsome young New Zealander known as "The Kiwi." She

caught him two-timing and responded like any sane woman by throwing his things out the window and climbing into bed with an old flannel nightgown and Oreos. Her friends Rita and Cleo decide that Cynthia's mourning has gone on long enough—as Rita says, "There is a palpable haze of self-pity enveloping you. I can barely make you out."— and come over to shake things up. Unfortunately, Cleo has just started dating Cynthia's ex-boyfriend Jake, and, in a masterpiece of bad timing, Cynthia catches them making out in her kitchen. She throws water in both of their faces, feels better, and agrees to go dancing with Rita. Cynthia's friends take off, and she contemplates her future.

CYNTHIA

The realization hits me heavily, like a .44 Magnum smashing into my skull. My heart starts beating with a quick dread and my blood freezes in my veins. My stomach does backflips. The ordeal I am about to face is one of the most chilling, grisly, and macabre experiences known to woman.

Dating. I will have to start dating again.

Please, God, no, don't make me do it! I'll be good from now on, I promise! I'll stop feeding the dog hashish! I'll be kind, thoughtful, sober, industrious, anything. But please, God, not the ultimate torture of dating!

That's why I stayed with him so long, probably. I couldn't stand going through it all again. Sure, he might be a trifle wild and intractable, I kept telling myself, but at least I know I'll get laid tonight, and tomorrow night. At least someone will go to the movies with me and not try to hold my hand.

Hand-holding. The WORST thing about dating. The fellow, or maybe even I, will decide that holding hands is a sweet, simple way to start. Hah! It's the most nerve-wracking experience of life! Once I start holding hands, I'm afraid to stop. If I pull my hand away, will he think I'm being cold, or moody? Should I squeeze his hand and kind of wiggle my fingers around suggestively? Or is that too forward? What if we're holding hands in the movies and I have to scratch my nose? If I let his hand go, then scratch the offending nose, and then not grab his hand again immediately will he think I'm rejecting him? Will he be relieved? What if my hand is clammy? A clammy hand is more offensive than bad breath or right-wing politics! A clammy hand means you are a lousy lay! Everybody knows that!

And what, dear spiteful God, will I wear? I'll need new dresses, new jewelry, new sweaters, trousers, underwear. And shoes! Shoes tell everything, shoes have to be perfect! Men like high heels, right? I can't walk in high heels. Well, I can try. For a really important date, I can just see myself spending $250 on a pair of drop-dead heels. This time will be different, I'll tell myself, this time I will be able to walk. But after an hour the ball of my foot will cramp up, I know it, and I'll hobble. "Is anything wrong?" he'll ask me solicitously, "you're limping." And I won't know where to look. I won't be able to say, "These fucking shoes are crippling me and if I don't take them off this minute I'll be maimed for life!" Because then he'll know I just bought them, that I bought them to go out on a date with him. And that will make him feel weird and pressured to know that this date was a big deal for me and he'll realize that I'm not as popular and sophisticated as he thought I was if I had to buy a special pair of shoes that I can't even walk in for chrissakes just for a date with *him*. So I have to explain the limping in such a way that it won't have to do with shoes. An old war wound?

What if my hair refuses to behave? What if it's all recalcitrant and cranky and goes all limp and flat on one side and then sort of bends at a right angle over one ear? I mean, sometimes I apply precisely the right amount of mousse and hang upside down when I blow-dry it and yet something still goes drastically wrong and I end up looking like Margaret Thatcher. Sometimes the suspense of what I will look like is so terrible that I have to take a Valium.

I have been known to apply four shades of lipstick, one on top of the other, in a pathetic attempt to achieve a certain I'm - not - actually - wearing - lipstick - I - just - naturally - have-pink-moist-luscious-lips effect. I have been known to put green eye-pencil below my lower lashes, look in the mirror, realize that I look like a gangrenous raccoon, quickly remove it, look in the mirror, realize that I'd rather look like a gangrenous raccoon than an anemic buffalo, and reapply the stuff. I have been known to start trying on outfits in an entirely tidy room and somehow when I am finished every single item of clothing I own is off the rack and on the floor and then when the phone rings there is no way on earth I can find it. I can't even find my *bed*. God, I hate dating.

And when he rings my doorbell and my stockings are still around my ankles because my garter belt is missing but with mad, deep, quick thought I finally remember it's in my black satin purse (don't ask) and I get it on and get the stockings up and answer the door smiling casually what precisely do I say?

WHAT WILL I TALK ABOUT ON A DATE? Not one thing that's on my mind will be a suitable topic of conversation. "Do you think we'll sleep together tonight?" "Are you one of those guys who can't make a commitment? Or can only make a commitment to a woman with really smooth, finely muscled thighs?" "Is my deodorant working?" "What kind of relationship did you have with your mother?" "How do you think we're getting along so far?" "Do you like me?" "How much do you like me?" "Are you sure you really like me?" "Dated any junkies?" "Any problems with impotence?" "You're not going out with me because you feel sorry for me, are you?"

No, we'll talk about movies. What we've seen recently. What if he tells me that he finally got around to seeing *Cocoon* and it turned out to be one of the greatest experiences of his life? Will I pretend to agree? I bet I will. I bet something slimy inside myself will cause me to nod my head encouragingly and say, "Yes, wasn't it lovely?" And then I'll hate myself because I've turned our date into a tissue of lies. I'll become distracted thinking about what a hypocrite I really am and my eyes will glaze over and I'll nod absently when he tries to draw me out and then he'll get all paranoid, thinking I hate him because he liked *Cocoon*. He'll be right.

But what if it turns out that his favorite movie is *His Girl Friday*, with *Slap Shot* a close second? Then I could fall in love. Then I'll really be terrified.

Glass Stirring
Eric Lane

Premiere: Orange Thoughts Theater Company, NYC, 1990
Publisher: Orange Thoughts
Setting: Small-town America, World War II

Glass Stirring is the story of an American family that loses its son in World War II. The play is divided into four monologues, with each member of the family speaking. The family consists of Agnes, the daughter who works in a dance hall; Johnny, the son who has died; Daddy, their father; and Jean, their mother in her mid- to late forties. Jean sits on a rocker with a crocheted blanket over her lap and legs. She holds a Bible.

JEAN

The Lord is my Shepherd; I shall not want.

I miss Johnny.

Church had a Bake Sale Sunday to raise money for a memorial they want to build, for all the boys. Everybody's been saving what they can but with the rations, cakes don't taste the same—except Mrs. Harris. Her Sister send her her canning points from the City, so her pies are sweet as before the War. One thing about a Bake Sale now, it all goes.

Mrs. Thompson, she made that apple pan dowdy she does. Her boy Jimmy was there wearing Johnny's coat. I gave it to him. I didn't think I was favoring him, I just knew they were the same size. Looked real good in it, too. I asked the Preacher, he said they'd give away the rest to boys in need. I still don't know what we're gonna do with Johnny's room. I go in there and it's like I feel him, in the walls, the headboard of that bed.

Preacher's talking Armageddon. I must've heard that passage a hundred times, then one day it just makes sense.

War's going on longer than anybody expected. Sunday night we had another air-raid drill. Whole house sealed tight, that blue army blanket over the window so no lights coming out. So the Japanese won't be able to tell us from the woods.

Agnes, she's trying to get us to come down to the dance hall. Daddy, he won't go. "Momma," he tells me. "You want to go you go alone." We went that one time—he just sat there looking out. Agnes and me, we danced. She's real good, too. Knows how to lead and everything. All those songs they're playing about you leaving me and dreaming the rest. Daddy thought it was loud, but not if you're dancing. I know Johnny liked to dance. I still don't know what we're gonna do with that room.

Preacher's giving out the clothes and the books, but I still feel him. I even knew when he died the moment it happened. Preacher's up there reading about Lot and his wife leaving the burning city. And just when he gets to the part where she turns to look back—everything stops. I see Jesus behind him on the cross looking down and it's like he's looking right at me and then he lights up—Jesus. None of the apostles or Mary—just Jesus. The light through the glass—pieces of red, blue, the brown in his beard, all lit. And looking down at me. I hear an airplane over and I know the Lord's taken my boy.

Nobody else sees. And I don't say nothing. I know if I

do they'll tell me it was just a cloud passing by or a shadow from the plane but I know it was Johnny—

Next day the telegram came.

We buried him out in the family plot. Agnes, she planted tulips. Goes every Sunday after church with me and Daddy to see if they come up yet.

Sometimes I feel like that house during air raid, all boarded up and no light showing through.

The Lord giveth; and the Lord taketh away. I know he told Lot's wife not to look back, but maybe she just couldn't see nothing ahead.

The Heidi Chronicles
Wendy Wasserstein

Premiere: Seattle Repertory Theatre, Seattle, Washington, 1988
Publisher: Harcourt Brace Jovanovich, Inc.
Setting: Multiple locations, New York and other cities, 1965–1989

Heidi Holland is an art history professor who specializes in the work of pre–twentieth century women painters. She came of age in the sixties, and *The Heidi Chronicles* details her progress from a starchy 1965 high school dance through a Eugene McCarthy fund-raiser, a women's consciousness raising rap group, a "Women in Art!" picket line outside the Chicago Art Institute, and into the Me-Decade eighties.

There are two principal men in Heidi's life. Peter Patrone, a gay pediatrician, is her dearest friend and soul mate. And against her better judgment, Heidi is romantically obsessed with Scoop Rosenbaum, the self-involved, outrageously confident editor of *Boomer* magazine. In this scene, Heidi is the featured guest speaker at an alumnae luncheon for the private girls' school she attended. It is 1986.

HEIDI

Hello. Hello. I graduated from Miss Crain's in 1965, and I look back on my education in Chicago very fondly. One of the far-reaching habits I developed at Miss Crain's was waiting until the desperation point to complete, or rather, start my homework. Keeping that noble academic tradition alive, I appear before you today with no formal speech. I have no outline, no pink notecards, no hieroglyphics scribbled on my palm. Nothing.

Well, you might be thinking, this is a women's meeting, so let's give her the benefit of the doubt. After teaching at Columbia yesterday, Miss Holland probably attended a low-impact aerobics class *with* weights, picked up her children from school, brought the older one to drawing with computers at the Metropolitan, and the younger one to swimming for gifted children. On returning home, she immediately prepared grilled mesquite free-range chicken with balsamic vinegar and sun-dried tomatoes, advised her investment banker/well-rounded husband on the future finances for the City Ballet, put the children to bed, recited their favorite Greek myths and sex education legends, dashed into the library to call the 22-year-old squash player who is passionately in love with her to say that they can only be friends, finished writing ten pages of a new book, brought the remains of the mesquite free-range dinner to a church that feeds the homeless, massaged her husband's feet, and relieved any fears that he "might" be getting old by "doing it" in the kitchen, read forty pages of the *Inferno* in Italian, took a deep breath, and put out the light. So after all this, we forgive Miss Holland for not preparing a speech today. She's exemplary and exhausted.

Thank you, but you forgive too easily. And I respect my fellow alumnae enough to know that I should attempt to tell you the truth. Oh, hurry up, Heidi. Okay. Why don't I have a speech for the "Women—Where Are We Going?" luncheon? Well, actually, yesterday I did teach at Columbia. We discussed Alexander Pope and his theory of the picturesque. And afterwards I did attend an exercise class. I walked into the locker room, to my favorite corner, where I can pull on my basic black leotard in peace. Two ladies, younger than me, in pressed blue jeans, were heatedly debating the reading program at Marymount Nursery School, and a woman my mother's age was going on and on about her son at Harvard Law School and his wife, a Brazilian hairdresser, who was by no stretch of the imagination good enough for him. They were joined by Mrs. Green, who has perfect red nails, and confessed to anyone who would listen the hardship of throwing her dinner party on the same night as a benefit at the Met. And in the middle of them was a naked gray-haired woman extolling the virtues of brown rice and women's fiction.

And then two twenty-seven-year-old hotshots came in. How do I know they were hotshots? They were both draped in purple and green leather. And as soon as they entered the locker room they pulled out their alligator datebooks and began to madly call the office. They seemed to have everything under control. They even brought their own heavier weights.

Now Jeanette, the performance artist/dancer/actress/ aerobics teacher comes in and completes the locker room. I like Jeanette. I've never talked to her, but I like her. I feel her parents are psychiatrists in the Midwest. Maybe Cedar Rapids.

Jeanette takes off her blue jeans and rolls her tights up her legs. I notice the hotshots checking out Jeanette's muscle tone while they are lacing up their Zeus low-impact sneakers, and Mrs. Green stops talking about her dinner party to ask, where did they find them? Everywhere she has looked on Madison Avenue is out. And the lady with the son at Harvard joins in and says she saw Zeus sneakers at Lord and Taylor and were they any good. Her daughter-in-law likes them, but she can't be trusted. The mothers with the pressed blue jeans leap to her rescue. Yes, they can assure her, despite the daughter-in-law, unequivocally, absolutely, no doubt about it, Zeus sneakers are the best.

It was at this point that I decided I would slip out and take my place in the back row of the class.

I picked up my overstuffed bag. But as I was just between Mrs. Green's raccoon coat and a purple leather bomber jacket, I tripped on one of the hotshot's God-damned five-pound professional weights, and out of my bag flew a week's worth of change, raspberry gum wrappers, and *Alexander Pope on the Picturesque* right on the gray-haired fiction woman's foot.

I began giggling. "Oh." "That's okay." "Excuse me." "I'm sorry." "I'm sorry I don't wear leather pants." "I'm sorry I don't eat brown rice." "I'm sorry I don't want to stand naked and discuss Zeus sneakers." "I'm sorry I don't want you to find out I'm worthless. And superior."

(Pause.)

I'm embarrassed, no humiliated in front of every woman in that room. I'm envying women I don't even know. I'm envying women I don't even like. I'm sure the woman with the son at Harvard is miserable to her daughter-in-law. I'm sure the gray-haired fiction woman is having a bisexual relationship with a female dock worker and driving her husband crazy. I'm sure the hotshots have screwed a lot of 35-year-old women, my classmates even, out of jobs, raises and husbands. And I'm sure the mothers in the pressed blue jeans think women like me chose the wrong road. "A pity they made such a mistake, that empty generation." Well, I really don't want to be feeling this way about all of them. And I certainly don't want to be feeling this way about "Women—Where Are We Going?"

I hear whispers. I hear chairs moving from side to side. Yes, I see. I have one minute left.

The women start filing out of the locker room. Jeanette ties her hair in a ponytail and winks at me. "See you in class, Heidi. Don't forget to take a mat this time."

And I look at her pink and kind face. "I'm sorry, Jeanette, I think I'm too sad to go to class."

"Excuse me?" she smiles and grabs a mat.

And suddenly I stop competing with all of them. Suddenly, I'm not even racing. "To tell you the truth, Jeanette, I think I better not exercise today."

"Is there anything I can do?" She puts her arm around me. "Are you not well?"

"No, Jeanette, I'm just not happy. I'm afraid I haven't been happy for some time."

(*She looks up at the audience.*)

I don't blame the ladies in the locker room for how I feel. I don't blame any of us. We're all concerned, intelligent, good women.

(*Pause.*)

It's just that I feel stranded. And I thought the whole point was that we wouldn't feel stranded. I thought the point was we were all in this together.

Thank you.

(*She walks off.*)

The House of Blue Leaves
John Guare

Premiere: Truck & Warehouse Theatre, NYC, 1971
Publisher: Samuel French, Inc.
Setting: Artie Shaughnessy's apartment in Queens, New York, October 4, 1965

Artie Shaughnessy is a zookeeper from Queens, New York, an aspiring songwriter who worries that he's "too old to be a young talent." Unhappily married to a mentally ill woman named Bananas, he has fallen in love with his neighbor Bunny Flingus, "a pretty, pink, electric woman in her forties." Bunny has had an endless series of jobs. She's the kind of woman who stuffs her plastic booties with newspaper to keep warm and wears a Beatles "I Love Paul"

button to Pope Paul's New York parade route. She sleeps
with Artie, but won't cook for him until after they're married: "We got to save some magic for the honeymoon. It's
my first honeymoon, and I want it to be so good, I'm aiming
for two million calories."

Artie has arranged for Bananas to be institutionalized,
and Bunny is eager to marry him as soon as he gets his
divorce. When they break the news to Bananas, she makes
Artie swear that she won't be given more shock treatments:
"At least the concentration camps—I was reading about
them, Artie—they put the people in the ovens and they
never took them out—but the shock treatments—they put
you in the oven and then they take you out and then they
put you in and then they take you out . . ." Bunny interrupts her.

BUNNY

Did you read *Modern Screen* two months ago? I am usually
not a reader of film magazines, but the cover on it reached
right up and seduced my eye in the health club. It was a
picture like this

(Clutches her head.)

and it was called "Sandra Dee's Night of Hell." Did you
read that by any happenstance? Of course you wouldn't
read it. You can't see anything. You're ignorant. Not you.
Her. The story told of the night before Sandra Dee was to
make her first movie and her mother said, "Sandra, do you
have everything you need?" and she said—snapped back,
real fresh-like—"Leave me alone, Mother. I'm a big girl
now and don't need any help from you." So her mother
said, "All right, Sandra, but remember I'm always here."
Well, her mother closed the door and Sandra could not
find her hair curlers anywhere and she was too proud to
go to her mom and ask her where they were—

[ARTIE

Bunny, I don't understand.

BUNNY]

Shut up, I'm not finished yet—and she tore through the house having to look her best for the set tomorrow because it was her first picture and her hair curlers were nowhere! Finally at four in the A.M., her best friend, Annette Funicello, the former Mouseketeer, came over and took the hair curlers out of her very own hair and gave them to Sandra. Thus ended her night of hell, but she had learned a lesson. Suffering—you don't even know the meaning of suffering. You're a nobody and you suffer like a nobody. I'm taking Artie out of this environment and bringing him to California while Billy can still do him some good. Get Artie's songs—his music—into the movies.

Lady Day at Emerson's Bar & Grill
Lanie Robertson

Premiere: Alliance Theatre, Atlanta, 1986
Publisher: Samuel French, Inc.
Setting: A small bar in south Philadelphia, around midnight, March, 1959

Lady Day at Emerson's Bar & Grill takes place at one of the last performances of the legendary jazz singer Billie Holiday. Forty-four years old, she has endured terrible pain: rape at age ten, racism, heroin addiction and "cold turkey" withdrawal, imprisonment, and denial of the "work card" that would allow her to sing in the clubs. Yet, the playwright states, "Joy and humor should be the prevalent emotions on stage. This is because singing was Billie's salvation."

Billie wears a white satin dress, bright red lipstick, and long fingerless gloves to hide her track marks. Here she tells of touring with Artie Shaw.

BILLIE

Easy livin'. Like the times I was singin' with Artie's band.
Artie Shaw. An' we toured, see. We started out in Boston
an' it was all downhill from that. In Boston, see, I had to
sit in the bus till it was time for my numbers 'cause they
didn't want no black bitch sittin' up on the bandstand with
all those fellahs in the band which was all-white, see, so
you can imagine when we got down to Virginia, North an'
South Carolina. Georgia. An' worse. Anyway, there was
this fancy restaurant we went into outside of Birmingham
an' Artie an' the boys just couldn't have been sweeter or
squarer with me. Places where they wouldn't let me in the
front door none of them'd use the front door neither. An'
if I had to sit out in the kitchen to get some eats the whole
bunch of them'd sit out there too. So that always pissed off
the ofays who ran the places anyway, see. So this one place
we went to we was all sittin' out in the kitchen with all the
colored help runnin' around us tryin' to do their jobs in
that place just like we wasn't there. An' it was hot as hell
in that kitchen anyway, and of course none of this treatment
was free you know. We was all payin' top price for this,
just like we was sittin' out front with all the grays. Only
we was in the kitchen because Artie Shaw had this black
bitch called Billie Holiday in his troupe. So everything was
smooth as silk till I realized all of a sudden I had to use the
bathroom in the worst way. I mean, my kidneys was almost
to bust an' float me outta there right into the main dining
room, an' I knew damn well they didn't want that. So I got
up an' asked this black dude who looked like he might have
had some sense where was the bathroom an' he asked me
why I wanted to know, thereby provin' he didn't have any
more sense than I had in askin'. I shoulda found it on my
own. Anyway, while I was tryin' to explain to him that I
didn't really need to go there to powder my nose, if that's
what was worryin' him. That it was for a more essential
reason than that, when this blond bitch comes in the kitchen
from the dining room. Somebody musta heard me askin'

this dude an' run off to get this bitch to bring her into the discussion. Now, she was the maitresse dee who wouldn't let me into the dining room to begin with. So she saunters up real big, still clutchin' all these big red plush covered menus under her left tit and says, "Just what exactly seems to be the trouble here?" an' I look at her, see, like where'd the fuck she come from an' go "The trouble seem to be that this dude can't answer a simple question." So then I knew somebody had ran to get her 'cause she says, "I'm sorry, Miss Day, but we don't have toilets for the colored." An' I said, "Listen, honey, you have me confused. I'm not Doris Day. I'm Billie Holiday. Lots of folks has said she an' me resembles each other, but this is the first time I know of where anybody's talked to the one an' thought they was talkin' to the other. Also I don't want to cast no aspersions on anybody workin' here or hurt anybody's feelin's or nothin' but ever body I see workin' here 'cept you is about as colored as they come. Now, where do they go?" So she gives me this sweet little smile out of one side her mouth an' says, "Yes, but they're males. We don't have a toilet for colored females." I said, "Honey, at this point I don't care if it's nothin' but a urinal or a dark corner of the room. Lead me to it, please. I'm about to bust." So she shifts her weight around slow, see, in this real tight black sequin-covered dress she's wearin' with sequin high-heel shoes to match, an' tells me, "We didn't want you comin' in our restaurant to start with. We don't allow colored here. We only let you in because Mr. Shaw agreed to pay twice as much for all of you if we'd let you eat out here in the kitchen. Otherwise you wouldn't even be here. Now, if Mr. Shaw wants to do that, that's his business. But he said nothing about letting you use the phone, or the bar, or the dining room or the men's toilet, and I'm not going to let you do that." So I said, "Listen, Mr. Shaw's been very sweet. He's done a lot of nice things like this for me, and I appreciate it. But one thing I know of he can't do for me and that's piss. So what do you propose I do about this situation?" An' she give me that sweet little twisted side of her mouth smile and clutched a firm grip on that stack of menus and said, "Why don't you sit on it!" I was so shocked. I just looked at her a minute and then I said, "No. I think I'll let you do that." An' I cut loose the biggest deluge all acrossed those sequined shoes of hers to come down the pike since Noah. You never seen a grown woman leap so high up in the air as she did in your life. Droppin' menus and screechin' like she'd been scalded all over the legs and feet by molten lead. An' all the boys in the band was on their feet ajumpin' up and down and hooting an carryin' on like we just won the second coming of the Civil War an' that was I assure you the high an' low of the whole tour for me. After that everybody in the band started sayin' "Watch out for Billie. She's got a secret weapon. She'll spoil your shoes quicker'n you can pay to get 'em polished" an' all kinda silly shit like that. But I loved 'em. They was pals to this black bitch an' I'll never forget it.

A Late Snow
Jane Chambers

Premiere: Playwrights Horizons, NYC, 1974
Publisher: Avon Books (in *Gay Plays—The First Collection*)
Setting: A country cabin by a lake

Ellie is a literature professor at a conservative college. She is a lesbian, but has kept her personal life in the closet for fear of repercussions on the job. Her grad-student lover, Quincey, disagrees with this choice on political grounds, but yields to Ellie's will. Quincey loves Ellie so much that she decides to surprise her by buying an antique Dutch cupboard—a piece that has great sentimental value for Ellie—from Ellie's ex-lover Pat. Pat won't sell the cupboard till Quincey agrees to let her deliver it to the weekend cabin she used to share with Ellie. As the play begins, Pat and Quincey are unloading the surprise present on a weekend when Ellie's away at a conference. They're soon faced with a surprise of their own, when Ellie comes home early—with another woman.

Margo is a brilliant novelist who rose to fame in her twenties and has since become a notorious recluse. Ellie hopes to lure her onto her college's faculty. The two women hit it off at the conference, but neither has broached the topic of sexual preference. Ellie insists that Margo's visit is strictly business, and Quincey, who worships Margo's work, tries to respect Ellie's privacy rules in spite of her jealousy. These four women, plus a fifth, "Perfect Peggy," are trapped overnight by an unexpected late snowfall. Pat, a severe alcoholic, gets very drunk and the innuendoes fly.

It's late at night. Peggy has fled upstairs, insisting that she's not a lesbian. Quincey has gone to bed. Pat drunkenly tries to woo Ellie back, then runs out into the snow. Margo, who's comes downstairs just in time for Pat's exit, asks Ellie point-blank if she loves Pat or Quincey. Ellie apologizes for bringing Margo into all this, and Margo reveals her own history.

MARGO

I was married to a man once, much like Pat. Worse, I guess. He was not only a drunk but a violent drunk. And I loved him. I loved him long after I left him. And I loved again. A woman. She died ten years ago.

[ELLIE
(Surprised.)

I'm sorry.

MARGO]

I haven't written a publishable book since that time. I haven't let another human being touch me since that time. Oh, I've slept with a few. I picked up a salesman in the bar downstairs from my hotel room. He was from Detroit. I never saw him again. Another time, a bellhop. And a woman reporter from a newspaper upstate. She was in town for the afternoon to interview me. But they didn't touch me: not emotionally, not really physically. I made love to them. . . . It's hard to make anything last, Ellie. A job, a talent, a marriage.

[ELLIE

A lot of people do it.]

MARGO

A lot of people hold on to dead things. But to make something last—and live . . . It's harder with a woman. There are no rules. And the stakes are so very high.

(They look at each other for a moment.)

We worked at it. We worked very hard at it. We brought new things into our relationship, we challenged one another with ideas, with goals. We weren't always successful. We had bad years, years when I was sure it was over, when I thought it should be over. But we survived them, somehow. It was good again, it was working.

(Pause.)

I think I hated her for dying, for leaving me. And I was very frightened. I still am.

Laughing Wild
Christopher Durang

Premiere: Playwrights Horizons, NYC, 1987
Publisher: Dramatists Play Service, Inc.
Setting: New York City

Laughing Wild is a play in three parts. In the first two, "Laughing Wild" and "Seeking Wild," characters identified only as a Woman and a Man address their monologues directly to the audience. In the third, "Dreaming Wild," they interact with each other in variations on a random attack at the tuna fish shelf of a New York City supermarket and a Sally Jessy Raphael interview with the Infant of Prague.

This section of "Laughing Wild" opens the play. (The entire monologue, in which the speaker eventually reveals herself as an opinionated, needy, and well-educated mental patient, runs fourteen pages.)

(A Woman enters and addresses the audience. She should be dressed fairly normally. She sits in a chair and talks to the audience. She can get up from the chair form time to time if the spirit moves her. The backdrop behind her should be nondescript—pretty much a limbo setting.)

WOMAN

Oh, it's all such a mess. Look at this mess. My hair is a mess. My clothes are a mess.

I want to talk to you about life. It's just too difficult to be alive, isn't it, and to try to function? There are all these people to deal with. I tried to buy a can of tuna fish in the supermarket, and there was this *person* standing right in front of where I wanted to reach out to get the tuna fish, and I waited a while, to see if they'd move, and they didn't—they were looking at tuna fish too, but they were taking a real long time on it, reading the ingredients on each can like they were a book, a pretty boring book, if you ask me, but nobody has; so I waited a long while, and they didn't move, and I couldn't get to the tuna fish cans; and I thought about asking them to move, but then they seemed so stupid not to have *sensed* that I needed to get by them that I had this awful fear that it would do no good, no good at all, to ask them, they'd probably say something like, "We'll move when we're goddam ready, you nagging bitch," and then what would I do? And so then I started to cry out of frustration, quietly, so as not to disturb anyone, and still, even though I was softly sobbing, this stupid person didn't *grasp* that I needed to get by them to reach the goddam tuna fish, people are so insensitive, I just hate them, and so I reached over with my fist, and I brought it down real hard on his head and I screamed: "Would you kindly move, asshole!!!"

And the person fell to the ground, and looked totally startled, and some child nearby started to cry, and I was still crying, and I coudn't imagine making use of the tuna fish now anyway, and so I shouted at the child to stop crying—I mean, it was drawing too much attention to me—and I ran out of the supermarket, and I thought, I'll take a taxi to the Metropolitan Museum of Art, I need to be surrounded with culture right now, not tuna fish.

But you know how hard it is to hail a taxi. I waved my hand, and then this terrible man who came to the street *after* I was there waved his hand, and the taxi stopped for him because he saw him first, and the injustice of it made my eyes start to well with tears again. So I lost that taxi. So I raised my hand again, and the next *three* taxis were already full, although one of them still had his "free" light on which made me angry, because if he had had it off, I probably wouldn't have raised my arm, which was getting tired now, I think hitting the man with the tuna fish used some muscles I wasn't used to using. And then this other taxi started to get near, and this woman with groceries came out, and she started to hail it and I went right over to her and I shouted smack into her ear: "If you take this taxi from me, I will kill you!" And she looked really startled, and then the taxi stopped, and I got in, and I said, I want to go crosstown to the Metropolitan Museum of Art, I must have culture, and quiet, and things of value around me, I have had a terrible time in the supermarket. And then the taxi driver, who was Greek or Muslim or Armenian or something, said to me, I have to go *down*town now, I'm about to get off work.

Well, I thought my head would explode. I mean, was his taxi available, or wasn't it? And wasn't it *law* that they can't refuse you, even if you want to go to Staten Island? But I just couldn't bear the thought of pressing charges against this man—it would take days and days of phone calls, and meetings, and letters, and all because he wouldn't bring me to the goddam Metropolitan. So I sat in his taxi and I wouldn't move. I thought for a while about going back and following through on my initial impulse to buy a can of tuna fish—tuna fish, mixed with mayonnaise, is one of the few things I can make in the kitchen—but then I realized that probably whoever was at the cash register would give me difficulties, probably because I was a woman, or because she was a woman, or maybe it was a man who hated women, or wished he was a woman—anyway it all started to seem far too complicated; so I thought, I'll just stay in this taxi cab, and I'll be damned if I get out.

Mama Drama

Leslie Ayvazian, Donna Daley, Christine Farrell, Marianna Houston, Rita Nachtmann, Anne O'Sullivan, Ann Sachs

Premiere: Ensemble Studio Theatre, NYC, 1987
Publisher: Samuel French, Inc.
Setting: Multiple locations on a mostly bare stage

Mama Drama, an evening of scenes and songs for women about issues of motherhood, "began in 1986 when Christine Farrell, newly pregnant and restless, realized that in five months there would be virtually no work for her as an actress. She gathered together other expectant mothers, experienced mothers, never-plan-to-be mothers and wish-I-could-be-a-mother friends and asked what we knew about being a mother, a daughter, and being pregnant." The following scene is called "The Lie."

ACTRESS #3

(Address the audience.)

When I found out I was pregnant I didn't even know who the father was. It was either David or Raoul—I knew that. I'd held onto my virginity until I was eighteen, I'd been to bed with two men and it was either David—bright, ambitious, generous but basically asexual David—or Raoul, a passionate but sleazy man.

I ended up spilling it all out to David, of course, because he listened to me and seemed to understand. He said he wanted to marry me and be a father to the child even if it wasn't his and oh-by-the-way he loved me and he was sure I would grow to love him. I didn't know. I couldn't go through with an abortion, I knew that, but I didn't think I could be a mother. I was a daughter. I wanted my mother. But my mother wanted me to give the baby up for adoption and get on with my life. I still didn't know. I never told Raoul, married David, and loved being pregnant. I even wondered for a while if the reason I was so happy was because I was in possession of two hearts.

When labor came it was in a great gush of warm water, soothing to the cramps that soon gave way to the dreaded pains of my dreams. I thought the attack on my body would never stop—that I could never survive this—until my baby girl was born. Perfect. Pefect.

I never even held her, because David and I had decided to give her up. "Stillborn," I lied. I lied to my friends, my family, my teachers at school. "Stillborn." I lied and lied and lied, and after David and I split up I almost began to believe it was true. Until I fell in love, got married again and gave birth to my second perfect child.

Now my first child haunts me. She's everywhere I look, including my own daughter's eyes. And I know she's here. David and I had specified to the adoption agency that she go to a couple in "the Arts" in New York City. But I can't get to her. They won't tell me anything about her except that when she turns eighteen she will have the right to find me. She'll be eighteen in August. And I'm here. I want her to know, I'm here.

More Fun Than Bowling
Steven Dietz

Premiere: Actors Theatre of St. Paul, St. Paul, Minnesota
Publisher: Samuel French, Inc.
Setting: A cemetery on a hill overlooking the small Midwestern town of Turtle Rapids

Jake Tomlinson, the owner of the Dust Bowl bowling alley, has been married three times. His first wife, Maggie, was an urban sophisticate who ran out on him, leaving him with five thousand dollars and a daughter named Molly. In quick succession, Jake married Lois, who died when lightning struck the bowling trophy she was holding, and her best friend, Loretta, who was crushed by a collapsing rack of bowling balls. Jake has decided his turn is up next, and he is practicing being dead by spending an afternoon underground in between his two dead wives' unmarked graves (he forgot which was which).

Neither wife is especially dead in the play. Loretta walks on and plants geraniums on her grave while telling the audience the story of her marriage. Lois soon follows suit. In this flashback scene, Lois is still alive and married to Jake, and her best friend, Loretta, is hoping to meet a man on the Duck Hollow Vo-Tech bowling team. Lois warns her to "keep your distance. You can hear those guys ticking."

LOIS
I went out with a guy from the Duck Hollow Vo-Tech.
[LORETTA
(*Not believing.*)
When?]

LOIS

About ten years ago. We went to a dance at the V.F.W.
hall on the Fourth of July. All the guys came dressed as
their favorite president. Half came as Washington. Half
as Lincoln. Vo-Tech's not long in the history depart-
ment. My date came as F.D.R. so he wouldn't have to
dance.

(Pause.)

We sat for two hours in the corner, eating mints. Then he
asked if I'd ever seen a "real . . . smooth . . . pickup." And
I said maybe not, and he lifted me up over his head and
took me out to the parking lot. That was pretty smooth, I
said, and he said "That wasn't it. This is it." He pointed to
his shiny silver Ford pickup truck with metallic green shell
on back. "Want to get inside and get to know each other?"
he said. Before I knew it, someone had sucked out all my
common sense with a straw and I said "Sure" and we sat
there smelling the fresh vinyl seat covers. He didn't say a
word. I turned on the radio. He turned it off. He said he
had something to show me and he unzipped his pants and
reached way down in them and pulled out a very . . .
small . . . key. "This key opens my gun rack" and sure
enough there was his twelve-gauge shotgun locked to a rack
behind our heads and he took down that gun and began to
clean it with his white handkerchief. He explained every
detail of that gun to me during the next hour as he caressed
it with that handkerchief. Then he loaded it. Then he lifted
the edge of my skirt with it and said "Now, what are *you*
gonna show *me*."

(Pause.)

[LORETTA

(Impatient.)

Okay, okay. So, what did you do?]

LOIS

(Pause.)

After showing him the entire contents of my purse . . . only
four minutes had elapsed. So, I started to unbutton my

blouse. And he started to smile. Then I stopped. I said "For the good stuff we need to get in the back." "Under the shell?" he said. "Yeah," I said. "I just put new carpeting back there," he said. "Your choice," I said, and after considering it for a moment . . . he nodded. "Take off all your clothes," I said. "Even my shorts?" he said. "Especially your shorts," I said. So there he was, naked in the back of the shell. And there I was, about to climb in—when I grabbed his clothes, slammed the cover shut, locked him in and drove the pickup to the front door of the V.F.W. Hall.

(Stands.)

I walked inside, grabbed the microphone from the stage and yelled "HEY, I GOT A KEG OF BEER IN THE BACK OF MY PICKUP. EVERYBODY HELP THEMSELVES." That metallic shell didn't last long, and F.D.R. would've been proud of how fast that boy ran away naked into the night.

Mrs. California
Doris Baizley

Premiere: Mark Taper Forum, Los Angeles, California, 1985
Publisher: Dramatists Play Service, Inc.
Setting: The stage of the 1955 Mrs. California Contest

Dot, a housewife from suburban Los Angeles, is one of four finalists in the 1955 Mrs. California Contest. The contestants compete in such activities as Table Setting, Meal Preparation, Ironing, Sewing, and Holiday Desserts, and must be prepared to answer questions in such areas as Family Fun and Proudest Moment. Dot's highly personal Proudest Moment is deemed inappropriate by her sponsor, who feels she should stress her achievements as a mother and wife. This monologue opens the play.

DOT

In the winter of 1943, I was an ensign in the WAVES, trained in Naval Communications and stationed in Cape May, New Jersey, to transmit messages from our head-quarters in Washington to our convoys at sea. On March 13th at midnight I got the report: seven German subs were shadowing UGS-6, a slow eastbound convoy taking strategic material to Europe on the North Africa route. The wolfpacks never attacked the fast-moving convoys, they'd wait for the slow ones. COMINCH picked up the German positions and I transmitted them to the escort commander at sea. He ordered an evasive change of course and sent out two destroyers as hunter-killers. They sank two of the subs. The others got away, but the convoy made it. They got our message in time.

(Leans forward, confidential.)

I shouldn't have known what that message was. I was only there to transmit. But I recognized the call signal and decoded it for myself. Strictly against orders in wartime, right? But I was quick. I could degarble a message like that.

(Snaps fingers.)

My husband, Jimmy, was on one of those destroyers. There I was, sitting in that little shore station in the middle of the night, sending that message out over the whole Atlantic Ocean to that ship at sea. Hoping that radio operator out there's on his toes. Hoping it works. There I am—one part of this huge system they're depending on for their lives—more than that, for Victory—for freedom—Europe—hell, for the world. And it all comes down to me in that room sending those radio waves out through my fingers to that ship in the middle of the ocean. And I saved it. Do you know what that felt like? Can you imagine how proud I was? I was the whole U.S. Navy that night. The whole U.S.A.

One Monkey Don't Stop No Show
Don Evans

Premiere: Crossroads Theatre Company, New Brunswick, New Jersey
Publisher: Dramatists Play Service, Inc.
Setting: Suburban Philadelphia

Myra Harrison (born Mattie Lou) is a middle-class black preacher's wife with transparently affected tastes. She belongs to a sorority and a garden club, keeps a five-hundred-dollar lapdog named Frou-Frou, and decorates in white-and-gold French Provincial. She is proud of her preppy son's aspiration to dentistry. When she finds his copy of *The Joy of Sex,* she can't bring herself to pronounce the last word of the title. Instead she gasps, "Lord, I wish I was white so I could faint." She acts horrified when her husband, Avery, takes an avid interest in the book and, spurred by a lusty beautician/masseuse named Miss Mozelle, starts coming on to his wife at all hours of the day.

But underneath all of Myra's pretentions and church-wife propriety is a vital woman waiting for an excuse to cut loose. Here she shares her secret self with the audience.

MYRA

OO . . . , ain't he somethin'? An' I wanna thank you' I ain't know the ol' rascal had so much life in him!
    (Moves to the audience with a funky-
           freedom to her gait.)
Yessir! Surprised me. An' don't you think I don't like it

either. I don't care how long you been together, you don't never let him know everything. Nevah! He think them rubdowns is somethin' new . . . shoot, Miss Myra ain't even in second gear yet. Y'see, I come up the old-fashioned way . . . the old-fashioned "colored" way. Soon as you hit that first danger sign, Momma call you aside an' lay it all out there for ya . . . "Keep your drawers up' an your dress down." That's what she say.

(Looks to make sure she is alone with her
audience.)

Now, I ain't sayin' Momma was right . . . an' I ain't tellin' you whether I followed her advice . . . but I sure learned how to *act* like I was followin' it whether I was or not.

(Points.)

Some o' you know exactly what I mean . . . 'cause you see, accordin' to the old folks women didn't have no sex drive no way. They "did their duty" . . . *after* the fact. The "fact" bein' marriage. Tell ya what I believe though . . . that gettin' happy took care of a whole lotta late night dreamin'. You ever notice who be doin' all the shoutin' and hollerin'? That's right . . . got the old and decrepit men . . . or they ain't got nobody. You check that out next Sunday . . . but this one here, Avery . . . I never would've believed it. I mean, I was willin' to do what I was s'posed to do. In fact, I was anxious. But . . .

(Checks around again. Speaks confiden-
tially.)

. . . truth be told . . . wasn't nothin' but routine. Got so I'd even pick the day in the week. Two days before my sorority meetin' an' five days after my last visit to the hairdresser. Then the old fool hit them middle years. Got curious an' got to readin' all them books, worryin' 'cause old age starin' him in the face. Gon try to get it all before it goes away. But lemme tell you . . . the best thing that *ever* happened to a middle-aged woman is male menopause! Everything up to that point ain't nothin' but rehearsal.

(Looks out cockily, sure of her footing.)

Am I lyin'? I ask you, Am I lyin'? Shoot . . . don't worry
about your hair. Do like Miss Myra . . . get yourself a
wig!

The Promise
José Rivera

Premiere: Los Angeles Theatre Center, Los Angeles, California,
  1988
Publisher: Broadway Play Publishing
Setting: The backyard of Guzman's home in Patchogue, Long
  Island

Lolin Alvarez is the next-door neighbor and friend of
eighteen-year-old Lilia Guzman. Lilia was to be married
against her will to the man of her father's choice, but on
the altar she was possessed, dybbuk-like, by the soul of her
dead lover, Carmelo. She is wasting away of anorexia, and
Lolin is trying to tempt both the souls in her body with
"sausage and yellow rice . . . black beans and tostones to
commit serial murder for."
  Lolin, "a single mother of three, is a lovely, lonely
woman approaching forty. She dresses to show off her
body." She addresses the following speech directly to the
audience.

LOLIN
I had another date last night. After dinner we're on the
sofa. The boys are in their rooms. And my date begins
exploring my unchartered terrain. Colonizing me. Putting
down resistance. Putting up the flag of his superpower. I
close my eyes, ready for the nuclear attack that will rip me
with shrapnel and spit. . . .
  (*A white flash of light.* LOLIN *laughs.*)

Then I hear laughing! It's my boys! They're in the living room taking Polaroids of Mommy about to go down on her date. And so help me, it strikes me as the funniest thing they've ever done. I start laughing. My boys are laughing. Then I notice my date's not laughing. He's adjusting his zipper, looking grim, and I ask him where his sense of humor is and he puts on a pair of brass knuckles that give his fist the density of a tank and he punches my oldest son in the face, sending his teeth all over the room. I start screaming. My son is unconscious. My other sons are trying to set my date on fire with kitchen matches and my oldest boy, my sweetheart, my love, is now in a hospital, swimming up to stable condition. For Chrissakes, I'm thirty-nine years old. I can't take another date like this.

Quartet Nights, or The Last Good Time We Had

Eleanore Speert

Premiere: 26th Street Performance Space, NYC, 1990
Publisher: —
Setting: A warm, favorite room; front porch; or bare stage

A woman named Jenny reminisces about her childhood in 1950s Baltimore. The play appears here in its entirety.

JENNY

This is pretty much the way it was, at least there and then. Our house was part of a progressive development, built in the 1950s. My parents moved in in '51, I came along after my sister, in '53, and by the time the quartet started and I was old enough to politely say hello—though in my pajamas and ready for bed—by that time, the hydrangeas were as tall as the porch and the dogwood branches touched each other, pink and white, at the side of the house. By then too, the carpet was worn just right for card games and lying on your stomach to watch Ed Sullivan. This was the fifties. I was 5 or 6, I don't remember. The world hadn't opened up to close in just yet. . . .

Anyway, the quartet arrived around 7 in the evening. Actually, only a trio arrived, my father rounded out the foursome. Sometimes I think this happened every week yet I don't remember it but a few times. It was so comfortable though, it must have occurred with some regularity. Perhaps I was already asleep some of the times, or I was too young to remember. Maybe I would just like it to be.

When the trio arrived I would usually find my spot. A spot which would later come to represent my life, my vantage point. Some kids run and hug the knees of familiar friends when they visit. Some definitely hide—retreat to rooms, or at least behind chairs, saying nothing, or suddenly crying for mother's attention. Me, I'd do something in the middle. I'd sit on the steps, behind the banister, and peek my head through the balusters; sometimes closer when no one saw me, but when someone smiled, I'd pull back. I'd blush, maybe giggle, mostly shrug and shrink down a little. When no one was paying attention again, I'd slide down a stair on my butt, still watching through my safety net; always able to observe, but not quite within reach.

The instruments would go right downstairs to the cellar. That's what we called the floor below the living room. Ours was a good example of 1950s bottom-floor family room. We had a phone down there, a bar, with clear glass shelves for highball glasses and martini shakers, and, the room was *paneled*. We had a built-in area my father made, also paneled, for the stereo, speakers and record holder. It had small paneled doors which were attached to little lights that went on automatically when the doors opened, and each compartment always had that wonderful smell of wood—

real wood—from the paneling—mixed with the odor of its own sap which would ooze through the cracks and harden into bubbles, and with the fumes of the heating elements inside the amplifier. There was comfort in that aroma. It was safe. It was home. . . . And the cellar was the place where my sister and I would go and put on one of maybe three records ever bought in our adolescence, and we'd dance our version of the jitterbug; first with each other, then with the pole that stood behind the piano bench to the left and almost in the middle of the room. Sometimes we'd take turns lying down on the vinyl sofa which made noise when you sat, and stuck to you if you rested after perspiring after dancing your version of the jitterbug. We'd take turns lying on this thing, watching the other one dance those new solo dances becoming so popular. But maybe all this was later, a little after the 50s, a little after the quartet evenings.

The instruments would go downstairs and the guys would chatter. I would follow at a distance, not saying anything, sometimes just standing, occasionally in the way, or peeking my head around the corner, watching some of the instruments come in through the side door, which made sense because it was much closer to the cellar anyway. Of course the side door was where the bees hung out, near the sweet flowers, so we were always instructed to move fast through that door, never keep it open. But mothers don't tend to have the same tone of voice when speaking to musicians, and it's hard to move quickly through that door holding a bass, so it was all a leisurely process, with the sun going down and the crickets starting. It's summer, in the 50s, in suburbia, in Baltimore, in a warm house and the music is about to start. No wonder I think back on those nights.

I watched them set things up. I don't remember drinks, but I'm sure there were beers and a few bourbon'ed ginger ales. Nothing big time. No one ever got drunk. I don't remember lights. In fact I can conjure up a picture of deliberate "atmosphere." No bright lights, just the side lamps that cast shadows with a yellow tint.

For some reason, I remember the drummer especially. Two reasons I think. One because I had never heard that sound before: the one where you hit this smallish, easy-to-carry-down-steps drum, with a fan of loose-fitting metal pieces. It's a great sound, and I remember being drawn to it. It was very exciting, daring, and new. I waited for it. . . . Secondly, because he often looked at me and smiled. He'd look around, get his cues from the guys, go with the conversation, but he'd always find me, sitting now on the basement steps, clutching the vertical holds and peering through. He'd find me and smile. Sometimes he'd make a face, sometimes he'd hit his drum harder and my stomach would jump. I loved that sound. I remember the drummer, and I think with some detail, but I don't remember the bass player, or the guitarist. Not at all. And I love those sounds too. I remember the music, or the feel of the music, or how the music made me feel. I remember hearing it all, but I don't remember the guys who played, except, of course, for the downbeat, fan man.

But the place didn't start hopping, no matter what the drummer could do, until my father sat down. We had his mother's old upright piano on the right-hand wall: A Baltimore-made Steiff, with ivory keys and a soul of its own. It's a gorgeous piece. We still have it, though it rests more often now, and it's out of tune. But then it could send you soaring. My father would sit down and just play. Simple. He knew the songs, he knew the words to the songs. I guess he used sheet music, goodness knows we had enough of it in the bench, but I don't remember how he did it. I've seen him play so many times without looking up that I can't separate the memories. I do remember watching his face as his hands flew. He'd bite his lip, he'd smile one of his goofy smiles, which come pretty naturally. He's not a prodigy, he's one of those people who knows how to play,

who sits down when asked and can duplicate the favorites.
No sweat. Well maybe there was some sweat, but I never
saw it, so I'm left with the magic. Oh, I remember him
practicing, but only occasionally and it didn't sound like
the times when I practiced: no red book with scales, and
simplistic tunes to repeat. No sir. We heard jazz and blues
and pop and lots of made-up original tunes, not necessarily
hummable, but awfully pretty.

This one night for some reason I was allowed to stay
down and listen. "Stay down": the local term for "staying
up late downstairs, as long as you're good and you're ready
for bed." We always had shorthand terminology . . . it
came with the era. I stayed on the steps most of the time,
perfectly content. I listened and was totally happy. During
a break, in the old-fashioned sense, meaning a little rest,
I ventured down and visited the drum. I got to hold the
fan stick and move it around on the stretched skin top. I
couldn't get the beat the drummer got, but if he held my
hand while I held the stick, I could pretend I did. In a few
minutes I returned to the stairs. The bass provided a beat
you could feel, traveling through the floor and up to where
I was sitting. Then my father would hit the keys running . . . no, I don't remember him taking anything from
the piano bench. He just played. Boogie, romance, rhythm
and nonsense. I stayed on the steps and let my eyes go
from drummer to piano, to bass to guitar, from smile to
smile to smile. I didn't hear anything but happiness. I
listened long. I remembered. It was one of the last good
times we had. It was the 50s, in Baltimore, a summer's
night, and a quartet evening of magic.

(The lights fade to black.)

Rupert's Birthday
Ken Jenkins

Premiere: Actors Theatre of Louisville, Louisville, Kentucky, 1980
Publisher: Dramatists Play Service, Inc.
Setting: A rocking chair

In this one-woman play, a woman mamed Louisa sits in a rocking chair sewing, telling the audience why she doesn't celebrate "public works holidays," but only Rupert's birthday. On the night of the full moon and Louisa's first period, her mother went into labor—and so did a cow named Miranda. Miranda was months premature, and, with her father and mother away at the hospital, it fell to Louisa to midwife the calf she names Rupert.

Louisa

The calf's nose had already appeared. I could see its blue tongue spilling over its chin where it rested on the front legs. In good position. Not breathing yet. Not using air. Still attached to its Momma. Breathing through her blood.

I thought, "What if I have to pull it?"

I had watched calves come before and once or twice I had seen Daddy pull them when the cow was having trouble.

In my mind's eye I saw Daddy's strong hands and arms clasp the slippery legs of the calf and pull out and down, in rhythm with the cow's contractions, until the head and shoulders of the calf were through the narrow opening of the cervix.

I looked down at my own small hands and thought, "These are no good. But, if push comes to shove, I'll try. I'll have to. I'm the one that's here."

Well, I watched Miranda closely for about an hour, stayed right by her side. She'd get up and walk around and then she'd lay back down and have another series of contractions. An every time she'd get to the point where the broad part of the calf's forehead would almost clear the cervix she wouldn't be able to get it out any further. And she would stop pushing and the calf would slip back inside her womb.

Now, cows are real strong, but the birthing muscles will wear out, and if the cervix doesn't stretch enough to let the calf through before the cow's muscles are too weak to push, then the cow will quit trying . . . and the calf will die inside her womb. Eventually, the cow will die, too.

Well, I was just beginning to realize that I was really going to have to do something when Miranda turned to me and seemed to say, "C'mon, you big dummy! I need some help! What are you waiting on? Christmas?!"

So, the next time she lay down, I took a couple of burlap feed sacks and got right up close behind her.

She was lying on her right side, with her legs sticking out, like this. So, I lay down on my right side, facing her rear end, like this. Then, I coiled up like a spring, with my knees bent up, and my bare feet flush against the muscles of her back legs.

Then I wrapped a feed sack around each of the calf's front legs and tied them on with doubled strands of baling twine.

Then, I looped the strands of twine together between the calf's legs so that there was just enough room for my two hands to grab ahold of.

Then, I got a firm hold—and waited.
When Miranda pushed—I pulled.
I pulled for all that I was worth.

Every time she'd got the calf's head in place she'd have to stop and rest. And every time she'd stop pushing the calf would start slipping back inside her.

"C'mon, Miranda, you can do it."

After a while I was dripping with sweat and every muscle in my body felt like it was on fire.

"It's now or never, Miranda, you hear? I ain't got much more strength left in me."

She pushed—and I pulled. I held my breath and pulled with all my might. I stretched my body taut like a bow string.

"C'mon, Miranda!"

And just when I thought I was going to explode, Miranda gave a great groan, and out sloshed the calf's head and shoulders and slid right up my naked body and came to rest with its head lying in my lap.

Its body and back legs were still inside Miranda.
Umbilical still attached.
Half in Miranda—and half lying on top of me.

I looked at the calf's head lying there, wet, between my legs—not yet quite alive, blue tongue lolling sideways out of its mouth, nose still full of birth, ears slicked back against its head, eyes dull and lifeless.

And—as I was looking at the calf's eye—Miranda stood up.
And—as she stood—the rest of the calf's body slipped out.
And—the umbilical broke.

And—as the umbilical broke—a *light* switched on in that
calf's eye.

I saw it.

It came to life. Life came to it.

As the umbilical broke—it became itself.
It became conscious. It *saw*.

And the first thing that it saw—was me.
Me—looking right at it. Looking right in at it.

I saw the first flash of life come into that calf's eye.
Saw it switch on—like a light in a dark room.

Seneca Hollow Rescue
Adam LeFevre

Premiere: Actors & Writers, New Paltz, New York, 1991
Publisher: —
Setting: Seneca Hollow Volunteer Rescue Squad Headquarters

Mona is married to George, a volatile mechanic in his
mid-forties who works for the local Volunteer Rescue
Squad. Her father died recently, and she is in an extremely
fragile emotional state. George doesn't know how to cope
with her grief and thinks she is having a breakdown. Mona's
main support has been a young minister named Lane. She
tells him, "You have such a beautiful face. A saint's face.
It shines. I wish you hadn't stopped coming by. You would
listen. In the longest silence, you would still keep listening."

The play begins with Lane passing his Volunteer Rescue
Squad test by correctly diagnosing a Resucit-Annie doll's

brain hemorrhage. As the squad members celebrate, Mona bursts in wild-eyed, babbling about an old man who fell out of the sky while she was gardening. She tells the squad he needs help: "This is the real thing! Code red!" George thinks she is "seeing things," but to calm her down he agrees to take the ambulance out to the site. He's joined by senior squad member Ace, leaving Lane to look after Mona. They will find out that Mona is telling the truth. An old man lies collapsed in the pole beans. When he finally comes to, he says he's an angel who fell from a tree. If he is an angel, he's certainly past his prime: his memory is shot and his laying on of hands no longer heals. But Mona believes in him. To George, this is proof that she's losing her grip.

In this scene, the ambulance has just left and Mona and Lane are alone. She tells Lane she misses his visits. He asks if she's still praying, and says that he knows her father is in God's hands. She wants to believe him.

MONA

I'm trying, Lane. I'm trying so hard. I couldn't sleep last night. I kept thinking about Daddy, riding with him in the back of the ambulance to the hospital, how his face looked so mean. He kept saying "Leave me alone. I'm turnin' into nothin', and I'm happy about it." I went outside. It was light from the moon. I walked way out into Blaisdell's pastures, sat down on a rock, closed my eyes, and I tried to pray. I asked God to give me a sign Daddy was all right, that he *was* somewhere. I sat like that for I don't know how long. When I opened up, there was all these cows around me, staring. Curious, I guess. I looked up into their eyes, so big and tender there in the moonlight, and I thought maybe God was trying to speak to me through the eyes of those cows. But I couldn't believe it. They were just stupid cows. They ran away when I clapped my hands. I just walked home. It musta been 4 A.M. I still couldn't get sleepy, so I paced around downstairs, around the loveseat, around and around, singing to myself. "Row, Row, Row Your Boat." That's the song Daddy used to sing me when I was little and couldn't sleep. So I sang it to myself.

(She sings.)

Row, row, row your boat. It woke Georgey up. He's worried about my mind.

Six Degrees of Separation
John Guare

Premiere: Lincoln Center Theatre, NYC, 1990
Publisher: Vintage Books
Setting: New York City

Flanders ("Flan") and Louisa ("Ouisa") Kittredge live on New York's Upper East Side, in an apartment that boasts a two-sided Kandinsky original and a luxuriant view of Central Park. Flan, a high-rolling art dealer, has a line on a Cezanne but needs a loan of two million dollars. Luckily, a "King Midas rich" friend from South Africa is in town. Flan and Ouisa invite him to dine, and during the small talk, the doorman brings up a young black man named Paul.

Paul is "in his early twenties, very handsome, very preppy. He has been beaten badly. Blood seeps through his white Brooks Brothers shirt." He tells Ouisa and Flan he's been mugged, that he goes to Harvard with their children Tess and Woody, and, eventually, that his father is Sidney Poitier. Paul fascinates the Kittredges and their guests with stories of his movie-star father, his international childhood, and his senior thesis reinventing of *The Catcher in the Rye*. None of this is true.

Paul is a compulsive liar, a con man who almost believes his own con. He's never met Sidney Poitier *or* the Kittredge children, but he does know Trent Conway, an embittered young gay man who grew up with Tess and Woody and was only too happy to "educate" Paul in return for sexual favors. Tess Kittredge has gotten a sort of confession from Trent, and Ouisa has just learned the truth about the young black man by whom she was so charmed. She is impressed that Paul learned so much in three months—even more so by the realization that "He wanted to be us. Everything we are in the world, this paltry thing—our life—he wanted it."

Ouisa

I read somewhere that everybody on this planet is separated by only six other people. Six degrees of separation. Between us and everybody else on this planet. The president of the United States. A gondolier in Venice. Fill in the names. I find that A] tremendously comforting that we're so close and B] like Chinese water torture that we're so close. Because you have to find the right six people to make the connection. It's not just big names. It's *anyone*. A native in a rain forest. A Tierra del Fuegan. An Eskimo. I am bound to everyone on this planet by a trail of six people. It's a profound thought. How Paul found us. How to find the man whose son he pretends to be. Or perhaps *is* his son, although I doubt it. How every person is a new door, opening up into other worlds. Six degrees of separation between me and everyone else on this planet. But to find the right six people.

Three Ways Home
Casey Kurtti

Premiere: Astor Place Theatre, NYC, 1988
Publisher: Samuel French, Inc.
Setting: New York City

Sharon is a white first-time volunteer caseworker, Dawn a black welfare mother, and Frankie her troubled sixteen-year-old son. Each of them talks directly to the audience in an opening monologue. The playwright urges actors not to shy away from the "in your face" style, and comments that "Dawn and Sharon are parallel characters from two very different worlds, yet they both share a rich cynicism and sense of humor. They are both 'tough bitches.' Dawn should not be played as some bitter, downtrodden welfare mother in second-hand clothing." She is thirty years old and has four children.

DAWN

I don't like other people putting their face into my business. There's always some agency on my ass. Spying, taking notes . . . I stay to myself. It's me and my kids. Period. You let the wrong person in you don't know what the fuck could happen. See, I'm in shit now because of my old man, James. He used to go with this crazy Puerto Rican bitch from the Bronx. She's found the number of the Bureau of Child Welfare and now my ass is grass. She tells a BCW worker that it's "Her duty to inform . . ." that I'm upstairs night after night beating the shit out of my four kids. The truth of the matter is that she pissed 'cause I'm living with her ex–old man. Them Puerto Rican chicks go crazy if you mess with their men. They'll come after you with a knife, throw acid in your face. Believe it. But this bitch is sneaky. She not going to go face to face with me. She knows I'll kick her ass. Word! So she drops a dime and now I got to drag my ass to Family Court. So, hey, Miss Puerto Rico gets her way this time. The fat-ass judge sentences me to this program—tells me this therapy's going to make me a better mother. He's giving me an opportunity, do I want to take it? So now I got to tell my life story to some worker once a week for God knows how long or he's going to take away my kids . . . And no one is going to take away my kids. Check it out. The worker they assign me to is this skinny-ass white bitch, Janet Churchill. The first thing she says is "Why don't you tell me a little bit about yourself?" I hate that fucking question. And besides, which little bit did she want to know? I told her to call my worker at Welfare and get a blow-by-blow account. She says, "I think you're feeling a little anger about being here?" Wow! What a brain-iac! I mean this THERAPIST got all that paper, diplomas and whatnot and she doesn't know how to talk to me. White people are whack! So she keeps talking her line. Looking at my file, keeping up with her Miss Nice Personality. All chit chat. Then she gets into my face, goes deep into my business and says, "When was the first time you noticed your father had a penis?" As far as I'm concerned that came out of nowhere. I said, "Look, bitch, I didn't look down there. Ever. You want to know what I remember about my father's body? The back of his neck, his shoulders. The suitcase he was carrying. That's all I remember. Him walking out the damn door." PENIS! JESUS CHRIST! So I don't show up for the second appointment. I'm afraid I'll punch the shit out of that worker. I've got to give myself the opportunity to chill. You dig? Anyway, when I do show up the next time, Ms. Whack Worker don't say shit about me missing the session. She all cooled out, must have got her some last night. Hair down on her shoulders. Not in that stupid ponytail. I tell her "I like your hair like that." She says, "You do? I usually don't wear it like this because it's such a bother." A bother? Right. Everything's so complicated with white people. It's all such a big deal. I tell her "You should try living my life for a day or two if you really want to see what being bothered is all about." Then I'm in for it, because that let's her jump right in there with her psycho shit. "Really, Dawn, why don't you tell me what your day is like? Why don't you start with this morning?" I tell her "Look, I gotta live it. That's bad enough. I'd kill myself if I had to run through it again on videotape for you." So the next couple of weeks was okay. Status quo. But then my oldest, Frankie, had to fuck everything up. See, I had to take my youngest, James Junior, to the hospital over the weekend because he fell out of bed. THAT'S FACT. I was out getting milk. Frankie was supposed to be in charge, watching the kids. But he left his twelve-year-old sister, Tawny, in charge and went up on the roof to read comics. All of a sudden he thinks he's King Fucking Tut. He's got a whole life going for himself up on that roof. He stores his stuff up there. Hey, I ain't insulted. I don't have enough room for all his shit down here. He's got a stack of comic books five feet high. That's just for starters. Ever since he turned sixteen, he's been acting whack. Slipping in school, disrespecting me and what not. And lately he comes home with all kinds of things . . . tapes, Sony Walkmen. Says his friends gave it to him . . . Yeah right. I tell him "If I catch you messing with them crack heads I will kill you." Anyway, check it out. I'm gone 20 minutes, 10 minutes to the A and P, 10 minutes back. I walk into that apartment and there's my baby on Tawny's lap screaming. Blood dripping down his little face. Oh, I broke. I wrapped the baby in his little blanket and I ran over to St. Luke's Hospital. They keep me waiting four fucking hours in that emergency room. Haitian nurses be scoping me, giggling. I feel like I got a big arrow pointing over my head saying, "YOU FUCKED UP." Finally the doctor gets his shit together. He takes one look at James Junior and says, "You're an abusive mother, you know that?" I explain that the baby has fallen out of bed. He says, "Yeah, sure." But he lets me take my baby. As soon as I sign some papers, I'm on the bus uptown to see Janet. I get there I tell her my side of the story and she believes me! Tells me that she'll stand by me if the hospital tries to mess with me. So I get ready to leave but she says, "It must have been painful to be treated like that." "Hey that's the story of my life. But I get over." She says, "Who else treated you like that?" "Well my mother used to tell me that I was found under a garbage can. That I wasn't born in a hospital. When she was angry, which was

all the damn time. She'd say 'Born the same way. Die the
same way.' You see I may not have too many 'feelings' but
one thing I do know, I ain't garbage." Janet gets up and
puts her arms around me and you know what? She starts
CRYING. I tell you this bitch is whack! . . . After she blows
her nose, she says, "Perhaps you'd like some more support
in your life." She wants to assign me a volunteer. Some
do-gooder who'll hang around with me, like a best friend.
I tell her I got enough agencies involved in my business as
is. And anyway I can't deal with another white bitch. But
Janet reminds me that she's saving my ass with the hospital
so could I "check it out for a month?" All right, send the
bitch over . . .

The Voice of the Prairie
John Olive

Premiere: Artreach, Minneapolis, Minnesota, 1986
Publisher: Samuel French, Inc.
Setting: Various locales in the U.S.A., 1895 and 1923

   In 1895, Poppy is an old Irish storyteller who travels
the backroads of the rural Midwest with his young grandson
Davey, passing the hat for nickels. After Poppy dies, Davey
runs into a blind girl named Frankie while trying to steal
a chicken from her barn. Her mother has just died too, and
her drunk, abusive father wants to put her in a home.
Instead, she runs away to ride the rails with Davey.
   In 1923, Davey has grown into David and has become
a new kind of storyteller. He has a pioneering radio show
called "The Voice of the Prairie," and he charms his lis-
teners with tales of his travels with Frankie the Blind Girl.
Eventually, "The Voice of the Prairie" is heard by a

woman named Frances. She's "a calm, contained, composed woman in her forties. She wears a conservative dress, carries a white cane and wears dark glasses." She is, of course, Frankie the Blind Girl grown up. She has just been reunited with David. He sees her, says, "Oh, my God!" and runs out of the room. Frances turns to the audience.

(*A spot fades up downstage.* FRANCES *steps into it. Although her demeanor is composed and self-assured, there's a strong current of emotional tension, audible in her voice.*)

FRANCES

I don't know what life is. And that's what life is.
(*Beat.*)
I said that to James and he was so upset, he couldn't even pray. James prays hard. I love him when he prays, he's like a tea kettle, just before it boils.
(*Beat.*)
Have you ever had a wonderful dream, or a horrible dream for that matter, and it leaves you with a feeling that you absolutely must tell someone about it, but when you try, you can't remember? That's what life is.
(*Beat.*)
So I try not to think about it. It's all just dreams, and what are dreams worth? James says we live only for the life to come and everything else is worthless. The devil lives in the past. Don't think about it, he says. But these voices from the past, these . . . phantoms and demons of my imagination, whatever they are, they shriek at me. Sometimes, I can't hear anything else.
(*Beat.*)
I try to tell James. But he just weeps, and prays, then goes for long walks and comes back all sweaty, then his asthma acts up, and his voice squeaks, and I laugh, and then it starts all over again. I can't help it. I'm terrible.
(*Beat.*)

I'm a very highly regarded member of my community. Everyone thinks the world of me. I've been written up in a number of publications. I'm the only blind schoolteacher in the entire state of Arkansas. I'm an inspiration to them all. The street I live on is dreamy and quiet, filled with honeysuckle, bougainvillaea, freesia, a layer cake of fragrances. That's what life should be.

When She Danced
Martin Sherman

Premiere: Yvonne Arnaud Theatre, Guildford, England, 1985
Publisher: Amber Lane Press
Setting: Isadora Duncan's home in Paris, 1923

The legendary modern dancer Isadora Duncan, now a matronly forty-six, is living in Paris with her tempestuous, brutal, and much younger lover, the Russian poet Sergei Esenin. The fact that Sergei speaks no English and Isadora no Russian does not seem to matter to either of them as much as their passion for art, sex, and drinking. But Isadora's manager, Mary, whom Sergei detests, decides she should have an interpreter "so you can understand what that slob is saying. It might just open your eyes."

Last night, Mary met a Russian translator at a party and asked her to come by and meet Isadora. When the shy, plain, self-effacing Miss Belzer arrives for her interview, Mary doesn't remember her. Belzer's first task is translating a torrent of verbal abuse between Sergei and Mary. She is embarrassed and shocked by the language, but tries to oblige. Finally both warring parties storm off and Belzer is left in the room with a weary, depressed Isadora. She asks Belzer, "Do you ever think of killing yourself?" Belzer simply says, "Yes." Isadora pours out her troubles—romantic,

financial, artistic—and goes to her room. Belzer addresses
the following speech to the audience.

BELZER

I saw her dance. I was very young, perhaps twenty. It was
her first tour of Russia—in St. Petersburg. We had heard
about this strange creature from America who danced barefoot on an empty platform, wearing only a tunic, and be-
having—well, they said in very strange ways. The audience
was there, I think, to laugh. When she first appeared they
made noises—you know, hissing noises. She was standing.
Simply standing. Standing still. The music was playing. It
was—I think—Chopin. And then—very slowly—she
began to move. But it was not the way anyone else moved
on a stage. I do not know exactly *what* it was—I think
perhaps she simply walked from one side of the stage to
another—and then it was hard for me to see, because my
eyes were burning—that is what happens when I cry—but
I do not know why I was crying. I thought I saw children
dancing, but there were no children. I thought I saw the
face of my mother as she lay dying. I thought I remembered
the rabbi's words. I thought I was kissing my child before
they took him away from me. I thought I felt the lips, the
lips of a man in a great white hat on the train to Kiev—
and all she was doing on the stage was walking, just a few
steps up, a few steps down, but this walk of hers, it was
like a comet shooting through my body—and then, suddenly, she stopped—and that was it—it was over—and the
audience that had been making those noises, this hissing,
were on their feet, cheering, but my eyes were still burning. And this is why I do not like to cry. And I never cry
since that night—since eighteen years. No matter what has
happened, I never cry. But sometimes when sleep does
not come or when the dreams have frightened me—sometimes . . . then . . . I make myself think of Isadora—dancing!

•

Approaching Zanzibar
Tina Howe

Premiere: Second Stage Theatre, NYC, 1989
Publisher: Samuel French, Inc.
Setting: Various cross-country locations and Olivia Childs's bedroom in Taos, New Mexico

Charlotte and Wallace Blossom and their two children drive across the country to visit Charlotte's beloved aunt Olivia Childs on her deathbed. Olivia is "an eminent site-specific artist" who creates immense environmental pieces in fabric. A vibrant, iconoclastic woman of eighty-one, she has made her artistic home in Taos, New Mexico. In the play's last scene, Olivia talks to her nine-year-old great-niece, Pony, who is frightened of death and has crawled into bed with her dozing great-aunt. Olivia wakes and tells the terrified girl, "I just had the most beautiful dream . . . No, it was a reverie, because it actually happened. Yes . . . It happened a long, long time ago."

OLIVIA
(Putting her arms around her.)

I was on this horrid train on my way to the Sahara Desert . . . Yes, there was something about the Sahara Desert back then . . . I wanted to get lost in it, fling myself face down in it . . . I'd been studying painting in Paris for the year. How could I have forgotten . . . ? I was all of 20. Mercy, this was 1,000 years ago. During my wild days.
(She roars.)
What I put my poor parents through! Well, you'll do it, too, you'll do it all, just wait and see . . . Poor thing, you're shivering . . .

[PONY
(*Whimpering.*)

I don't want to die, save me, save me!

OLIVIA

What's all this talk about dying all of a sudden? . . .] I was
on a train somewhere between Paris and Tangier . . . we'd
stopped at some God-forsaken town in the middle of nowhere, and standing on the platform was the most beautiful
man I'd ever seen—tall, with olive skin and a thrilling
mouth. He wore a white suit and was pacing up and down
the platform carrying this enormous bouquet of poppies
that stained his face crimson. I couldn't take my eyes off
him. He was like something out of *The Arabian Nights*. I
kept expecting to see peacocks and jeweled elephants
stamping in the distance. Finally he caught my gaze . . . I
pressed my face against the window and whispered, "My
name is Callisto!"

(*She laughs.*)

Do you believe it? I used to call myself Callisto in those
days . . . The train suddenly started up. We pulled out of
the station. I watched him get smaller and smaller. Then
I fell into a deep sleep. I began having nightmares . . . I
was being chased down this long tunnel . . . I started to
scream. Someone grabbed my hands. I opened my eyes.
It was him! He'd jumped on the train at the last minute
and was sitting across from me, eyes laughing, poppies
blazing . . . He didn't speak a word of any language I knew,
but he held me spellbound. I never made it off the train.
He wrapped me in his flying carpet and wouldn't let me
go. You've never seen such feverish carryings on . . . He
rocked me over mountains, sang me through rain forests
and kissed me past ancient cities. Oh, what a ruckus we
made! Well, you'll do it, too, you'll do it all, wait and see.
We ended up in Zanzibar, island of cloves.

(*She removes her nasal canula.*)

I was so full of him, I thought my heart would burst. Zanzibar!

As the Crow Flies
David Henry Hwang

Premiere: Los Angeles Theatre Center, 1986
Publisher: TCG (in *Between Worlds: Contemporary Asian-American Plays*)
Setting: Living room of an upper-middle-class home, the present

Mrs. Chan is an upper-middle-class Chinese woman in her seventies. She is married to P.K. and has been having her house cleaned for over a decade by Hannah, a black woman. Mrs. Chan believes in many superstitions, such as that a ghost cannot kill a man if there is a goldfish in the room, nor can it enter a house if there is a raised step in the doorway. Today she was visited by a warning ghost. Her husband is afraid she will die. But she says she will resist. She must care for her husband and see her grandchildren grow, and she has too many responsibilities to die.

CHAN

I arrive in American one day, June 16, 1976. Many times, I have come here before, to visit children, but on this day, I arrive to stay. All my friends, all the Chinese in the Philippine, they tell me, "We thought you are stupid when you send all your children to America. We even feel sorry for you, that you will grow old all alone—no family around you." This is what they tell me.

The day I arrive in America, I do not feel sorry. I do not miss the Philippine, I do not look forward live in America. Just like, I do not miss China, when I leave it many years ago—go live in Philippine. Just like, I do not miss Manila, when Japanese take our home during wartime, and we are all have to move to Baguio, and live in haunted house. It is all same to me. Go, one home to the next, one city to another, nation to nation, cross ocean big and small.

We are born traveling. We travel—all our lives. I am not looking for a home. I know there is none. The day I was marry, my mother put many gold bracelets on my arm, and so many necklaces that the back of my head grows sore. "These," she tells me. "These are for the times when you will have to run."

Blind Spot
Michael Sutton

Premiere: West Bank Theatre, NYC, 1990
Publisher: —
Setting: Various locations in small-town Virginia

Jimmy, who lives in New York, has just gone home to Virginia for his father's funeral. As he waits for his much-delayed flight back to civilization, he muses about his eccentric Southern family, and the audience meets them in a series of linked scenes and monologues. Aunt Leota is the first to appear. (This monologue is her only scene in the play.)

Aunt Leota

Well, I'm the one that everyone in town has been talking about. And they can just go on talking about me, because they know I'm special, and they're miffed about it. They think that I've gotten above my raisings, haughty and uppity ever since I found out *Time* magazine was coming down. They're going to "check out" my story, and—believe you me—it is a darn sight better than that story they ran on those people that thought they saw Mary Magdalene on a highway overpass in San Antone. I mean, what is the big surprise that they would come down here to Radford? I mean, I have Jesus, right here on my refrigerator. And I don't know about you, but in my book, that makes me pretty darn special.

You see, I came downstairs late Sunday night to get me some buttermilk. My supper wasn't sitting easy and I couldn't sleep. I turned on the light and it was the first thing I saw. This stain, this big brown stain, right in the middle of my new Harvest Gold refrigerator, which I had just cleaned with Bon Ami the day before. Then I looked closer and I realized that this stain was in the shape of someone's face. At first I thought it was Elvis, but I looked closer, and it wasn't Elvis. It was Him. Plain and simple— it was Jesus.

Well, it made me kind of nervous. So I went into the living room to sit a spell and calm down, and there I sat the whole rest of the night, trying to figure it out. Why me? Of all the refrigerators in Radford, why mine? Then around dawn it came to me.

When I was about seven years old, I was playing in this big, vacant lot full of garbage, next to the Hickmans' house, which was the house next to ours. I know it seems kinda filthy for a little girl to be playing in a garbage dump, but it sure was a lot more fun than playing with Suzy Hickman 'cause she lied and all she ever wanted to play was school. So I was having a big time, pretending that I was a nurse in this big war. I had my little doctor's kit with me and this old towel wrapped around my neck like Florence Nightingale. Well, I got up to this freezer that was out on the dump, and I pretended that it was a trench and that I had to climb down in and save this wounded soldier. Well, I no sooner got down in that freezer when everything went pitch black. I tried to stand up. I tried kicking and screaming and pushing and knocking. But I was trapped. Like a fish on a hook, if you know what I mean. And I just started crying and crying. And then, I started praying.

Now, the amazing thing is, my parents didn't go to church. I had never been to a church, we didn't have TV back then so I hadn't seen it on TV. I couldn't read so I hadn't read about it. Either I had seen someone do it and forgot about it, or it was just instinct, but either way—I prayed for my life. I prayed, "Please dear God, don't let me die, if you let me live I promise I will be the best girl in the whole wide world, and I promise I will go to church for the rest of my life. Just don't let me die." I said it over and over and over eight million times, and each time I said it I meant it more than I did the time before. And all of a sudden, the lid just popped open, and I jumped up—half expecting to meet an old bum who was rummaging around in the dump and had opened the freezer looking for something.

(Whispering.)

No one was there. There was not a soul on that lot. No one you could see . . . if you know what I mean.

So you can imagine where I was the next Sunday and every Sunday afterwards. Right there on the third pew, right beside the stained glass picture of Jesus raising Lazarus from the dead. Just like I promised. For forty years now. But last Sunday I didn't go to church. I had the worst headache you could ever imagine, and I don't get headaches. Why I couldn't even get up, it was like being in a coma. Miss Hutchinson brought me in some supper around five. And I guess that helped because my headache lifted at about 6:02. Then I came down for some buttermilk. And look what happened. Jesus decided that if I couldn't go to his house, he'd come to mine. And that is what prompted me to remember that other time he had come to me. Twice in my life he has come to me. Twice. 'Course, I saw Elvis too. I was digging potatoes last summer, and Lord, I pulled up a big spud, and I mean to tell you if you would have told me that that potato could sing "Jailhouse Rock," I'd have believed it. I ain't going to tell *Time* magazine about Elvis. I'm going to just stick with Jesus, 'cause he's here on the refrigerator. But I will tell you one thing I've never told anyone. It was the weirdest thing that ever happened to me: I once saw Mel Tormé on a potato chip, and he ain't even dead yet.

Don't You Ever Call Me Anything but Mother
John O'Keefe

Premiere: Padua Hills Playwrights Festival, Claremont, California, 1983
Publisher: Theatre Communications Group (in *Shimmer and Other Texts*)
Setting: Lower-class Midwestern home

In this one-woman play, Doris is a serious alcoholic who talks incessantly to her school-age son, John E, as she moves from room to room in the offstage semi-darkness. The playwright describes her first appearance, several minutes into the play: "She is dressed in a faded yellow-and-blue terrycloth bathrobe. She wears a pink shower cap. She has fluffy white slippers on and they are not so fluffy and not so white. She is a woman in her mid to late sixties. She is very thin. Her face is freckled and wrinkled and bony. She has no teeth. Her lower jaw juts out and her mouth looks like a little shrunken trunk. She has a can of beer in one hand and a glass in the other. A cigarette sticks out of her mouth like a nail." Clearly, John E has long since grown up and gone, and Doris is in her own world. She is playing the country-western record "I'm Sending You a Big Bouquet of Roses."

> *(She draws the kitchen window shade down and the room goes dark except for the light coming from the refrigerator as she opens it to get another beer. She pours herself a can by refrigerator light. She closes the door and crosses through the hall into the bedroom.)*

DORIS
Oh look at this place, John E. It looks like a casket. I shouldn't see the bedroom in the daylight.

*(She draws the window shade down and the
room goes dark. She turns on the night-
light.)*

Oh, it looks so much better now, like the thirties. The
thirties should only be seen at night, John E, at night when
it's black and gold. That's when I had such red hair it'd
burn your heart out. And I did, John E, I burned a lot of
hearts with my hair. You can still see parts of the red in
my hair. They glisten and glow.

(Suddenly enthusiastic.)

Let me doll up for you, John E! Let your mother doll up
for you and show you her stuff.

*(A light clicks on just behind the bathroom
door. The record continues with "I'm Sending You a Big Bouquet of Roses.")*

Let me see here now.

*(We hear bottles clanking as she rummages
through the cabinet.)*

Oops.

(She drops a bottle. It breaks.)

I just haven't done this in such a long time I get slippery
fingers. You should help me, John E, you should help me
clean this up. Oh, all right, I'll just do it later. I keep this
house up, don't you think? That's more than I can say for
your grandmother, my mother. Did you know she couldn't
even cook pancakes? Stab a fork into them and goo would
run out of the center. She never made the beds. Even
when your grandfather was alive. She didn't do a thing,
but she always looked busy. And she didn't take care of
herself either. Oh, she smelled! I mean, sometimes she
smelled like she had been lying in bed with a man all of
her life. You know what I mean, don't you? She smelled
"that way." Stay away from women that smell "that way."
They're dangerous. Oh, darn this hair. It's always had a
mind of its own. But that's why it's so beautiful, John E,
that's why it's like wave-water. There we are. Now just a
little on my face and I'm through.

*(The record has ended and the needle
swishes in eerie syncopation on the tail-out
groove. The bathroom door slowly opens
and brilliant white light breaks from the
room. Gradually the figure of* DORIS
*emerges. She is bathed in bright light. Her
old face is painted with white powder. Her
cheeks are covered with bright red rouge.
Lipstick is smeared over her lipless, toothless
mouth. Dark green eye shadow and long,
false eyelashes make her look as if she has
two black eyes. Her frail body is covered
with a wrinkled, stained nightgown. She
speaks in a soft, shy voice.)*

Hello, John E, this is your mother. Do you like me? I can still draw an eye or two. Do you remember what I looked like with those shoulder pads and the Scottish plaid? I'm Irish, you know, but I look good in things like that with my hair all piled up like on a Coca-Cola sign out of the forties. I had slim legs and a lithe body and champagne breasts and my skin was creamy white with warm little freckles on it. John E, look at me. I'm going to tell you something you should know about. Look at this body. Do you know what this body is for? It is for the lust of God to have his way with me. All . . . the . . . way, John, all the way. To plant a baby inside of me. To plant a baby in me. That's where you were. You were up inside of me.

(She cups her hands between her legs.)

Up here. Haven't I ever told you about that stuff? Let me tell you, my darling son. A man, John E, a man put his thing in me. And it made him feel terribly good. That thing, that big thing of his. It made him want to come. Do you know what "want to come" means? It means that he can't stand the pleasure of it so much that he dies in me. He dies in me. He dies in me, John E, and when he does his whole body gets hard and starts to shudder and he starts pumping and pumping and he makes these strange cries like a baby wanting his mother and his face gets red like a poor sweet thing and he begins to weep and then, John E, then he comes.

(Mysteriously.)

He comes inside of my body and I hold him and I say, "Yes, yes, my sweet darling," and I rock him and caress him and he gets all soft and cuddly and he just curls up and goes to sleep. But I don't sleep, John E, no, I don't sleep. I lie there in the dark and feel his cum go sticky, feel it up inside of me, sending its magic into me, red and wanting and hurting for the magic that will wear your eyes and dress in your skin.

(She smiles knowingly, almost winking.)

Someday you'll come, John E. You'll know when you come. You'll know it for sure.

Lettice & Lovage
Peter Shaffer

Premiere: Theatre Royal, Bath, England, 1987
Publisher: Harper & Row
Setting: Grand Hall of Fustian House

Lettice Douffet is a Preservation Trust tour guide assigned to show groups around Fustian House, a gloomy, unheated sixteenth-century hall in which nothing historically significant has ever happened. The tourists are understandably bored, and Lettice (whose extravagantly theatrical mother taught her to "Enlarge! Enliven! Enlighten!") begins to embellish the story of Fustian House with ever-wilder tales of her own invention. This is Lettice's fourth and most extravagant variation on the history of Fustian House's Grand Staircase.

LETTICE

The incident I have just described to you—in which the
Virgin Queen Elizabeth was saved from almost certain
death by a feat of daring completely unachievable today *by
even the greatest Olympic athlete*—is only one of many
deeds of high drama which have been enacted upon the
stage of this historic staircase.

(Pause.)

Not all of them, alas, were so happy in their outcome. The
ensuing century was in every way darker, and the doings
on its staircases were correspondingly more murky . . . It
was upon these very stairs one hundred years later, that
the most *terrible* of all events connected with this house
occurred—on Mid-summer morning, sixteen hundred and
eighty-nine.

(All look expectant. LETTICE *warms to her
tale.)*

This day was intended to celebrate the marriage of Miss
Arabella Fustian to the handsomest young lordling in the
region. The bride was a radiantly beautiful girl of eighteen—"the catch of the County," as she was called. On the
morning of her wedding her father, Sir Nicholas, stood
exactly where I stand now—waiting to escort his only
daughter to the church. The door of the bedchamber
opened above

(She points; all look eagerly.)

and out stepped this exquisite creature in a miasma of white
samite. It is not hard to imagine her father staring up at
her, tears welling in his old eyes—she about to descend
these stairs for the last time a maiden! And then—ah, suddenly! a terrible drumming is heard! A frantic pounding
along the oak gallery—and toward her, galloping at full
speed, is Charger, the faithful wolfhound of the family, wild
with excitement at smelling the nuptial baked meats roast-
ing in the kitchen below! In his hurtling frenzy he knocks
the girl aside! She staggers—flails the air—shoots out her
hand for the banister, which alas is too far from her, and

falls headlong after the beast! . . . her lovely body rolling
like a cloud down the fifteen stairs you see, until at last
with one appalling jolt it comes to rest at her father's
feet! . . .

(She points to the spot, at her own.)

No Mercury he, but ancient and arthritic, he stoops to touch
her. Is she dead? No, the Saints be praised! Her neck is
unbroken.

(A pause.)

In a dreadful echo of the gesture with which his ancestor
won the family title, he catches the girl up in his arms and,
watched by the agonized dog, carries her upward to her
room. A room she was never to leave again. Arabella regained consciousness, yes, but her legs, which had danced
the Gavotte and the Scotch Jig as no legs had ever danced
them, were now twisted beneath her in mockery of the
love-knots which grace the plaster ceiling above you!

(All look up.)

By her own choice the girl immured herself in that chamber
up there for life, receiving no visitors but howling incessantly the Marriage Hymn which had been specially composed for her by Henry Purcell himself! . . . The Family
Chronicle records that her attendants were all likewise dis-
torted. I quote it for you. "The wretched lady would employ
as domestics only those who were deformed in the legs and
haunches: knotted women, bunchbacks, swivel-hips, and
such as had warpage and osseous misalignment of the
limbs." Servants of all shapes clawed their way daily up
this staircase, which was now known no longer as the Staircase of Aggrandizement, but the *Staircase of Wound and
Woe!* This name it has retained ever since.

Nunsense
Dan Goggin

Premiere: The Baldwin Theatre, NYC
Publisher: Samuel French, Inc.
Setting: Mt. St. Helen's School Auditorium, Hoboken, New Jersey

When the Little Order of Hoboken's cook, Sister Julia—Child of God, serves some vichyssoise, she accidentally kills fifty-two nuns with botulism. The entire order would have been wiped out had not some of the sisters been out playing Bingo. By selling greeting cards, they raise money to bury the dead sisters. They bury forty-eight of them; then the Reverend Mother buys a Beta-Max for the convent. In order to raise money to bury the remaining four sisters, who are currently stashed in the convent's freezer, the Reverend Mother and her most talented nuns put on a show on the set of the eighth-grade production of *Grease*.

Before the first act finale, one of the sisters finds a brown paper bag with poppers in it, in the girl's locker room. Reverend Mother takes command. While she may try to appear strict, everyone knows "her bark is worse than her bite. She loves the spotlight and is an outrageous, quick-witted soul who knows how to get a laugh." She takes the bag and shoos the sisters off to prepare for the finale.

REV. MOTHER

I'm terribly sorry for this delay, they'll only be a moment. Now what is this she's fussing about?
(REV. MOTHER *sits down at the counter stool closest to* C. *The spotlight fades up on her. She discovers a small bottle of liquid in the bag and holds it up. It contains a substance called "Rush" which, if inhaled, causes an almost instant "high" feeling. It, like airplane glue, etc., is the type of thing*

that today's students might be fooling
around with, much to the chagrin of the
nuns.)

Well, it's called "Rush"—it must be something for peo-
ple in a hurry—
(*She examines the bottle.*)
—I guess you take a spoonful after every meal—let's see—
no—it says here: "Remove cap, allow to stand, aroma will
develop." Aroma? What kind of aroma?
(*She opens the bottle and takes a whiff.*)
Oooohhh—Good Lord it smells awful. Why would any-
one want this stuff? R U S—Oh!
(*It has hit her. She puts her finger inside the*
edge of her headpiece as if to loosen it a
bit—she starts to laugh.)
Is it warm in here? I'm awfully warm—It must be the—
(*She indicates her headpiece.*)
I don't know what the girls are doing with this stuff but
it can't be good for you.
It smells just awful.
(*She opens the bottle and takes another*
whiff. She's laughing much more now.)
Is it hot in here? It must be the lights!
All right, in a few monents, minents, moments
(*Hysterical laughter.*)
we'll get back to Nundance—No—FLASHNUN
(*She flips her scapular as if to flash the au-*
dience—more hysterical laughter.)
—Butch Cassidy and the Sundance Nun—no, that's not
right.
(*She turns to the band.*)
What show is this? Never mind. I'm all right, I'm all
right.
(*To audience.*)
Okay, let's get back and watch a couple of butch nuns dance!
(*Pause.*)
Did I say that? Oh, that's not right.

(Laughter continues.)

You know, this stuff is absolutely marvelous! I'm gonna take some of this back to the convent.

*(She holds one finger to the side of her nose
   while she takes a huge snort.)*

Whooooaaaaaaa!

Do you want to try this?

(She gets up and goes toward band.)

Have you guys tried this? It's wonderful.

(She moves toward the audience.)

Have you tried it?

It's hot in here!!

(She falls to the floor, laughing hysterically.)

Wings
Arthur Kopit

Premiere: Yale Repertory Theatre, New Haven, Connecticut,
 1978
Publisher: Hill and Wang
Setting: The world of a stroke patient

Wings is a theatrical depiction in sound and images of
the dual realities of stroke patient Emily Stilson: the hospital ward where she undergoes rehabilitation therapy, and
the mysterious inner world of one who has lost control of
portions of her brain. Mrs. Stilson suffers from a stroke-
induced language disorder called aphasia, the inability to
match words and objects. In her youth, she was an aviatrix
and wing-walker. Now she has to work to remember the
word "plane." Throughout the play, the audience hears
brief passages of Mrs. Stilson's lucid thought as well as her
heartbreaking struggle toward lucid speech. At the end of
the play, after Mrs. Stilson tells her speech therapist Amy
that she left her body last night and looked down at herself

from the ceiling, we hear her thoughts again: "It comes now without my asking . . . Amy is still beside me but I am somewhere else. I'm not scared. It has taken me, and it's clear again. Something is about to happen." The lights change to a narrow spot on Mrs. Stilson, with darkness all around, for the following monologue.

MRS. STILSON

I am in a plane, a Curtiss Jenny, and it's night. Winter. Snow is falling. Feel the tremble of the wings! How I used to walk out on them! Could I have really done— . . . Yes. What I'd do, I'd strap myself with a tether to the stays, couldn't see the tether from below, then out I'd climb! Oh my, but it was wonderful! I could feel the wind! shut my eyes, all alone—FEEL THE SOARING!

(The wind grows stronger. Then the wind
dies away. Silence. She notices the change.)

But this is in another time. Where I've been also . . . It is night and no one else is in the plane. Is it . . . remembering?

(Pause.)

No . . . No, I'm simply there again!

(Pause.)

And I'm lost . . . I am lost, completely lost, have to get to . . . somewhere, Omaha I think. The radio is out, or rather for some reason picks up only Bucharest. Clouds all around, no stars only snow, don't possess a clue to where I am, flying blind, soon be out of gas . . . And then the clouds open up a bit, just a bit, and lights appear below, faint, a hint, like torches. Down I drop! heart pounding with relief, with joy, hoping for a landing place, I'll take anything—a field, a street, and down I drop! No place to land . . . It's a town but the smallest—one tiny street is all, three street lamps, no one on the street, all deserted . . . just a street and some faint light in the middle of darkness. Nothing. Still, down I go! Maybe I can find a name on a railroad station, find out where I am! . . . But

I see nothing I can read . . . So I begin to circle, though I know I'm wasting fuel and I'll crash if I keep this up! But somehow, I just can't tear myself away! Though I know I should pull back on the stick, get the nose up, head north into darkness—Omaha must be north! But no, I keep circling this one small silly street in this one small town . . . I'm scared to leave it, that's what, as if I guess once away from it I'll be inside something empty, black, and endless . . .

(Pause.)

So I keep circling—madness!—but I love it, what I see below! And I just can't bring myself to give it up, it's that simple—just can't bring myself to give it up!

(Pause.)

Then I know I have to. It's a luxury I can't afford. Fuel is running low, almost gone, may be too late anyway, so—

(Pause.)

I pull the nose up, kick the rudder, bank, and head out into darkness all in terror! GOD, BUT IT TAKES EFFORT! JUST DON'T WANT TO DO IT! . . . But I do.

(Pause. Suddenly calm.)

Actually, odd thing, once I did, broke free, got into the dark, found I wasn't even scared . . . Or was I?

(Slight laugh.)

Can't remember . . . Wonder where that town was . . . ?

(Pause.)

Got to Omaha all right.

(Pause.)

Was it Omaha . . . ?

(Pause.)

Yes, I think so . . . Yes, Topeka, that was it!

(Pause.)

God, but it was wonderful!

(Slight laugh.)

Awful scary sometimes, though!

The Young Lady from Tacna
Mario Vargas Llosa

Translated by David Graham-Young

Premiere: Gate Theatre, Notting Hill, England, 1989
Publisher: Hill & Wang (in *Three Plays by Mario Vargas Llosa*)
Setting: A writer's study; his grandparents' house in Lima, Peru,
  during the 1950s

A writer named Belisario, struggling to write a fictional
love story, finds his work interrupted by unbidden memories of his Peruvian grandparents and the little old lady
who lived with them, Mamae. Mamae was his grandmother's cousin Elvira, a woman who broke her youthful en-
gagement to a Chilean officer when she met his married
lover, and decided to spend her life single.

As a child, Belisario sat at Mamae's feet while she told
him stories, stories that started as memories and gradually
edged toward fiction. Now Belisario realizes his own memories are doing the same thing. He decides to write the
"love story" of Mamae's young life. This is one of the tales
he remembers her telling.

MAMAE:
(To an imaginary BELISARIO *still at her
feet.)*

When your Grandma Carmen and I were children together
in Tacna, we went through a phase of being very pious.
We did penances severer than the ones imposed at confes-
sional. And when your grandmother Carmen's mother—
my aunt Amelia—fell ill, we made a vow, so that God would
save her. Do you know what it was? To have a cold bath
each day.

(Laughs.)

At that time, it was considered madness to have a bath
every day. That habit came in later when the foreigners
arrived. It was quite a performance. The servants heated

up pails of water, the doors and windows were all bolted, the bath was spiced with salts, and when you got out of the tub, you went straight to bed so you didn't catch your death of cold. So in our efforts to save Aunt Amelia, we were ahead of our time. Every morning for a whole month, we got up as quietly as mice and plunged into icy cold water. We'd come out, our skin all covered in goosepimples, and our lips purple. Aunt Amelia recovered and we believed that it was all because of that vow we made. But a couple of years later she fell ill again and was in the most agonizing pain for months on end. She finally went out of her mind with all the suffering. It's hard sometimes to understand God, my little one. Take your Grandpa Pedro, for example. Was it fair that everything should have turned out so badly for him, when he'd always been so upright and so good?

MEN
TEENS—20s

•

All Night Long
John O' Keefe

Premiere: Magic Theatre, San Francisco, California, 1980
Publisher: Performing Arts Journal Publications (in *Word Plays 2*)
Setting: Inside of a house

Eddie is a seventeen-year-old high-school student who has just come home from school. He carries his books in a book strap, tosses them on the sofa, then heads for the refrigerator. This monologue opens the play.

EDDY

Hi, Mom, I'm home!
*(He pulls out the fixings for an enormous
sandwich and begins to build one.)*
Had a hard day today. Georgie Gessel beat up on me as soon as I got in the building. He told me to get off Buddha Row. I told him that I wasn't on Buddha Row. And that got him real mad. I'm pretty sure that he was thinking about hitting somebody before he got to school, especially me. I guess I got the face you like to punch. But I covered my cheeks with the sides of my hands like Dad told me to do and he only got me on the forehead and temples, sure protects the eyes though. Anyway, Georgie left in a huff after some of the cheerleaders gave him the read out. He got real red in the face and his eyes started to water and he snorted up his nose a lot and got me up against the lockers so that I made a big bang and I saw stars pouring out of my eyes and I felt all alone in the center of the universe like a big blob of nothing, shrinking all of the stuff of creation out of my head, and Karen Minataur bent real

close to my face so that I could smell her perfume and I
could see her big green eyes and her full red glisteny lips
and her pearly white teeth and I could feel her warm, moist
breath. And she said in the sweetest voice, "Are you okay,
Eddie? Georgie didn't mean it personally. It's just that he's
from the other side of the tracks and his dad beats him up
a lot." I understood, Mom, I did. And I told her that. I
said I had a lot of liberal guilt to deal with myself so I could
understand the value of a psychotherapeutic perspective.
And then she left and I heard Georgie's big Chevy roar off.
I worried about her all day. If she keeps missing school she
won't be able to go to Springfield Junior C.O. this fall and
she has a fine alto voice.

> (EDDY *has now finished making his huge
> sandwich and does a California roll over the
> back of the couch and onto the cushions.*)

But one thing I didn't do, Mom. I didn't cry. I know that
that might make me tighten up my facial muscles and lock
my solar plexus so that I breathe wrong, but it did something for my leadership capacities. I *know* I won't go down
in mixed chorus this year!

Asinamali!
Mbongeni Ngema

Premiere: U.S.: *Woza Afrika!* Festival at Lincoln Center, NYC,
   1986
Publisher: George Braziller, Inc. (in *Woza Afrika!*)
Setting: A jail cell at Leeuwkop Prison, outside Johannesburg

   "Out of the anger and passion of the residents of the
Lamontville township came the leader Msizi Dube. Passionately demonstrating against proposed rent increases,
he led the masses with the cry 'Asinamali!'—'We have no
money!' This rallying phrase provided a focus for the dis-

enfranchised as well as a poignant description of the condition of blacks throughout South Africa."

Bhoyi Ngema is one of five prisoners in the jail cell. A young activist from the Lamontville township, he worked with Dube, and helped rid the streets of government informers.

BHOYI

Thousands of people gathered in an open field in Lamontville Township. My friend, Bhekani, and I were among the first people who heard Msizi Dube shout: ASINAMALI for the first time. And after that gathering, the whole township understood . . .

[ALL
(In a powerful, slow deliberate whisper.)
ASINAMALI.]

BHOYI

We the youth went into the streets. It was finally happening, my friend Bhekani and I were in front. That guy, Bhekani, Bhekani he was a beautiful stone-thrower. He never missed an informer with a stone. One day soldiers and police came to our school. Bhekani picked up a stone and hit one soldier who was on top of a tank. That was the beginning of shit. We scattered. I threw myself under the barbed-wire fence and I saw Bhekani's feet passing over my head running down the vegetable garden, a policeman right behind him. Ay, that policeman was running like Zola Budd man.

[*They all laugh.*]

He caught Bhekani by his shirt. Bhekani came out of the shirt and this policeman had Bhekani's shirt, in his hands. His police hat was flying up, his boots were heavy and he was running. We were laughing.

[*They all laugh and scream.*]

Bhekani was laughing too. Just around the corner, I saw one policeman pick up a machine-gun. Tratatatatata-tata.

(Pointing it towards SOLOMZI who then falls in response.)

And then I saw Bhekani taking long strides, lifting up into the air, over the vegetable garden fence and then a somersault. And then he hit the ground. That man, my friend, he lay there and he was no longer the man I knew.

The Author's Voice
Richard Greenberg

Premiere: Ensemble Studio Theatre, NYC, 1987
Publisher: Dramatists Play Service, Inc.
Setting: The author's lair, a shadowy New York apartment

Todd is a callow but photogenic young novelist. His beautiful and seductive editor, Portia, trails him home from a party. She's surprised by the House of Usher atmosphere and the curious smell that emanates from behind a closed door: "Tell me the truth—those aren't neighbors behind that door. Behind that door, there's some horribly twisted gnome who does all your writing for you." Todd tells her she's had too much to drink and rushes her out. The door opens and out comes a horribly twisted gnome with a sheaf of manuscript pages.

The gnome is named Gene. Todd picked him up, as he says, in the gutter. Gene does the writing and Todd is the front man, the book jacket photo, the one who gets taken to lunch. Their already fragile and envy-filled relationship goes into tilt when Gene gets a glimpse of Portia through his keyhole and falls madly in love. Gene breaks Todd's rules and leaves the apartment. Todd is terrified. When

Gene returns, Todd quietly asks to hug him, then wrestles
him down to the ground in a rage, screaming, "SON-OF-
A-BITCH! NEVER DO THAT AGAIN!" Gene crawls into
his room and tells Todd through the door, "We're over."

> (TODD *stands at the door, a liquor bottle in*
> *his hand. From* GENE's *room, an incessant*
> *keening, a mournful, animal sound.* TODD
> *knocks his palm against the door. Again.*
> *Again. Again. Again.)*

TODD

Christ, I'm sorry!
> (*Beat.*)

I didn't mean to hurt you. Please come out.
> (*Beat.*)

Please come out.
> (*Beat.*)

I'm not a cruel person. I'm not . . . I don't . . .
> (*Beat. The keening subsides.*)

Gene?
> (*It starts again.*)

Gene, I'm sorry, I'm sorry, I'm sorry, I'm sorry, I'm . . .
> (*He is now almost climbing the door, almost*
> *caressing it, pacifying.*)

Listen . . . Listen . . . Listen . . . Gene?
Gene? . . . Gene? . . .
> (*The keening subsides again.*)

Gene, are you all right, now?
> (*Beat. Still quiet.*)

Are you better?
> (*Still quiet.*)

Are you better?
> (*Still quiet.*)

You sound better . . . Gene, what can we do? Can we be
friends? Can we . . . ?
> (*Beat.*)

Gene, listen, I'm going to do like we used to, okay? Remember? I'm going to tell you something that happened to me and you can tell me what it means, remember? Okay?

(Beat.)

Is that okay?

(Beat.)

Is that okay?

(Beat.)

Okay.

(He sits with his back against the door.)

This happened the other day at the Health Club. You know, where I go?

(Beat.)

Right. Well, I was going to take a swim. I'd never used the pool there before but I wanted to swim. So I was getting suited up when a man at the row of lockers across from me started talking to his friend. This man, he was balding, but he seemed pretty fit, and he was pleased with himself, you could tell, like he didn't even mind being bald, and I thought, well, if I feel like that at his age, I won't be doing half-bad. And his friend looked pretty good, too, and it sort of cheered me up. Anyway, they went to the pool. I finished getting ready, and then I went to the pool. It was just the three of us and an attendant. The attendant yelled at me, "No trunks!" I didn't understand. Then I looked at the two men swimming in the pool. They were naked. It was policy. When they were naked like that, they didn't look so good. They looked fat. They looked like fish— large . . . extinct . . . fish . . . I bent to take off my trunks. As I did, the bald man came up for air. For a second, he was completely still, frozen solid in the water. He looked at me and kept looking. I dove in, a perfect dive with a flip and a spin. When I came up for air, the bald man wasn't in the pool anymore. He was standing by the poolside, crying hysterically. His friend was next to him, trying to calm him down, but the bald-headed man wouldn't stop crying. "Why are you crying?" his friend kept asking. "It was the dive," he said. "It was the dive."

(Beat.)

Gene . . . ?

(Beat.)

Gene, why did that make him cry?

(Beat.)

Why? . . . Why did that make him cry?

(Beat.)

Gene . . . ? Gene . . . ? Why?

I need you to tell me these sorts of things, Gene. I can't figure them out on my own.

(Beat.)

My life isn't good. You think it is, but it's not. Once it was, but it's not anymore.

(Beat.)

I used to be made happy by . . . stupid things. Parties! People around me. I was vain. I was a peacock. I looked in the mirror. I looked so hard I didn't recognize myself. I didn't recognize anything. I forgot why I did things. I got scared, Gene! I got scared outside, I got scared in my room. I didn't know where I was half the time. I wanted to drown, I wanted to be covered over . . . Then I found you.

(Beat.)

Make me famous, Gene. I want to be famous. People will photograph me and write about me. I'll study how they see me and live inside it . . . Fame will be a kind of home. But I need you to get it for me. Only they can't know it's you, they can't know it's you; if they ever see you, it will die like *that*.

(Snaps his fingers. Beat.)

It panics me when you leave and it panics me when you're here. You're the whole problem of my life, but without you I don't have any life.

(Beat.)

I'll give you what you want. I won't deny you any more. Anything I can, I'll give you.

Biloxi Blues
Neil Simon

Premiere: Neil Simon Theatre, NYC, 1985
Publisher: Samuel French, Inc.
Setting: An army boot camp barracks and other locations in Biloxi, Mississippi, 1943

Five young recruits travel by train to Biloxi, Mississippi, for basic training. One of them, Eugene Morris Jerome, wants to become a writer and keeps a journal describing his companions. The first three are typical grunts: smelly, horny, and flatulent. Eugene describes the fourth: "Arnold Epstein of Queens Boulevard, New York, was a sensitive, well-read, intelligent young man. His major flaw was that he was incapable of digesting food stronger than hard-boiled eggs. . . . I didn't think he'd last very long in the army because during wartime it's very hard to go home for dinner every night."

Sure enough, Arnold is an immediate target for Drill Sergeant Toomey when he requests permission to go to the bathroom (not "the latrine") during the sergeant's first intimidation speech. Later, when Arnold refuses to eat "slop," he is assigned five straight days of KP, including cleaning the latrines. Bitter and humiliated, he tells Eugene he's planning to leave the army, go AWOL, and spend the war in Mexico.

ARNOLD

I was in the latrine alone. I spent four hours cleaning it, on my hands and knees. It looked better than my mother's bathroom at home. Then these two non-coms come in, one was the cook, that three-hundred-pound guy and some other slob, with cigar butts in their mouths and reeking from beer . . . They come in to pee only instead of using the urinal, they use one of the johns, both peeing in the same one, making circles, figure-eights. Then they start to walk out and I say, "Hey, I just cleaned that. Please flush the johns." And the big one, the cook, says to me, "Up your ass, rookie," or some other really clever remark . . . And I block the doorway and I say, "There's a printed order on the wall signed by Captain Landon stating the regulations that all facilities must be flushed after using" . . . And I'm requesting that they follow regulations, since I was left in charge, and to please flush the facility . . . And the big one says to me, "Suppose you flush it, New York Jew Kike," and I said my ethnic heritage notwithstanding, please flush the facility . . . They look at each other, this half a ton of brainless beef, and suddenly rush me, turn me upside down, grab my ankles and—and—and they lowered me by my feet with my head in the toilet, in their filth, their poison . . . all the way until I couldn't breathe . . . then they pulled off my belt and tied my feet on to the ceiling pipes with my head still in their foul waste and tied my hands behind my back with dirty rags, and they left me there, hanging like a pig that was going to be slaughtered . . . I wasn't strong enough to fight back. I couldn't do it alone. No one came to help me . . . Then the pipe broke and I fell to the ground . . . It took me twenty minutes to get myself untied . . . Twenty minutes! . . . But it will take me the rest of my life to wash off my humiliation. I was degraded. I lost my dignity. If I stay, Gene, if they put a gun in my hands, one night, I swear to God, I'll kill them both . . . I'm not a murderer. I don't want to disgrace my family . . . But I have to get out of here . . . Now do you understand?

Boys' Life
Howard Korder

Premiere: Lincoln Center Theatre, NYC, 1988
Publisher: Dramatists Play Service, Inc.
Setting: Various locations in a large city

Three male friends in their twenties hang out in each other's apartments and compare notes on women. Don starts the play single, has a nightmare first date with a difficult waitress, and marries her. Jack is already married with a young son; he can't stand his wife and is dying to start an affair. Phil's history with women is so pathetic that Jack figures he must be gay and not know it.

At a party, Phil runs into Karen, a troubled and self-hating woman he slept with twice, left before dawn, and hasn't called since. He realizes he's fallen in love with her and pours out his heart: "I'm dying without you, Karen. I'm serious." Karen says she's not worth it, but Phil persists. Jack describes their relationship to Don: "This girl, he's been seeing her a week, every night he goes to her place, right, they talk about the whales or something, he gets to sleep on the couch. She says she's frigid. He says it doesn't matter. She says her uncle raped her when she was ten. He says I love you. She says maybe you shouldn't come by anymore. He says let's give it time. She says I'm screwing somebody else. He says it's all right, we can work around it. Isn't that so *typical*?"

Here, Phil tells Jack his own version. They are sitting on a park bench near a playground where Jack's son plays.

PHIL

I would have destroyed myself for this woman. Gladly. I would have eaten garbage. I would have sliced my *wrists* open. Under the right circumstances, I mean, if she said, "Hey, Phil, why don't you just cut your wrists open," well, come on, but if *seriously* . . . We clicked, we connected on so many things, right off the bat, we talked about God for *three hours* once, I don't know what good it did, but that *intensity* . . . and the first time we went to bed, I didn't even touch her. I didn't *want* to, understand what I'm saying? And you know, I played it very casually, because, all right, I've had some rough experiences, I'm the first to admit, but after a couple of weeks I could feel we were right there, so I laid it down, everything I wanted to tell her, and . . . and she says to me . . . she says . . . "Nobody should ever need another person that badly." Do you *believe* that? "Nobody should ever . . ."! What is that? Is that something you saw on TV? I dump my *heart* on the table, you give me Joyce Dr. Fucking Brothers? "Need, need," I'm saying I *love* you, is that wrong? Is that not allowed anymore?

(Pause. Jack looks at him.)

And so what if I did need her? Is that so bad? All right, crucify me, I needed her! So *what!* I don't want to be by myself, I'm by myself I feel like I'm going out of my mind, I do. I sit there, I'm thinking forget it, I'm not gonna make it through the next *ten seconds,* I just can't *stand* it. But I do, somehow, I get through the ten seconds, but then I have to do it all over again, 'cause they just keep coming, all these . . . seconds, floating by, while I'm waiting for something to happen, I don't know what, a car wreck, a nuclear war or something, that sounds awful but at least there'd be this *instant* when I'd know I was alive. Just once. 'Cause I look in the mirror, and I can't believe I'm really there. I can't believe that's me. It's like my body, right, is the size of, what, the Statue of Liberty, and I'm inside it, I'm down in one of the legs, this gigantic hairy leg, I'm scraping around inside my own foot like some tiny fetus. And I don't know who I am, or where I'm going. And I wish I'd never been born.

(Pause.)

Not only that, my hair is falling out, and that really *sucks.*

Dalton's Back
Keith Curran

Premiere: Circle Repertory Company, NYC, 1989
Publisher: Dramatists Play Service, Inc.
Setting: Simultaneously Dalton's present-day apartment in Boston and his suburban home in the 1950s

Dalton Possil was raised by an unpredictable, often violent mother and still suffers nightmares that cause him to talk in his sleep. He works as a teacher and is increasingly obsessed with becoming a parent himself. He presses his lover Teresa to have a baby. She isn't ready, nor is she convinced that the traumatized Dalton would make a good father. Throughout the play, Dalton's past is literally with him. Scenes of his childhood abuse coexist in the same room with scenes of his present-day life with Teresa.

The playwright describes Dalton as follows: "twenty-nine years old. Initially shy, playful, amazed. Then unpredictable, joyous, angry. Dalton can never be self-pitying, or too self-aware. His feelings surprise, rush on, take over, overwhelm. A man of great charm and vulnerability. Childlike, impulsive. He is taller, bigger, more attractive than he knows. His body contradicts him, his voice can break— there is something of the adolescent about him—not a childishness, but a wonder, a defenselessness."

Dalton has just woken up from one of his dreams. Teresa tells him he talked in his sleep: "This and that, you said 'Hi' a lot—but you were smiling. Till the end it was a happy one."

DALTON
(Smiling, remembering.)

Yeah . . . The same dream I had all the time as a kid. I'd written about it in the journal, I guess that sparked it again.

[TERESA

Tell me.

DALTON

Uh . . .] The place is . . . very different. That's the point
of the place. Everything is different just for the sake of it.
People are strangely shaped and animals wear clothes and
dance. Flowers sing in harmony, like on the Broadway show
albums I had as a kid. That's it, that's the dream. Oh, once
I tried to get there.

[TERESA

Yeah?]

DALTON

I was six or seven. *Small*. I packed my red knapsack with
Hostess products and comic books and got on a *bus*. I sat
in the back and pictured my triumphant arrival in the very
different place. I pictured banners saying: "Welcome
John"—because in the very different place my name would
be John.

[TERESA
(Laughing.)

Mmmm . . .]

DALTON

There would be a huge Christmas tree and Pilgrims slicing
a turkey and huge rabbits hiding colored eggs—because,
in honor of my arrival, the residents would be celebrating
every major holiday at the same time. There would be a
marching band playing my favorite song, which at the time
was "A Boy Like That" from *West Side Story*. I even
planned to make a speech. I would say smart things and
then all the strangely shaped people in the very different
place would hug me. I'd hug them back—but I'd hug them
back all at *once* because my arms would grow and grow,
stretching out longer and longer—longer than anyone else's
arms had ever grown in the very different place's history.
And one by one, every strangely shaped person I held in
my arms would . . . would disappear into me. Go right
inside me with a "thwump" noise. They'd look up at me
and say—before they went inside me—they'd say:
"Thanks, John. Thanks for finally coming." Thwump.

(Pause.)

It was, of course, a local bus. Didn't even *stop* at the "Very Different Place"—wasn't even on the schedule. I figured it out, got off at the stop near my house, went home, I hadn't been missed—and nothing was very different.

(Long pause. DALTON *thinking,* TERESA *looking at him. A moment very full of feeling.)*

Foolin' Around with Infinity
Steven Dietz

Premiere: Brass Tacks Theatre, Minneapolis, Minnesota, 1988
Publisher: Samuel French, Inc.
Setting: A fallout shelter and the command post of an underground missile silo, both in Nevada

Arthur "Mac" McCormick and John "Jesse" Randall work the night shift in a missile silo a mile beneath the Nevada desert. These men are empowered to push the button that activates nuclear missiles—after an elaborate system of checks and procedures that, among other things, instructs each man to shoot the other if he suspects him of balking. Meanwhile, they pass the time with an endless game of Monopoly. Mac is the crew commander, a taciturn, questionably stable man in his fifties whose daughter, Luke, is so obsessed with nuclear threat that she's set up housekeeping in a public fallout shelter. Jesse is new on the job, and already starting to have his doubts.

JESSE
(Steps into an area of light downstage and speaks to the audience.)

I used to live in an old house in a college town. I had nine roommates. We did what the times told us to do. We ate mushrooms and wore bandanas and wrote FUCK on things that were not moving. We drank tequila and beer and drove around with Lou Reed to sober up. I am not proud of those days, but they reside in me. They are the days I first bordered on realism. They are the days I first flirted with maturity. And avarice. And cowardice. And helplessness.

(JESSE *moves to his seat in the Command Post. The only light is a shaft of light on him. The rest of the Command Post, including* MAC *at his chair, is in darkness.*)

Eight of us are crammed into a 1961 Rambler. We are coming home from a concert. My ninth roommate, Henry, has stayed at home. My friend Connie is driving. Three in front. Five in back. We have done a lot of mushrooms and smoked a lot of dope. The Moody Blues spew pop philosophy through the tiny in-dash radio. We are eight bodies in a metal box moving seventy miles an hour. And, as always at this point in the evening, the conversation consists of talking about *just how stoned we are.* We are laughing riotously at our lack of motor skills. And upon experiencing any new visual sensation—a billboard, a bumper *sticker,* windshield *wiper*—we scream in joy at the top of our lungs. It was at this moment that Connie—with both hands still propped up on the wheel—very softly said: "God, this is good shit. I'm so glad I'm not driving."

The rest of us froze. Connie, with both hands still propped up on the wheel, was wearing a beatific smile and navigating us down the highway. We heard only soft asphalt and loud Moody Blues: *"Breathe deep the gathering gloom. Watch lights fade from every room . . . "* The rest of us are absolutely silent. Staring at Connie, staring at the wheel, staring at the road. And each of us is terrified to tell her that she *is* driving—for fear she'll panic, lose control and kill us all. *"Cold hearted orb that rules the night. Removes the colors from our sight. Red is gray and yellow white . . . "* I am in the seat next to Connie. Frozen. Uncertain whether to grab the wheel. *"But we decide which one is right. And which is an illusion."*

The miles went by in silence as we barreled through
the twilight. And there we sat. Seven panicked faces in a
metal box moving seventy miles an hour. And Connie,
happy and serene, holding the wheel. Secure in the knowledge that someone else is driving.

Kathie and the Hippopotamus
Mario Vargas Llosa

Translated by David Graham-Young

Premiere: Gate Theatre, Notting Hill, England, 1989
Publisher: Hill & Wang (in *Three Plays by Mario Vargas Llosa*)
Setting: An artist's attic in Paris during the 1960s

A rich Peruvian woman with the pen name Kathie Ken-
nety has hired writer Santiago Zavala to ghostwrite a mem-
oir about her travels through North Africa. They work
improvisationally in Kathie's Parisian attic—Kathie tells
stories, and Santiago puts them into flowery prose. At times
the two impersonate characters in the stories; at other times
they are joined by two fictional characters named Ana and
Juan. Eventually, Kathie's memoirs begin to include other
characters from her past, including her ex-husband Johnny,
a passionate surfer with no other interests in life. Santiago
asks Kathie, "Did he really devote his life to riding waves?
Didn't he feel ashamed?" Juan, as Johnny, responds.

(As he surfs, JUAN *keeps his balance by pad-
dling with his hands, and by leaning from
side to side to steady himself as the waves
tug him along tossing him up and down.)*

JUAN

Ashamed? Quite the reverse. It makes me feel proud, I
like it, it makes me happy. Why should I be ashamed?

What's wrong with surfing? I've surfed all over the world—
in Miraflores, Hawaii, Australia, Indonesia, South Africa.
What's wrong with that? It's the most fantastic thing there
is! I enter the water slowly, smoothly, gliding along, teasing
the waves, outwitting the waves, then suddenly I dive, I
slice through them, I cut across them, harnessing them,
taming them, on, on I go, further and further, pulled by
the undertow right up to the rollers after they've broken.
I get onto my board, and like a jockey on the starting line,
I size them up, getting their measure, calculating, guessing.
Which of these little crinkles will grow and grow and become the best wave to ride? That one! That one there! I
can hardly wait. It's thrilling. My muscles tingle! My heart
pounds! Pum, pum, pum. There's not a second to lose,
Johnny! I get into position, I wait poised, now, I slap the
water, and we're away, it's got me, it tows me along, I
caught it just at the very moment before it broke, I jump,
I stand on the board, I stretch up, crouch, stretch up again,
it's all in the hips now, it's all balance, experience, stamina,
a battle of wits. No, little wave, you won't knock me over!
I've ridden waves which could topple a skyscraper, I've
tunnelled under waves as sheer as cataracts, like gaping
caverns, like soaring mountains, I've ridden waves which,
had I lost my balance, would have smashed me to pieces,
torn me limb from limb, pulverized me. I've ridden waves
through jagged coral reefs, in seas infested with marauding
sharks. I've nearly been drowned a hundred times, nearly
been deafened, paralyzed, maimed. I've won champion-
ships on four continents and if I haven't won any in Europe
it's because the waves in Europe are lousy for surfing. Why
should I be ashamed of myself?

Keyhole Lover
Keith Reddin

Publisher: Dramatists Play Service, Inc. (in *Desperadoes, Throwing Smoke* and *Keyhole Lover*)
Setting: Bare stage

A spot comes up on a young man named Warren, sitting on a stool. He tells the audience how he became a voyeur, and eventually a fervent customer of live-sex peep shows. This monologue opens the play.

WARREN

She didn't spot me the first time. Or the second. Watching her like taking baths and just brushing her hair, stuff like this. I didn't think too much about, like you know, you open the bathroom door and she's standing in front of our big mirror looking at herself, and touching herself, and you know like checking herself out, and such. This is normal things. Then I try to find these excuses to come in on accident and take a quick look, you know. I mean there's nothing weird about this, you know, but like she would smile too. I know this. I saw her smile at me. And so I know it's all right. True she is my sister, but I don't want to screw her or such things like that, but you know, she is pretty good looking, so the other guys tell me and she knows it, and so she doesn't mind when I came in on accident and would look at her. Then like when her boyfriend Marty or *MARTIN* as she has to say, them on the couch and he puts his hands all over her and she knew I was watching from the kitchen, making the excuse me, pardon me, I have to pass through here to the kitchen or to the TV room to watch this particular program at this real specific time, and again, she would smile at me, she knew. There was like this understanding between us. *MARTIN* and her get very quiet, and passionate, and he wants to like go all the way, that is his expression, I don't say jerky things like that. And I would look. I would look and not get excited. I was just studying the both of them and I would not jerk off or something weird I would only watch. And even when there was no way she could know I was watching her, I knew that she knew, understand?

Love Letters
A. R. Gurney, Jr.

Premiere: Long Wharf Theater, New Haven, Connecticut, 1988
Publisher: Dramatists Play Service, Inc.
Setting: Bare stage

Two actors sit at a table together, reading a lifetime's correspondence between Andrew Makepeace Ladd III and Melissa Gardner. Through the letters, we see the characters progress from a polite little boy and a mischievous girl to a tragically repressed politician and an alcoholic, self-destructive artist. Here, Andrew writes to Melissa from college.

ANDY

O.K. Here goes. The reason I'm writing Angie Atkinson is because I just don't think I can stop writing letters, particularly to girls. As I told you before, in some ways I feel most alive when I'm holed up in some corner, writing things down. I pick up a pen, and almost immediately everything seems to take shape around me. I love to write. I love writing my parents because then I become the ideal son. I love writing essays for English, because then I am for a short while a true scholar. I love writing letters to the newspaper, notes to my friends, Christmas cards, anything where I have to put down words. I love writing you. You most of all. I always have. I feel like a true lover when I'm writing you. This letter, which I'm writing with my own hand, with my own pen, in my own penmanship, comes from me and no one else, and is a present of myself to you. It's not typewritten, though I've learned how to type. There's no copy of it, though I suppose I could use a carbon. And it's not a telephone call, which is dead as soon as it is over. No, this is just me, me the way I write, the way my writing is, the way I want to be to you, giving myself to you across a distance, not keeping or retaining any part of it for myself, giving this piece of myself to you totally, and you can tear me up and throw me out, or keep me, and read me today, tomorrow, any time you want until you die.

Love Minus
Mary Gallagher

Premiere: Capital Rep Art Awareness, Lexington, New York, 1988
Publisher: Dramatists Play Service, Inc.
Setting: Various locations in New York City

Love Minus charts the crisscrossing involvements of four young people who've come to New York to make their mark. Nick, a successful TV actor, picks up Karla, an aspiring novelist, in a park along the Hudson River. The affair starts hot and heavy, but Nick pulls back abruptly, saying he wants to stay friends. Heartbroken, Karla consults her friend Lydia, who calls Nick "an emotional mugger" and forbids her to him again. Karla says Nick has her unpublished manuscript, and Lydia arranges to get it from his roommate Alan.

Alan has just come back from a month-long children's theater tour of the rural South. He's humiliated by the job, but relieved to have acting work and willing to plug along until things get better. Alan's the kind of guy who sends postcards of the Last Supper with moving eyeballs and somehow finds joy in no-name beer and a part-time job as

a messenger. He sits down with a bowl of aging leftovers
and tells Nick about the tour.

ALAN

The first day, we all loved each other so much, we hugged
all day long in the car. And then . . . four weeks, nine
states, forty-seven shows. By the end of the tour, we were
hugging the doors, I've got bruises from the handles. Plus
this new techie—*Rory,* his name is—got to drive. Which
woulda been all right, I mean at least he had a license, but
he never had to piss. So he wouldn't make the rest stops.
And he was such a rude creep that the girls were afraid to
tell him when they had to go. So they'd tell this other guy
and me and we'd put the muscle on Rory. By the third day
out, we didn't even talk to him. We'd see a rest room sign,
this other guy would strangle Rory . . . and I'd steer us off
the road.
        (Acts out this whole maneuver.)
                [NICK
            (Gloomy, preoccupied.)
Sounds like a whole tour about toilets.]
                ALAN
Every tour is a tour about toilets! You have to eat and you
have to piss, and you cling to that! . . . You also have to
drink—what else was there to do in a town like Cannery,
Missouri?—and we'd get stinking drunk, because we had
nothing to say to each other. And the next morning, we'd
rise at dawn to do "Foofoo and the Princess of the Sunflower
Town." I'd walk into this silo, or wherever they'd penned
up the kids, and I'd say . . .
        (Very weary and hungover.)
"Hi, kids . . . I'm Mr. Magic Man . . . can you say Hi?"
And they'd all holler, "HIIIIIII, MIIIIIISTER
MAAAAAAAGIC MAAAAAAAN!!!!!"
        (Clutches his head.)
If there's a hell where actors go, it must be children's
theatre.

Lydie Breeze
John Guare

Premiere: American Place Theatre, NYC, 1982
Publisher: Dramatists Play Service, Inc.
Setting: Nantucket, 1985, a house out on the Madeket Road

Fifteen-year-old Lydie Hickman and Beaty, the Irish maid, enact a dark ceremony in remembrance of Lydie's mother, Lydie Breeze, who hanged herself. In the next scene, Lydie's older sister Gussie, the private secretary to Senator Amos Mason, returns home on William Randolph Hearst's private yacht. And there is another, unexpected visitor, a young man named Jeremiah Grady. He is looking for Lydie Breeze.

Jeremiah, an actor who made his career as the monster in a London production of *Frankenstein,* is described by the playwright as "in his late twenties. He affects the pose of a dandy, a ragged Byronic mien. But his face betrays a real anguish. His speech is markedly English. His whole manner is histrionic, except—that anguish, that pain—that is authentic." Jeremiah's father Dan Grady, Lydie Breeze, and her husband Joshua were all members of a post-Civil War Utopian commune that dissolved after Joshua killed Dan Grady in a fight. The tragedy that has brought Jeremiah back to Nantucket is not his father's, but his own. He is infected with syphilis, which he got from Lydie Breeze.

JERE

I watched my father die. The police took you away. Amos went into town with you. The house was empty except for Lydie Breeze and me. I heard her footsteps coming up the stairs. Slow. Heavy. Her hair was down. She sat on the edge of my bed. She leaned over me. She held me. She had been weeping.

[JOSHUA

Bam bam bam. Where have those hunters gone . . .]

JERE

Her hair fell over me like a tent. Her hair smelled . . . Oriental. Omar Khayyam. *The Rubaiyat*. She whispered to me, Are you awake? Yes. I loved your father. I did too. She said, You fool, I loved him. And she began beating the walls and crickets were in them and began squawking. She was so angry. He betrayed me. How? You were all friends. I have somehting for you, she said. She reached under the sheet. Why were we whispering? Her hair made it all so quiet. And she began touching me. I became frightened. What was happening? Oh yes, she said, you're his son. You're a man. And she rolled me onto her and I wanted to run away because I felt a power in me that had never existed in me before. I was thirteen. I did not know what that feeling was . . . She pushed me aside. And then she put her hair back and held me, all shaking, and began holding me like a mother. What have I done to you? What have I done to you? And she cried and she cried and she cried. At my father's funeral, she did not look at me. Then I was sent to England. Before I went, it began to hurt down there where she had taken me.

[JOSHUA

Hurt?]

JERE

I was afraid to tell anyone how much it hurt. I was afraid the people in England might send me back. Put me in jail. So I didn't tell anyone. The English relatives were so nice. The English school was so nice. Christ! I was even disappointed in the lack of horrors. The only horror was the pain coming out of me. And then the doctors diagnosed me and put me on medication of arsenic treatments which did not poison me but almost did. And I was told I could never have a normal life and must never touch a woman because of how infected I was and I began to live in that tent of hair and suffocate and dream only of Lydie Breeze who had poisoned me and I went with whores because I had to release this need in me. And then a series of murders began

in London. Brutal murders. Prostitutes. Tarts. Useless bits
of humanity. Murders on streets that I had been
on . . . and I became terrified and to save myself and stop
the bad dreams said I will become other people who are
not afraid and I became an actor . . . and I had success . . . and now I want to face that woman and meet her
as an equal. Because I am no longer afraid of her. I want
myself back. I want to kill Lydie Breeze or make love to
Lydie Breeze. But I come back and find she is dead. And
there can be no—revenge? I don't want that. I want her
to see her poison. I don't want to be this monster. I am
sick of playing this monster and if I am asked to play it for
the rest of my life I have to have a whole human being to
come back to when the curtain comes down. A human being!

Medal of Honor Rag
Tom Cole

Premiere: Theatre Company of Boston, Cambridge, Massachu-
setts, 1975
Publisher: Samuel French, Inc.
Setting: An office in Valley Forge Army Hospital, 1971

A young black soldier named "D.J." Dale Johnson has
been awarded the Medal of Honor for his bravery in Vietnam. He is suffering from acute depression and has been
hospitalized in an army hospital. The army doctors bring
in a civilian psychiatrist from New York, a specialist in
"impacted grief" who is himself a Holocaust survivor, to
examine him. D.J. is resistent, but after the doctor reveals
his own struggle with survivor guilt, he begins to open up.
He tells the doctor about his first day in Vietnam, when
he was an "F.N.G." (Fucking New Guy) hitching a ride to
Danang on an army truck.

D.J.

Well, uh . . . we were riding along, in the truck. Real hot, you know, and nobody much was around . . . and we see there's a bunch of kids, maybe three, four of them crossing the road up ahead. . . . You know?

[DOC

How old were they?

D.J.

Well, it's hard to tell.] Those people are all so *small*, you know?—I mean, all dried-up and tiny, man . . . Maybe ten years old, twelve, I don't know . . .

[DOC

And?]

D.J.

Well, we see they're being pretty slow getting out of the road, so we got to swerve a little bit to miss them. . . . Not a lot, you know, but a little bit. This seems to make the guys in the back of the truck really mad. Like, somebody goes, "Little fuckers!" You know? . . . Then those kids, as soon as we pass, they start laughing at us, and give us the finger. Know what I mean?

(D.J. *gives the* DOCTOR *the finger, to illustrate. The* DOCTOR *starts to laugh, but then puts his hand to his head, as if knowing what is to come.*)

Yeah. So I'm thinking to myself, "Now where did they learn to do that? That ain't some old oriental custom. They musta learned it from our guys." . . . Suddenly the guys on the truck start screaming for the driver to back up. So he jams on the brakes, and in this big cloud of dust he's grinding this thing in reverse as if he means to run those kids down, backwards. The kids start running away, of course, but one of 'em, maybe two, I don't know, they stop, you see, and give us the finger again, from the side of the road. And they're laughing. . . . So, uh, . . . everybody on the truck opens fire. I mean, I couldn't believe it, they're like half a platoon, they got M-16s, automatic rifles, they're blasting

away, it sounds like a pitched battle, they're pouring all
this firepower into these kids. The kids are lying on the
ground, they're dead about a hundred times over, and these
guys are still firing rounds into their bodies, like they've
gone crazy. And the kids' bodies are giving these little
jumps into the air like rag dolls, and then they flop down
again. . . .

                [DOC

             (Very quiet.)

What happened then?]

                D.J.

They just sorta stopped, and me and these guys drove away.

             (DOC waits.)

I'm thinking to myself, you know, what *is* going on here?
I must be out of tune. *My first day in the country,* and we
ain't even reached the Combat Zone! I'm thinking, like,
this is the enemy? Kids who make our trucks give a little
jog in the road and give us the finger? I mean, come on,
man! . . . And one guy, he sees I'm sort of staring back
down the road, so he gives me like this, you know—

     (D.J. simulates a jab of the elbow.)

and he says, "See how we hose them li'l motherfuckers
down, man?" Hose 'em down. You like that? . . . And
they're all blowing smoke away from their muzzles and
checking their weapons down, like they're a bunch of gun-
slingers, out of the Old West. . . .

    (D.J. shaking his head. He still has trouble
            believing he saw this.)

Men Inside
Eric Bogosian

Premiere: Public Theatre, NYC, 1982
Publisher: Vintage Books (in *Drinking In America*)
Setting: Bare stage

Men Inside is a one-man performance of nine varied character monologues. Bogosian describes its origins: "The best thing about being an actor is that you can be somebody you never were and never would be. Like a soldier. Or a cowboy. Even more interesting is how you figure out how to act like a cowboy. I've never met one in my life. I must have learned how to act like a cowboy from John Wayne, an actor." This monologue is called "Rodeo."

(Very fast-paced, jittery, jumping around
the stage. High-pitched "cowboy voice.")

Whooooeeeee! Boy you shoulda been there, we took that sucker down! It was good, it was real good!

(Moves his hands as if he's steering a car.)

RRRRRMMMMM!!! Ninety-five miles an hour—BOOM! I hit that Winnebago, guy never knew what hit'er! Just pushed 'im right off the side of the road.

I'm lookin' in my rearview mirror and I see that guy—he's jumped out of his car, jumpin' up and down, pissed off! I couldn't resist: I bang a U-ey, come back beside him and get out. Guy says to me,

(In deep Texas accent.)

"Come here boy, I wanna talk to you!" I said, "I wanna talk to you too!"

(A right, a left.)

BING! BANG! Guy never knew what hit him! Left enough rubber on that road to make a new set of tires!

I tell you, when it gets goin' that fast and hard I get high! Musta been doin' two, three hundred per. . . . Billy was pullin' 'em so fast he broke a knuckle. . . . You know that Billy when he starts pullin' those beers, pullin' those beers . . . jus' sittin' in the backseat like a hog in a corncrib, suckin' down that brew, half-naked, covered with sweat and stink. . . .

The beer cans rollin' aroun' on the floor and I musta been doing a hundred and fifty m.p.h.! . . . All of a sudden, I see this girl walkin' down the street, right? I couldn't resist. . . . I hit the brakes and start followin' her in the car, real slow like. Real Playboy-bunny type of girl, you know? I'm followin' real slow, givin' her my "evil eye" and she's jus' a-walkin' down the sidewalk like she don't notice! . . .

All of a sudden, Billy pops out the back window: "Hey baby, hey baby, come 'ere, I wanna kiss your face!" She says, "Kiss my ass!" So Billy, you know what Billy says??? You know what he says? "I can't tell the difference!" I can't tell the difference! Pretty good, huh? That Billy's some kind of comedian, huh? Some kind of comedian. "I can't tell the difference!" WHOOOOEEEE!

(With no warning, he violently starts miming shooting a rifle three times in three different directions.)

BOOM! BOOM! BOOM! Wish I had a machine gun, coulda killed me even more deer. . . . Killed me three deer, had to leave two behind! Didn't have room on the car for 'em! I jus' took this one big bloody buck, took him and strapped him onto the front of the car, tied him right onto the bumpers. So I'm goin' down the highway, musta been doin' three, four hundred miles per hour. . . . Billy's passed out in the backseat, and the blood starts comin' right up onto the windshield! I had to use my windshield wipers jus' so I could see!

(Laughing.)

I come into this gas station—car's all covered with blood, right?—come into this gas station and the boy says to me? "You boys look like you been busy!" Billy hangs his head out the window like some kind of old dog, he says: "Sure have!" and pukes all over the guy's shoes! Whooooeeeee!!! We know how to have a good time!

Remedial English
Evan Smith

Premiere: Young Playwrights Festival, Playwrights Horizons, NYC, 1986
Publisher: Grove Press (in *Out Front: Contemporary Gay and Lesbian Plays*)
Setting: Cabrini Catholic Academy and Vincent's home

Vincent Ryan is an extremely bright gay senior with a C average at the Cabrini Academy, a private high school for boys in a medium-sized Southern city. He has a *huge* crush on Rob Andrews, a drop-dead beautiful but dense classmate. He does not know Sister Beatrice is about to ask him to tutor Rob in English. She wants Vincent to see what it is like trying to teach a blank wall, hoping this will inspire him academically.

Having waited quite some time for her to finish correcting papers, he delivers what is essentially an interior monologue that opens the play.

VINCENT

Sister, I think it's very rude of you to keep me waiting like this. It's been fifteen minutes since you said, "I'll be finished in a minute," and unless I'm doing worse in algebra than I thought, you're off by fourteen minutes. Fourteen minutes may not seem like much to you—time moves pretty quickly after your hundredth birthday—but this is *supposed* to be my study hall. I have many important things to do during my study hall. I am developing a fascinating abstract pattern to fill the margins of my chemistry book, I'm right in the middle of *Lake Wobegon Days*, and I have almost finished my project of inserting the complete works of Judith Krantz into the library's card catalog. This is a school, after all, Sister. You of all people shouldn't want to see me wasting my time.

What did I do to merit such treatment? Is it because of that little tiff we had in English yesterday? Sister, we all say things in the heat of argument which we later regret. I'm sorry I called T.S. Eliot a "social-climbing Yankee papist." I don't even remember what I *meant* by that!

Have you forgotten all the good times we have had together? Don't you remember Dramatic Literature when I was a sophomore? We read aloud to the class . . . I was Jean . . . you were Miss Julie . . .

Oh, good grief, *please* don't tell me you found the Sister Beatrice Virgin Vote! God, how could I ever explain that? But if you *did* find it, you should at least be pleased with the results! Fifty-eight percent of my music class said that they thought you were a virgin. Sister, you've got to understand, such a large part of my life is spent in your company, and yet I hardly know anything about you! You've got to expect a certain amount of healthy curiosity and speculation. Do you ever wish you hadn't become a nun? What would you have done instead? Do you have any regrets? *Are* you a . . . ? Never any answers from this woman of mystery. Oh, well, you take your time, Sister, I don't mind waiting.

Sideshow
Miguel Piñero

Publisher: Arte Público Press (in *Outrageous*)
Setting: The inner city

Sideshow concerns the street world of drug dealers, addicts, pimps, prositutes, hustlers, and con men. Henry Clearnose is a thirteen- to fifteen-year-old Puerto Rican glue sniffer. He got his name because he always clears his nose before he "blows his mind." He says he chooses glue because it's cheap, less dangerous than other drugs, and the sight of needles makes him faint. It is night. He is high and on the roof.

CLEARNOSE

The city is drowning under tons of tubes of glue. Wow, the
sky has backed away and the stars are doing the bugaloo
blues. The buildings look like giant tubes of glue and the
garbage cans hold mountains of jewels sparkling for my eyes
to see. Man, I is a prophet. I am Jesus Christ reincarnated,
one of the most outasight images I've pulled from my dream
brown paper bag. Can you imagine a world without glue?
You gots to have glue, you need it to hold the world together . . . and it's store bought. I better keep my imagination open for the cops. They found out I was with
Frankie. He was my gluehead partner. We used to paste
the world together up on the roofs, in the school toilets,
in the subway trains. Oh, yeah, I was with him when he
jumped into the tracks. That's the day the A-train became
the B, dig it, B for blood. Wow, don't you git it? It's a
heavy joke. I mean, like the dude was all over the place:
head one way, arms another, leg on the platform, a very
untogether person. Man, like it ain't like I pushed him into
the tracks. Like I don't know what they want me
for . . . you know like . . . you know what I mean, you
know? Right, take me a short visit into my dream brown
paper bag. Yeah, that's cool. Losing much of its power now.
Oh, I wish everybody would stop saying how much they
care and love.

(*Lights dim while* CLEARNOSE *mumbles.*)

Six Degrees of Separation
John Guare

Premiere: Lincoln Center Theatre, NYC, 1990
Publisher: Vintage Books
Setting: New York City

Flanders ("Flan") and Louisa ("Ouisa") Kittredge live
on New York's Upper East Side, in an apartment which

boasts a two-sided Kandinsky original and a luxuriant view
of Central Park. Flan, a high-rolling art dealer, has a line
on a Cezanne but needs a loan of two million dollars. Luckily, a "King Midas rich" friend from South Africa is in
town. Flan and Ouisa invite him to dine, and during the
small talk, the doorman brings up a young black man named
Paul.

Paul is "in his early twenties, very handsome, very
preppy. He has been beaten badly. Blood seeps through
his white Brooks Brothers shirt." He tells Ouisa and Flan
he's been mugged, that he goes to Harvard with their children Tess and Woody, and, eventually, that his father is
Sidney Poitier. Paul fascinates the Kittredges and their
guests with stories of his movie-star father, his international
childhood, his senior thesis reinventing of *The Catcher in
the Rye*. None of this is true.

Paul is a compulsive liar, a con man who almost believes
his own con. He's never met Sidney Poitier *or* the Kittredge
children, but he does know Trent Conway, an embittered
young gay man who grew up with Tess and Woody and
was only too happy to "educate" Paul in return for sexual
favors. The Kittredge children are furious at their parents'
gullibility. After a growling family fight, Ouisa stretches out
on the couch and Paul appears in her dream.

PAUL

The imagination. That's our out. Our imagination teaches
us our limits and then how to grow beyond those limits.
The imagination says Listen to me. I am your darkest voice.
I am your 4 A.M. voice. I am the voice that wakes you up
and says this is what I'm afraid of. Do not listen to me at
your peril. The imagination is the noon voice that sees
clearly and says yes, this is what I want for my life. It's
there to sort out your nightmare, to show you the exit from
the maze of your nightmare, to transform the nightmare
into dreams that become your bedrock. If we don't listen
to that voice, it dies. It shrivels. It vanishes.

(PAUL *takes out a switchblade and opens it.*)
The imagination is not our escape. On the contrary, the imagination is the place we are all trying to get to.
(PAUL *lifts his shirt and stabs himself.*)

So Slow It Whirls
Eric Lane

Premiere: Orange Thoughts Theatre Company, NYC, 1989
Publisher: Orange Thoughts
Setting: Various locations

So Slow it Whirls is a collection of monologues depicting different aspects of American life. Here, Jimmy Stone, a gay seventeen-year-old high-school senior, tells of being singled out and tormented in school.

JIMMY

It's 6½ months to graduation. I'm graduating a year early. You see, I have enough credits, I just had to double up on English, Sophomore and Junior last year, and I'm clear. My SAT's are fine and I'll be hearing from colleges in April so.

I don't know how—Scratch that.

You ever have a moment where everything stopped? Sounds around you. People. Noise. It's like you know it had to've kept going. I mean those fluorescent bulbs don't just stop, but for that moment you could've sworn they did. The hum gone silent.

What am I talking about, you're asking. You see, that's how I remember it. In 8th grade. Art. See all the kids are mixed together in the class. Not like English where you got tracks "A" "B" "C," but everyone mixed up together in Art. And so what winds up happening is the "A" track

kids sit together at one set of tables and the "B" and "C."
And so I'm sitting with some guys I know at a table and
Keith Friedman he sits with us, too. You see, he's into
magic. He brings in cards and handkerchiefs and quarters
he's always pulling out of somebody's ear. And you see,
what happens is the greasers they eat it up. Not like it, I
mean. But love to watch Keith perform and watch him,
over him, waiting for him to fuck up. So like they can laugh
and call him a fag and that's what they do. And every day
they call Keith over and he goes, and then the same every
day. Sometimes they punch him, and Mr. Gladden'll
pretend he doesn't see, or one time he told them to sit
down.

So anyway, Keith, he sits with us and so long as he's
getting beat on, they leave the rest of us alone. Well, maybe
they call out "fag" or whatever but it's Keith they want to
get really.

Well, till— You see, this one day I'm painting, we're
painting at this time, and I need to get to the sink. And
it's behind them, the greasers. And so I walk past and this
one Jimmy Kincaid, he calls out my name and before it
yells out the word "duh"— Well, I don't have to do it for
you but you get the idea. And so I get some water and head
back to our table, but this time instead of walking past him
I head around the other way. So I don't need to pass him.
I don't even think about it, I just do it. And this is what I
was talking about before, how time stopped—and they look
from one to the other and smile almost, not outside but I
could see it, 'cause in that moment they knew they had
me. That it hurt.

And so from then on it's my name shouted with "duh"
in front of it anytime they see me. And not just in this class
but the hall, on the way to school, home. See and even
though I pretend like it doesn't bother me, too late. You
see, 'cause they already know. And when I sit back down,
Keith, it's like he looks at me and he doesn't say anything

but I can see he's relieved. 'Cause even though they still call him "fag" and tear his cards, now they got me to attack, too.

And Mr. Gladden, he pretends like he doesn't see. The other teachers, too. But how could they not? You see, it gets so big, this "duh" thing with my name, that one time this 8th grader, by now I'm in 9th, this 8th grader sees me and says to his friend, "There he is, Jimmy Stone." And his friend's surprised. You see, he didn't realize I existed. He'd been saying my name for a year now every time someone answered a question wrong, or said something faggy, but he never knew there was a person attached to the name.

6½ months and I'm out of here. You see, I have enough credits. I've done my time.

Talley & Son
Lanford Wilson

Premiere: Circle Repertory Company, NYC, 1985
Publisher: Farrar, Straus & Giroux, Inc.
Setting: Formal parlor of the Talley place, just outside Lebanon, Missouri, 1944

It's the Fourth of July, 1944. The members of a wealthy and quarrelsome Missouri family gather together for the funeral of its patriarch and a powwow over the future of the family business, a clothing mill called Talley & Son. Even the two Talley grandsons, both fighting in World War II, have been granted leave to come home for the funeral. But things do not go as planned. The feisty patriarch gets off his deathbed and goes for a drive in the family Packard. And the younger grandson, Timmy, is killed in action the day before his leave.

Timmy is the play's narrator, addressing the audience directly. He is onstage throughout the play, watching the family anticipate his arrival and receive the telegrammed news of his death. Here he describes what happened.

TIMMY

Dad said he didn't even know where I fell. That official "fell." Like a lotta people he gets very—not just correct, but formal—under pressure. Hell, "fell" isn't the half of it. Splatted is more like it. Didn't feel a thing. Shock and whatnot takes care of that. I felt a force all against me and suddenly I've got a different angle on the terrain. I'm looking up into the trees instead of out across the jungle floor. I thought, How am I looking at that? Then I thought, Oh, sure, I'm flat on my ass looking up. Some squawking parrot up there looking down at me; gonna drop it right on my face. I figgered, all right, this part is easy. I just lay here till some corpsman comes up and does his job. You get very philosophical. Then the corpsmen come and, oh, Daddy, I knew from the look on their faces that this is bad. This young recruit, couldn't be sixteen, turned around and I thought he was gonna puke, but he flat out fainted before he had the chance. You could tell he'd enlisted in this thing ten minutes after seeing *To the Shores of Tripoli*. Then all of a sudden I'm on a stretcher and they're rushing me off to somewhere. You understand, you don't feel the stretcher under you, you just know they're rushing you to somewhere. You're looking up into the sun; some guy is running along beside you, trying to keep his hand over your eyes, shade them from the sun; you'd kinda rather see it. And all the corpsmen are still looking so cut-up I said, "Hey, do you raggedy-asses think I don't know you're razzing me? I got a pass to go home, you're trying to make me think I won't get there." Or, actually, I thought I said that; then I realized nothing had come out. I thought, Well, hell, if this isn't a lousy predicament. You always wondered if it comes will you fall all to pieces, and now it's come and I'm doing fine and damned proud of it and nobody is gonna know.

> (TALLEY *enters from the kitchen and exits*
> *out the front door.*)

Granddad Talley would say, "Pride goeth before a fall, sir." Should have known it. Of course, you do know that the body is doing what the body does. You can feel—barely, a little bit—that your body is urinating all over itself and your bowels are letting go something fierce. You try to get ahold with your mind of the muscles down in your belly that you use to hold it off, but your mind can't find 'em.

> (*Pause.*)

If those guys hadn't looked so bad, you might have gone all to pieces, but they're so torn up, you feel somebody has got to take this thing lightly.

Three Ways Home
Casey Kurtti

Premiere: Astor Place Theatre, NYC, 1988
Publisher: Samuel French, Inc.
Setting: New York City

Sharon is a white first-time volunteer caseworker, Dawn a black welfare mother, and Frankie her troubled sixteen-year-old son. Each of them talks directly to the audience in an opening monologue. The playwright urges actors not to shy away from the "in your face" style, and comments that "Frankie should be played primarily as an uncomfortable adolescent kid, not as some psycho ready to come apart at the seams." Over the course of the play, Frankie starts to fence stolen goods and hustle gay johns for money. He will also drift further and further away from reality and into his "X-Men" fantasy world.

(Loud rap music begins as FRANKIE *enters.*
He "sneaks" downstage center. Music ends.
Silence. He removes sunglasses and speaks.)

FRANKIE

Yo, what's up? My Mom's got all these people now, first
James, then her psycho worker, now this new other one.
Soon you're going to see the whole Secret Service pull up
here and act as her damn body guard. I mean WORD, she's
got all these people around her so now I got to climb in
the back seat? I used to be Numero Uno around here till
James came on the scene. Dude shows up smack dab on
my thirteenth birthday. Ruins my whole life. 'Cause he got
between me and my Moms. We used to be like this. But
he messed up something that can't be put back together.
Now I'm just supposed to hang around and do household
chores? Yo, do I look like Mary Poppins to you? I got things
to do, so let James watch the kids. I hate that guy. He
doesn't do anything anyway. Just leans on my ass. It's not
like he's my damn father! It's because of him I can't stand
it around here, so I'm changing things around . . .

(Pulls out an X-Men comic book.)

. . . See I'm modeling myself after the X-Men. You ever
hear of them? I'll tell you a little bit about them. My older
brothers and a couple of sisters started making their appearance around 1967 in a comic book about their lives.
They're stationed on this here planet. Sometimes they
travel to other worlds, secret locations. They're all mu-
tants . . . Fucked up. Bent out of shape. But they're not
just fucked up. They got some kick-ass powers. That's why
after some serious research I hooked up with the X-Men.
See, you got some sleeping creatures hiding in these here
buildings.

(Leaps onto fire escape.)

One time, three years ago, they tried to grab ahold of my
sister Tawny. I saved her but they got ahold of my ass.
They messed me up—tried to do me like a girl—so my

Moms took me to this place where they ask you a lot of questions you don't want to explain. I went back twice. Then I cured myself. Started reading the X-Men and I learned how to get my guard up.

(Begins "acting out" Wolverine fantasy.)

See this here world fears them because they're different. I dig them 'cause they're not all good or bad. That's the way I am. Not all good or all bad. You dig? Well take Wolverine . . . Man . . . He's a hairy ass Mother Fucker with razor sharp claws. They're made of adamantium, that's the strongest metal known to mankind. Wolverine is all messed up in the face, but basically a very nice person. Sometimes I go over to Central Park and listen to my sounds. Think about them coming to life, making an appearance. To teach me about the powers. So I can prepare for my life, take care of James and some other things. They could show up one of these days. It's possible. Then I won't have to be alone. Learning all about life by myself. But I'm doing okay. Right now I'm teaching myself how to disappear. Check it out.

Women and Wallace

Jonathan Marc Sherman

Premiere: Playwrights Horizon, NYC, 1988
Publisher: Dramatists Play Service, Inc.
Setting: Multiple locations

Women and Wallace spans twelve years in the life of Wallace Kirkman, ages six through eighteen. In the play's second scene, Wallace's mother fixes her son a peanut butter and banana sandwich, then slits her throat with the knife. Wallace comes home from the second grade and discovers the body, along with a suicide note that reads "Cremate the parasite."

As Wallace grows up, he interacts with various women including his grandmother, classmates, a psychiatrist, crushes, and girlfriends. Interspersed with these scenes are pieces of Wallace's writing performed as monologues directly to the audience.

WALLACE

"My Mother's Turtlenecks." By Wallace Kirkman. Age sixteen. My mother loved my father and hated her neck. She thought it was too fleshy or something. If I hated *my* neck, I'd have it removed, but my mother never trusted doctors, so she wore turtlenecks. All the time. In every picture we have of her, she's wearing a turtleneck. She had turtlenecks in every color of the rainbow, she had blacks, she had whites, she had grays, she had plaids, she had polka dots and hound's-tooth checks and stripes and Mickey Mouse and even a sort of *mesh* turtleneck. I can't picture her without a turtleneck on. Although, according to Freud, I *try* to, every moment of every day. We have a photograph of me when I was a baby wearing one of my mother's turtlenecks. *Swimming* in one of my mother's turtlenecks is more like it. Just a bald head and a big shirt. It's very erotic in an Oedipal shirtwear sort of way. It's a rare photograph, because I'm smiling. I didn't smile all that much during most of my childhood. I'm taking lessons now, trying to learn again, but it takes time. I stopped smiling when my mother stopped wearing turtlenecks. I came home from a typical day in the second grade to find her taking a bath in her own blood on the kitchen floor. Her turtleneck was on top of the kitchen table, so it wouldn't come between her neck and her knife. I understood then why she had worn turtlenecks all along. To stop the blood from flowing. To cover the wound that was there all along. They tried to cover the wound when they buried her with one of her favorite turtleneck dresses on, but it didn't matter. It was just an empty hole by then. My mother wasn't hiding inside.

(Pause.)

She wrote a note before she died, asking to be cremated, and I asked my father why she wasn't. He said my mother was two women, and the one he loved would have been scared of the flames.

(Pause.)

I look at that photograph of little me inside my mother's shirt all the time. It's the closest I can get to security. There are no pictures of me inside mother's womb, but her turtleneck is close enough.

Yankee Dawg You Die
Philip Kan Gotanda

Premiere: Berkeley Repertory Theatre, Berkeley, California, 1988
Publisher: Dramatists Play Service, Inc.
Setting: Various locations in and around Hollywood

Two Asian-American actors meet at a party in the Hollywood Hills, at an audition, and again in an acting class. It's a spiky relationship. Vincent Chang, "a youthful, silver-maned late sixties," began his career as a hoofer on the "Chop Suey Circuit" and later broke into movies, playing a variety of Oriental villains, inscrutable servants, and other clichés. He is gay, but has spent a lifetime in the closet out of fear for his career. Bradley Yamashita is an ambitious young theater actor with one independent film credit and a chip on his shoulder about Asian-American consciousness. He tells Vincent that he grew up watching him on TV ("you were sort of my hero"), but later takes him to task for acting like "a Chinese Stepin Fetchit." Vincent defends his pride and craft, and lambastes Bradley for the shallowness of his acting. An acting class improv leads to the following revelation.

BRADLEY

I think I killed someone.

[VINCENT

Like in a person? A human being?

(BRADLEY *nods*.)

My God.]

BRADLEY

I'm not sure. I may have. But I'm not sure. It was stupid. So stupid. I was about 16. I used to hang around a lot with some Chinatown boys, gangs and that sort of thing. I was walking down Jackson Street with my girlfriend, we were going to see the movies, when these two guys—they must have been college students come to gawk at all the Chinese people—turned the corner. Well, as they walked passed, one of them looked at my girlfriend and said, "Hey, look at the yellow pussy." So I walked over to the one guy, "What did you say? What did you say?" He just laughed at me. So I pulled a knife and stabbed him.

(*Shocked silence*.)

[VINCENT

What happened then?]

BRADLEY

We went to see the movie.

(*Pause*.)

I don't know. Sometimes it just builds up. The anger.

(*Pause*.)

That was over 10 years ago. I hope he's OK. I hope with my heart he's OK.

(*Dim to darkness*.)

The Boys Next Door
Tom Griffin

Premiere: McCarter Theatre, Princeton, New Jersey, 1986
Publisher: Dramatists Play Service, Inc.
Setting: An apartment in New England

Arnold Wiggins lives with three other men in a group home for retarded adults. Though "the boys" are functional enough to live on their own (with frequent visits from a social worker named Jack), much of everyday life overwhelms them. Arnold, who works as a part-time janitor in a movie theater, has a series of linguistic tics and an obsession with moving to Russia. When the play opens, he is sitting on the apartment floor with four supermarket bags.

ARNOLD
(Directly to the audience.)
My name is Arnold Wiggins. I'm basically a nervous person. People call me Arnold because I don't have a nickname. So I pretend that Arnold is my nickname so that when people call me Arnold, I pretend that they are close personal friends who know me by my nickname: Arnold. I live here at the Stonehenge Villa apartment complex in a group apartment with three other guys. Did I mention I'm a nervous person? Well, frankly, I am. Today I went to the market at the end of the street to get some Wheaties. But I couldn't remember whether I wanted one box or more boxes, so I asked the manager how many boxes I should get. "For just you?" he said. "Yes, sir," I said. "Seventeen," he said. "Thank you," I said. But, and this is what I want to emphasize by nervous, I could only find nine boxes. So what could I do?

(Pause.)

I got nine boxes of Wheaties.

> *(He removes various sized boxes of Wheaties*
> *from the bags.)*

And seven heads of lettuce.

> *(He removes the lettuce, studies the situa-*
> *tion.)*

That made sixteen.

> *(Pulls out a bag of charcoal.)*

And one bag of charcoal briquets. That made seventeen.

> *(He takes out the milk.)*

And a quart of milk. You know, for the Wheaties. But the more I thought about it, the more I thought I didn't get enough . . . what? Was it (A) lettuce? (B) Wheaties? (C) charcoal briquets? This concerned me. So I asked a girl in line what she thought. I forget what she said, but it was pretty thorough. And then I came home.

> *(Pause.)*

Do you think I did the right thing?

Burn This
Lanford Wilson

Premiere: Circle Rep/Mark Taper Forum, Los Angeles, California, 1987
Publisher: Farrar, Straus & Giroux, Inc.
Setting: A residential loft in lower Manhattan

Anna is a dancer. In the play's first scene, she has just returned from the appalling funeral of her roommate and dance partner, Robbie, who was drowned with his lover in a freak boating accident. Robbie had not seen his huge Midwestern family for over five years, and none of them ever saw him dance—or knew he was gay. Anna describes a nightmarish incident in which she was wakened by butterflies in a nephew's not-yet-dead collection, pinned to her bedroom wall and fluttering frantically. She started screaming hysterically and ran downstairs wrapped in a sheet. A "glowering older brother" fetched her clothes and took care of the butterflies.

The next scene, more than a month later, begins with somebody pounding on the door in the middle of the night. Anna lets in a wired and furious man who spins off a white-hot tirade about parking spaces before she can ask who he is. He's Robbie's brother Pale—"the one who saved you from the ferocious butterflies." Pale is a New Jersey restaurant manager, unhappily married, explosively sexual. He got his nickname from his choice of brandy—V.S.O.P. (Very Special Old Pale) and dresses in expensive suits and lizard shoes. He claims to have come to pick up Robbie's things, but he's also attracted to Anna. Pale speaks in dense free-associative riffs and Anna has just apologized for losing the thread of one of his stories.

PALE

Now, see, that I can't take. I can't stand that.

[ANNA

I'm sorry, really, but—]

PALE

Well, see, fine, you got these little social phrases and polite-nesses—all they show me is this—like—giganticness of unconcern with your "I'm sorrys," man. The fuckin' world is going down the fuckin' toilet on "I'm sorrys." I'm sorry is this roll of toilet paper—they're growing whole forests, for people to wipe their asses on with their "I'm sorrys." Be a tree. For one day. And know that that tree over there is gonna be maybe music paper, the Boss is gonna make forty million writin' some poor-slob-can't-get-work song on. This tree is gonna be ten-dollar bills, get passed around, buy things, *mean something*, hear stories; we got sketch pads and fuckin' "I don't love you anymore" letters pinned to some creep's pillow—something of *import*. Headlines,

box scores, some great book or movie script—Jack Nich-
olson's gonna mark you all up, say whatever he wishes to,
anyway, out in some fuckin' desert, you're supposed to be
his *text*, he's gonna lay out this line of coke on you—Tree
over there is gonna be in some four-star restaurant, they're
gonna call him parchment, bake pompano in him. And
you're stuck in the ground, you can't go nowhere, all you
know is some fuckin' junkie's gonna wipe his ass and flush
you down the East River. Go floating out past the Statue
of Liberty all limp and covered with shit, get tangled up
in some Saudi Arabian oil tanker's fuckin' propellers—you
got maybe three hundred years before you drift down to
Brazil somewhere and get a chance to be maybe a coffee
bush. "I'm sorrys" are fuck, man.

The Chickencoop Chinaman
Frank Chin

Premiere: American Place Theatre, NYC, 1972
Publisher: University of Washington Press
Setting: Oakland district of Pittsburgh, Pennsylvania, the late
   sixties

Frank Chin describes Tam Lum as "a Chinese American
writer filmmaker with a gift of gab and an open mouth. A
multi-tongued word magician losing his way to the spell
who trips to Pittsburgh to conjure with his childhood friend
and research a figure in his documentary." Tam stands
downstage center in a spotlight as his friend, Kenji, tunes
a large old-fashioned radio.

TAM

Did ya hear that . . . ? Listen, children, did I ever tellya,
I ever tellya the Lone Ranger ain't a Chinaman? I ever

tellya that? Don't blame me. That's what happens when you're a Chinaman boy in the kitchen, listening in the kitchen to the radio, for what's happenin in the other world, while grandmaw has an ear for nothing but ancient trains in the night, and talks pure Chinamouth you understood only by love and feel. She don't hear what a boy hears. She's for the Chinese Hour and chugablood red roving, livin to hear one train, once more. I heard "Jack Armstrong, All-American Boy" fight Japs, come outa the radio every day into our kitchen to tell me every day for years that "All-American Boys" are the best boys, the hee-rohs! the movie stars! that "All-American Boys" are white boys every day, all their life long. And grandmaw heard thunder in the Sierra hundreds of miles away and listened for the Chinaman-known Iron Moonhunter, that train built by Chinamans who knew they'd never be given passes to ride the rails they laid. So of all American railroaders, only they sung no songs, told no jokes, drank no toasts to the ol' iron horse, but stole themselves some iron on the way, slowly stole up a pile of steel, children, and hid there in the granite face of the Sierra and builded themselves a wild engine to take them home. Every night, children, grandmaw listened in the kitchen, waiting, till the day she died. And I'd spin the dial looking for to hear "Anybody, Chinese American Boy," "Anybody, Chinese American Boy" anywhere on the dial, doing anything grand on the air, anything at all. . . . I heard of the masked man. And I listened to him. And in the Sunday funnies he had black hair, and Chinatown was nothin but black hair, and for years, listen, years! I grew blind looking hard through the holes of his funnypaper mask for slanty eyes. Slanty eyes, boys! You see, I knew, children, I knew with all my heart's insight . . . shhh, listen, children . . . he wore that mask to hide his Asian eyes! And that made sense of me. I knew he wore a red shirt for good luck. I knew he rode a white horse named Silver cuz white be our color of death. Ha ha ha. And he was lucky Chinaman vengeance on the West . . . and silver bullets cuz death from a Chinaman is always expensive. Always classy. Always famous. I knew the Lone Ranger was the "Chinese American Boy" of the radio I'd looked for.

(*Music up. Rossini's* William Tell *Overture.*)

Chug
Ken Jenkins

Premiere: Actors Theatre of Louisville, Louisville, Kentucky, 1980
Publisher: Dramatists Play Service, Inc. (in *Rupert's Birthday and Other Plays*)
Setting: A small mobile home somewhere in southern Indiana

Chug is a one-man play, a shaggy dog story told by a genial man named Cardwell Hoover Ubell Garnett Evers, who's trying to figure out how in hell he got himself up to his eyeballs in the bullfrog-breeding business. This is how it all began.

CHUG

I was in this bar down in Louisville with a buddy of mine by the name of Drunken Rush. His name is really Duncan, but we all call him Drunken . . . 'cause he is. Anyway, we were settin' there in this bar . . . watchin' this . . . ah . . . lady fiddle player . . . ah . . . fiddle? . . . when in through the door walks this red-headed woman in a frilly yella dress wearin' high-heeled shoes. 'N she is accompanied by a totally bald-headed guy with a beard. Wearin' a white robe . . . covered with beads and rhinestones and pieces of broken mirror.

'N these two walk straight over to me and Drunken, and the redhead says, "I'm Freda."

'N I says, "You're something else."

'N she says, "My guru, Moo-Moo here, feels that you represent a great 'resonance' for me. Do you mind if we sit down?"

Well . . . what the hell. I been around some. I am *not* a child. What's the pitch, I'm thinkin'? Where's the gimme?

But, I says, "Please do. Drunken, meet Freda and her Guru, Moo-Moo. This is my buddy, Drunken Rush. How do. How do. My name is Chug. Actually, my name is Cardwell Hoover Ubell Garnett Evers . . . but, I'd appreciate it if you'd call me Chug."

'N the Guru looks at me 'n says, "Mooooooooo."

'N Freda looks at me 'n says, "You're cute."

'N Drunken looks at me 'n says, "This is too crazy for me!"

'N he went off to find a "hill-billy bar with some straight *people* in it."

So I looks at Freda 'n says, "What's the catch?"

'N she looks right back at me 'n says, "How high is up?"

And the Guru, he looks at both of us 'n says, "Moo-oo-oo."
                    (*He crosses to tape deck.*)

Anyway . . . that's how we met. In a bar. We resonated.
            (*Punches "play." "Tintinabulation."* Evironments. *Bells*)

Resonated. Get it? Sonar? Sound? Vibrations. Very big into "vibrations," and "harmony," and "rhythm," and "resonance" was Freda. And me? I was very big into Freda. Now don't get me wrong. I liked her for other things than her body. There was her car, her credit cards, her private plane . . . nah . . . I'm just shittin' ya.

I liked Freda because she made me *aware*. Yeah. She really made me aware of . . . my ears. She made me aware of my whole body, but . . . she really made me aware of "listening."

She would say to me, "Listen, Chug. Really listen. Just stop. Stop twitchin' around 'n makin' noise. Just stop. Stop thinkin'. Just listen."

(He listens.)
And I would. I would do it.
                    (He listens.)
I really got to like it.
                    (He listens.)
You know . . . you listen to something for a long time 'n
you start to feel like you understand it. You start thinkin'
that you know the story behind what you hear.
Like . . . you listen to ocean waves, 'n you hear stories
about fish, and ships, 'n sailors, 'n storms, 'n deep, secret
places. You listen to them glass wind chimes? . . . wind
might come all the way from China. Or another galaxy.
And music? Brahms. Bach. Beethoven.
'N . . . Bullfrogs.

The Colored Museum
George C. Wolfe

Premiere: Crossroads Theatre Company, New Brunswick, New
    Jersey, 1986
Publisher: *American Theatre* magazine
Setting: A stylized museum

An ensemble of two men and three women portray a
gallery of living "exhibits" in what the playwright describes
as "a museum where the myths and madness of black/
Negro/colored Americans are stored." The following exhibit
is called "The Gospel According to Miss Roj."

(The darkness is cut by electronic music.
Cold, pounding, unrelenting. Lights flash on
and off, pulsating to the beat. A neon sign
clicks on which spells out The Bottomless
Pit. There is a blast of smoke and from the
haze MISS ROJ *appears. He is dressed in*
striped patio pants, white gogo boots, a hal-

*ter and cat-shaped sunglasses. What would
seem ridiculous on anyone else* MISS ROJ
*wears as if it were high fashion. He carries
himself with total elegance and absolute
arrogance.)*

MISS ROJ

God created black people and black people created style.
The name's Miss Roj . . . that's R-O-J thank you, and you
can find me every Wednesday, Friday and Saturday nights
at The Bottomless Pit, the watering hole for the wild and
weary which asks the question, "Is there life after Jherri-
curl?"

(A waiter passes by and hands MISS ROJ *a
drink)*

Thanks doll. *Yes,* if they be black and swish the B.P.
has seen them, which is not to suggest the Pit is lacking in
cultural diversity. Oh no. There are your dinge queens,
white men who like their chicken legs dark. And let's not
forget, "Los Muchachos de la Neighborhood."

But the speciality of the house is, The Snap Queens.

(He snaps his fingers.)

We are a rare breed.

For you see when something strikes our fancy, when
the truth comes piercing through the dark, well you just
can't let it pass unnoticed. No darling. You must pronounce
it with a snap.

Snapping comes from another galaxy, as do all snap
queens. That's right. I ain't just your regular oppressed
American Negro. No-no-no! I am an extra-terrestrial, and
I ain't talkin none of that shit you seen in the movies. I
have real power.

(He stops the passing waiter.)

Speaking of no power, will you please tell Miss Stingy
with-the-Rum, that if Miss Roj had wanted to remain sober,
she could have stayed home and drank Kool-aid. Thank
you.

Yes, I was placed here on earth to study the life habits of a deteriorating society, and child when we talkin New York City, we are discussing the Queen of Deterioration. Miss New York is doing a slow dance with death, and I am here to warn you all, but before I do, I must know . . . don't you just love my patio pants? Annette Funicello immortalized them in *Beach Blanket Bingo,* and I have continued the legacy. And my gogos? I realize white after Labor Day is very gauche, but as the saying goes, if you've got it flaunt it, if you don't front it and snap to death any bastard who dares to defy you.

(Laughing.)

Oh-ho! My demons are showing. Yes my demons live at the bottom of my Bacardi and Coke.

Let's just hope for all concerned I dance my demons out before I drink them out 'cause child, dancing demons take you on a ride, but those drinkin demons just take you, and you find yourself doing the strangest things. Like the time I locked my father in the broom closet.

Seems the liquor made his tongue real liberal and he decided he was gonna baptize me with the word "faggot" over and over. Well he's just going on and on with "faggot this" and "faggot that," all the while walking toward the broom closet to piss. Poor drunk bastard was just all turned around.

So the demons just took hold of my Wedgies and forced me to kick the drunk son of a bitch into the closet and lock the door.

(Laughter.)

Three days later I remembered he was there.

(Laughter.)

(The waiter enters, hands MISS ROJ *a drink.*
He downs it.)

Another!

Oh yes-yes-yes! Miss Roj is quintessential style. I cornrow the hairs on my legs so that they spell out M-I-S-S

R-O-J. And I dare any bastard to fuck with me because I will snap your ass into oblivion.

I have the power you know. Every time I snap, I steal one beat of your heart. So if you find yourself gasping for air in the middle of the night, chances are you fucked with Miss Roj and she didn't like it.

Like the time this asshole at Jones Beach decided to take issue with my culotte-sailor ensemble. This child, this muscle-bound Brooklyn thug in a skintight bikini, very skintight so the whole world can see that instead of a brain, God gave him an extra-thick piece of sausage. You know the kind who beat up on their wives for breakfast. Well he decided to blurt out when I walked by, "Hey look at da monkey coon in da faggit suit." Well, I walked up to the poor dear, very calmly lifted my hand and . . .

(He snaps in rapid succession.)

A heart attack, right there on the beach. You don't believe it? Cross me! Come on. Come on.

(The waiter hands MISS ROJ *a drink. He*
downs it.)
(Looking around):

If this place is the answer we're asking all the wrong questions. The only reason I come here is to communicate with my origins. The flashing lights are signals from my planet way out there. Yes girl, even farther than Flatbush. We're talking another galaxy. The flashing lights tell me how much time is left before . . . the end.

(Very drunk and loud by now.)

I hate the people here. I hate the drinks. But most of all I hate this goddamn music. That ain't music. Give me Aretha Franklin anyday.

(Singing.)

"Just a little respect. R-E-S-P-E-C-T." Yeah! Yeah!

Come on and dance your last dance with Miss Roj. Last call is but a drink away and each snap puts you one step closer to the end.

A high-rise goes up. You can't get no job. Come on everybody and dance. A whole race of people gets trashed and debased. Snap those fingers and dance. Some sick bitch throws her baby out the window 'cause she thinks it's the devil. Everybody snap! *The New York Post.* Snap!

Snap for every time you walk past someone lying in the street, smelling like frozen piss and shit and you don't see it. Snap for every crazed bastard who kills himself so as to get the jump on being killed. And snap for every sick muthafucker who bored with carrying around his fear, takes to shooting up other people.

Yeah snap your fingers and dance with Miss Roj. But don't be fooled by the banners and balloons 'cause child this ain't no party going on. Hell no! It's a wake. And the casket's made out of stone, steel and glass and the people are racing all over the pavement like maggots on a dead piece of meat.

Yeah dance! But don't be surprised if there ain't no beat holding you together 'cause we traded in our drums for respectability. So now it's just words. Words rappin. Words screechin. Words flowin instead of blood 'cause you know that don't work. Words cracklin instead of fire 'cause by the time a match is struck on 125th Street and you run to Midtown, the flame has been blown away.

So come on and dance with Miss Roj and her demons. We don't ask for acceptance. We don't ask for approval. We know who we are and we move on it!

I guarantee you will never hear two fingers put together in a snap and not think of Miss Roj. That's power baby. Patio pants and all.

> (*The lights begin to flash in rapid succession.*)

So let's dance! And snap! And dance! And snap!

> (*There is a blast of smoke. When the haze settles,* MISS ROJ *is gone and in place of him is a recording of Aretha Franklin singing "Respect.")*

Crossing Delancey
Susan Sandler

Premiere: Jewish Repertory Theatre, NYC, 1985
Publisher: Samuel French, Inc.
Setting: New York City

Isabelle "Izzy" Grossman is an educated, contemporary young woman who works in a literary bookshop and regularly visits her Bubbie (Yiddish for grandmother) on the Lower East Side. Izzy is single, though she daydreams about a narcissistic novelist named Tyler Moss, who frequents the shop. Bubbie doesn't approve: "You live alone in a room. Like a dog. A dog should live alone. Not people." Without consulting Izzy, she sets up an appointment with a marriage broker. Appalled, Izzy tells her, "Bubbie, this isn't the way I live. This is a hundred years ago. This isn't me." But she agrees to keep the appointment to make her grandmother happy.

The marriage broker's prospect, Sam, owns a pickle stand on Delancey Street. The playwright describes him as "a pickleman and a poet, an inhabitant of the Lower East Side, in his early thirties, gentle, intuitive, appealing, and very wise for his years." Izzy is frank with Sam about her distrust of such arrangements, but Sam will not be put off. He spotted Izzy with her grandmother two years ago, and has wanted to meet her ever since. He is willing to woo her and be patient—even when Izzy breaks a date for an ill-fated rendezvous with Tyler. She has just arrived at Bubbie's after that encounter, and finds Sam still waiting and Bubbie asleep.

SAM

You should write down what she tells you. All of it. These are diamonds she gives you—I keep a little notebook for this purpose.

(*He picks it up from the table.*)

I put it down whenever the idea is clear to me. I put it down. And questions, too. When they are clearly in my mind. I like to see them on the page. I leave room for the answers. Here, you see—this is a question I have been looking at—" How do I talk to Isabelle?"

(He puts the pad down and paces about the kitchen.)

It's hard this business of getting acquainted. You want to say the right thing. You want to show the other person the best you got. Like in the market when I go to buy the cukes—They got the samples on display—always the tastiest looking, perfect sizes. One summer when I was a boy my Papa got me a job working at the wholesale produce market so I would know the other side of the business better—also to see the world a little, I think—And the guys who run the stands they put these samples out for each kind of vegetable and fruit they're selling—so you know what you're getting when you buy your bushel basket. And these samples they call flash. And at the end of the day when the market's closing down, the boss comes around and says, "okay, work the flash!" That means—you can sell it, you can let it go, the flash, the best stuff you got. . . . I want very much to show you the best I got. Isabelle. Please let me do that.

(IZZY crosses to the sink with some dishes from the table.)

Maybe I talked too much—but I been saving up.

The Day You'll Love Me
José Ignacio Cabrujas

Translated by Eduardo Machado

Premiere: Caracas, Venezuela, 1979
Publisher: *American Theatre* magazine
Setting: The Ancizar family patio, Caracas, Venezuela, 1935

Pio Miranda and Maria Luisa have been engaged for ten years. Pio, a night-school teacher and a fervent Marxist-Leninist, has filled Maria Luisa's head with naive dreams of moving to a *kolkhoz* (collective farm) in the Ukraine, and she has decided tonight is the night they must leave. Tonight also marks the arrival in Caracas of the legendary film star and tango singer Carlos Gardel, who will make a surprise visit to the Ancizar's patio before the evening is out. ("The Day You'll Love Me" is one of his songs.)

Maria Luisa is still a virgin at thirty-seven. Pio declares, "I believe in a world where ideas can be shared with female comrades. In the name of the new humanity, I stand opposed to all this macho courtship." As Maria Luisa's more cynical sister Elvira observes, "That fellow is incapable of an erection inside our national borders. Even his biology will only work in the Union of Soviet Socialist Republics." Pio tells Elvira how he became a Communist.

PIO

Now, I'm going to talk about this for the last time.
(Pause.)
In the thirty-nine years of my life, I have been a school-teacher, a printing shop cashier, a secretary for an emerald buyer on the Rio Magdalena, a spiritualist, a Rosicrucian, a Freemason, an atheist, a libertarian and a Communist. I'm a Communist because when I was a boy, in Valencia, my sainted mother, Ernestina, the widow of Miranda, a retired nurse at the Lepers' Hospital, and a constant reader of *The Count of Monte Cristo*, hanged herself in her room.

Do you know how she hanged herself? She piled up on her floor *Les Misérables* by Victor Hugo, *The Thirteenth Coach* by Xavier de Montepin, *The Lady of the Camelias* by Alexander Dumas, *Anna Karenina* by Leo Tolstoy and an illustrated edition of the Bible. She got up on the pile of books and, God damn it, didn't even leave me a word of explanation. She just leapt from romantic literature with an all-consuming fury. Now it seems a joke, and I surprise myself sometimes laughing when I tell it. But from that day on I was afraid! I would wet the bed from sheer anxiety. I didn't dare cross the patio after eleven for fear of meeting up with her under the lemon tree, or in the dining room, or in the kitchen. You ask, what the hell am I afraid of? I'm afraid she'll tell me why she did it. I'm afraid of ending up on the same beam under the same roof.

(Small pause.)

I read the books from that scaffold Mama had made in her room, looking for some key, some answer, any explanation whatsoever! And I found nothing. Pages and pages . . . of fluff!

(Pause.)

I joined the seminary of the archdiocese and began to masturbate every night. One day they discovered me in the middle of a lark with a statue of Santa Rita. And they had me declared afflicted and insane! So I stopped believing in God. Because how the fuck can I believe in God if a statue of Santa Rita turns me on? Don't you understand that they expelled me from this provincial life?

[ELVIRA
Praised be to the merciful Lord.]

PIO

There is no merciful Lord! You are in the world with your hands and your tongue. . . . And there is no merciful Lord! I could try to tell you that I'm a Communist because of the ballsiness of the *Manifesto,* or the courage of Marx, or the thinking of Engels! But I am a Communist because of the statement of Aura Celina Sarabia who was the cook in the Hotel Bolivar where my mother died. And do you know why my mother hanged herself? Because they reduced the budget of the Ministry of Health, and there was a mistake in the list of people with pensions! Aura Celina told me. A mistake in the list of pensioners, and six weeks without any money. She died of shame. . . . And I asked myself, how can I destroy these institutions and somebody told me, "Read this." And here I am, talking to you about my revolutionary life.

Division Street
Steve Tesich

Premiere: Ambassador Theatre, NYC, 1980
Publisher: Samuel French, Inc.
Setting: An apartment house on Division Street, Chicago

Chris Adrian, a radical leader of the sixties, is trying to put his past behind him and join in the "me-decade" eighties under a new I.D. His cover is blown when a news photographer recognizes Chris puking stuffed cabbage outside a Serbian restaurant and plasters his photo all over the paper. Among the various blasts from the past who respond to the photo and hunt Chris back down are his ex-wife Dianah, a vibrantly beautiful woman who has a strange habit of talking in song lyrics, and her legal aid divorce lawyer, Sal Kellogg. Sal is small, slight, and so unprepossessing that people—including Dianah—literally don't notice him. He is frantic to make human contact.

SAL

Look at me, Dianah. I'm right here. I'm easy to see. Look at me, please.
> (*She looks but not really at him, through him and beyond.*)

You are looking at a desperate, homeless, friendless creature, Dianah. I just can't seem to make an impression on
anyone. Even my parents. I was conceived on a Castro
convertible at their friend's house. They never had sex at
home. When I was a baby they'd leave me at home with
a baby sitter and go and have sex in a motel, or in a hotel,
or at a friend's house. They had friends everywhere and
they never introduced me to any of them. One day they
just didn't come back. They just forgot about me. I was
raised by a baby sitter, Dianah, who charged six seventy-
five an hour. My old man, Kellogg, that rotten old man of
mine, paid her seven years in advance. But when the money
ran out she left. I got a job to try and keep her, but I got
laid off. I was ten. Out of a job at ten! The older I grew,
the more I craved love and friends, the less the world
seemed to care. I am nobody's memory. Nobody gets together on a rainy day and wonders: How's Sal Kellogg
doing? What's Sal Kellogg up to? Pigeons starving to death
will not eat my bread crumbs in the park. Dogs facing
certain death in a dog pound will not go home with me. I
send letters and checks to the starving of Guatemala but
they don't write back. Scientology doesn't want me. Moon-
ies don't want me. I could be had for a song but the world
stops humming when Sal goes by. I would become a flasher
but who would look? I talk to myself and even I don't listen.
Are you listening, Dianah?

(*He cries, kneeling to Dianah, sobbing.*)

This is the single longest uninterrupted speech I have ever
made, Dianah, and I hope it moved you.

Elliot Loves
Jules Feiffer

Premiere: Promenade Theatre, NYC, 1990
Publisher: Grove Press
Setting: Near North Side of Chicago in the mid-eighties

Elliot is a neurotic man in his forties, whose girlfriend, Joanna, is a neurotic twice-divorced real-estate broker with two kids. They go to a party to introduce her to his closest friends. When the evening doesn't go as he planned, Elliot becomes depressed and Phil, an accountant and friend since high school, decides to cheer him up. Phil is in his forties, separated, and a recovering alcoholic. They talk while out on the terrace of a high-rise.

PHIL

Everyone talks about support groups for alcoholics. You know? Somebody should talk about countersupport groups. "Come on, one little drink won't hurt you." I've never been offered so many drinks in my life since I went on the wagon. The shit you get away with drunk. You know? You can't drop water bags off a terrace sober.

[ELLIOT

You never did that.]

PHIL

Not here. A couple of years ago. Condoms filled with water. I can't remember the name of the girl I woke up in bed with that night. You know? But I remember the condoms filled with water. That's what I have nostalgia for. The freedom. I'm a tightass sober; I'm a free man drunk. You know? I talked women into bed I wouldn't have the nerve to open my mouth to sober. I made friends. You know? I could never talk up to people the way Larry does. You know? But five or six bourbons, I could tell jokes. I don't know how to tell a joke, but I could tell 'em drunk. You know? I was better at everything drunk . . . except marriage and work. You know? And I prefer drinking to both. I bet JFK could put it away. Bet he could hold his liquor too. I bet he was a couple of sheets to the wind all through the Cuban missile crisis. I know I'd be. Adlai Stevenson and the Joint Chiefs in one room, Judith Exner in the next. You know? Can you imagine me peeing off a balcony with JFK? Teddy maybe, not Jack. Jack was a classy drunk. I'm more like Teddy. Black guys—they really pull out the jams drunk. Hispanics too. They get crazy—you know?—the music and everything. Crazy. They get high on the noise. Not Jews, though. When Jews get drunk they confuse it with their role in the universe. They don't have fun, they have insights. You can just bet that Einstein had a bag on the night he came up with $E = MC^2$.

(ELLIOT *laughs*.)

You think that's funny? You want to put money on Freud being smashed the night he came up with the Oedipus complex?

(ELLIOT *turns away, smiling*.)

Karl Marx—he came up with communism tanked. You know, Elliot? Four in the morning, bombed out of his mind. If he hadn't made notes, he would have forgotten it the next morning and we're all better off. Right? Right. You know? Wasps drunk—Wasps drunk are no different from Wasps sober. You know? Upper-class Wasps, I mean, upper-class. Lower-class—they know how to have a good time. But upper-class Wasps, you know—you know?—they get paranoid drinking that, that they'll lose control. Right? Right. An ex-altar boy like me, you know, I only feel in control when I'm drunk; but Wasps, who really are in control, when they get drunk they get afraid that they'll lose it. You're not smiling. That's okay too. This is the best time I've had since I quit drinking, and it's because you don't care if I'm alive or dead. If you're just holding that glass, Elliot, and not drinking on account of me, you don't have to. I'm past that.

The Film Society
Jon Robin Baitz

Premiere: Los Angeles Actors Theatre, Los Angeles, California
Publisher: Samuel French, Inc.
Setting: Durham, Natal Providence, South Africa, 1970

Jonathon Balton teaches at Blenheim, an underendowed South African private school. His passion is film, and he runs an extracurricular Film Society for interested students. Two of his colleagues, Terry and Nan Sinclair, bait the conservative establishment of the school by inviting a black guest speaker, the Reverend Elias Bazewo, to speak at Centenary Day. Bazewo is arrested. Jonathon's response? "Politics, Terry. I'm the last person to talk about politics. I can't even get a print of *Touch of Mink*."

But politics are forced upon Jonathon when Bazewo dies of "a heart attack" in prison. Conservative parents yank their pupils from school, and the headmaster, hoping to bury all strains of "bohemianism," fires Terry and shuts down the Film Society. Through the manipulations of Jonathon's mother, "a brutal and savage woman" with colonial airs and a great deal of money, Jonathon is appointed assistant headmaster. When the headmaster dies, he is offered that job as well—on the condition that he fire Nan Sinclair.

Jonathon, Terry, and Nan have just returned from the headmaster's funeral. After this speech, Jonathon will tell Nan that he's been made headmaster, and she is fired.

BALTON

This was only my second funeral. My father's the only other. You were very fond of my father, weren't you, Terry? Horses, and all that. But you didn't really know him. Did you?

[TERRY

. . . No. I mean, the public version only. Right? You look like you could use a drink, Jonathon.

BALTON

No. Just tired out.] I was thinking of the farm. Every Saturday night, father'd give one of the cows to the natives. A treat. Few farms did that. But actually, it was no sacrifice, just a small feeble animal. And yet, cane-cutters, herd boys, all of them . . . would look forward to Saturday night. The compound would come alive. That mad Zulu pop music on the Bantu radio. I'd sit in nanny's lap, watching. It was all very festive.

(Beat.)

I was mostly interested in the killing of the cow. Used to be, they used a knife, and that was vivid, very much a thing of the bush. To see the creature's dull eyes flashing, hooves scraping at the dirt as the knife was led across the throat— and the blood running into a gourd on the ground. But the part that fascinated me the most, was when it was dead. Its evisceration. The skin drawn slowly back, and the veins exposed, black blood clotting into the reddish dust of the compound, which would be dead quiet, sombre. Little ivory-coloured and purple-hued sacks filled with bile and acid and urine. Balloons of undigested grass, bones cracked, and muscles pulsing gently, as a fire was readied, and the tongue, the great curled muscle, unravelled, cut out, and the teeth and jaw laid bare.

(Pause.)

But it is one Saturday in particular that I remember. It was my birthday, and I was given the honour of killing the cow. I was eleven. The knife was dispensed with, and my father gave me a pistol with tiny silver-tipped bullets. I was to blow out the brains from a little spot between the eyes, and this death had none of the ritual of the knife. It was an assassination and I believe the natives knew this. Unbearable to have this cow led to me, docile, and uncomplaining. She was tied to a post, with a little strand of rope, and I tried to do the thing very quickly. But you see, I did not do a proper job of it. And the bullet ricochetted off her skull and down into the jaw—this shattered pulp of bone

and blood, through which she screamed, you see, as I recall
it. And tore loose from her feebly tied rope. And there she
was, with saliva, and plasma all about, bolting into the cane
fields, everyone stunned. She was gone. And I stood there.
Frozen.

(Pause.)

And I looked up, and saw my father standing on the ver-
andah of the main house with my mother—and he said
something to her, and went inside, and nanny came to me.
And of course, by this time, I was crying. The natives
staring at their feet—mortified. No laughter—which might
have been preferable.

(Pause.)

And then my father came out of the house with his shotgun,
got on his horse, and rode into the field, and there was a
single muffled blast, and nanny put me to bed. A quiet
supper that night, no singing or dancing, and of course,
not long after, we moved into the city—my mother's idea.
So I was just thinking about my father, and all.

Goose and Tomtom

David Rabe

Premiere: Lincoln Center Theatre, NYC, 1986
Publisher: Samuel French, Inc.
Setting: An apartment in the underworld, recently

Goose and Tomtom are small-time hoods in a surreal-
istic underworld. They are passing the time in a well-bar-
ricaded apartment and scheming a way to get back the
diamonds stolen from Tomtom's moll Lorraine. Lorraine
has decided to find out which of the two men is tougher
by sticking pins in their arms. After ten pins apiece, she
declares, "You guys are both tough," and storms into the
bedroom. Goose has had a dream that disturbs him. He

says to Tomtom, "Sometimes I still got like these frog feelings from when I was a frog."

GOOSE

I mean, it was before I lived around here. I don't know
where it was, but I was in this room, and I couldn't get
out. But I don't give a fuck. It's happened before. And
then, all of a sudden, there's all this dark behind me that's
different than all the other dark, and in this different dark,
there is the reason that it's different, and the reason is it's
a ghost behind me, and when I turn to look he just moves
so he stays behind me, and then he says like into the back
of my head, "Don't you wanna know the secret?" And I
say, "No, I don't." An' he says, "It's a secret about you,
don't you wanna know it?" And I say, "No," an' I'm wishin'
he would go away, and he hears my thinkin', so he's angry.

(TOMTOM *spasms, getting sicker, and* GOOSE
goes to the downstage crates from which
TOMTOM *got the aspirins.* GOOSE *gets a
thermometer, a stethoscope, aspirin, perhaps something for the pins. Going back to*
TOMTOM, *he tends him.*)

All of a sudden in his anger I can't move anymore, and
then I can, but I can't stand up, or talk. And all of a sudden
I know why all the other little kids in the neighborhood
hate me, 'cause they do, and tease me, 'cause they do, and
it's 'cause I'm a frog. 'At's the secret about me. And now
he's brought it up outa the secret places in me and into my
body; this ghost with these eyes has looked at me an' turned
me into a frog in me.

(Pause.)

Well, I'm cryin'—I'm not afraid to tell you, Tomtom, I'm
cryin' an' beggin', I'll do anything he wants—I don't know
what it is—but I can't move or speak, all green and spotty.
So the night is on and on, and it's truer than anything else.
I belong on my belly. Out of doors an' wet and cold. Out
by green scummy ponds unable to talk all my feelin's or

thoughts but burstin' with 'em. Layin' inna wet slimy grass, hopin' to lick some fly outa the air. Worms around me an' spiders. The night seems so long. As years an' years. And then there's light, an' I see my body's a person again, 'cause I made the ghost a promise I don't know what it was.

(Slight pause.)

An' sometimes, I still get feelings of a frog an' I gotta look around and check everything real good an' make sure I'm not layin' in green wet grass wantin' to eat flies, 'cause I'm cold in my heart sometimes. I'm all spotty an' green in my heart. In my heart I know where I belong, an' I got big buggy eyes.

(Pause.)

That fuckin' promise to a ghost, I made it—I don't know what it was, but I know I'm keepin' it. He said I would be a frog as long as he was a ghost, and blood was red and mud wet an' secrets secrets. You ever made a promise to a ghost? Tom . . . tom?

Hurlyburly
David Rabe

Premiere: Goodman Theatre, Chicago, Illinois, 1984
Publisher: Samuel French, Inc.
Setting: An upscale house in the Hollywood Hills

Phil is an unstable, out-of-work Hollywood actor in the throes of a marital crisis. As his casting director friend Eddie describes it, "you two are in the middle of this bloodbath— the goddamn climactic go-round of your seven-year career in, you know what I mean, marital carnage." Phil's wife, Susie, thinks having a baby together will save their marriage, and Phil, who already has three children by a failed marriage, is not so sure. Unable to face his wife's desperation, he is pretending to try to get her pregnant while taking a drug that renders his sperm ineffective. Phil has come to Eddie's house for comfort and advice. Both men are heavy before-breakfast users of cocaine, weed, and bourbon. Eddie has just advised Phil, "All I'm sayin' is, don't have a baby thoughtlessly."

PHIL

Eddie, for god sake, don't terrify me that you have paid no attention! If I was thoughtless would I be here? I feel like I have pushed thought to the brink where it is just noise and of no more use than a headful of car horns, because the bottom line here that I'm getting at is just this—I got to go back to her. I got to go back to Susie, and if it means havin' a kid, I got to do it. I mean, I have hit a point where I am going round the bend several times a day now, and so far I been on the other side to meet me, but one a these days it might be one time too many, and who knows who might be there waitin'? If not me, who? I'm a person, Eddie, and I have realized it, who needs like a big-dot-thing, you know—this big-dot-thing around which I can just hang and blab my thoughts and more or less formulate everything as I go, myself included. I mean, I used to spend my days in my car; I didn't know what the fuck I was doin' but it kept me out of trouble until nothin' but blind luck led me to I-am-married, and I could go home. She was my big-dot-thing. Now I'm startin' in my car again, I'm spendin' days on the freeways and rain or no rain I like the wipers clickin', and all around me the other cars got people in 'em the way I see 'em when they are in cars. These heads, these faces. These boxes of steel with glass and faces inside. I been the last two days without seeing another form of human being in his entirety except gas station attendants. The family men in the day with their regular food and regular hours in their eyes. And then in the night, these moonlighters; they could be anything. In the wee hours of the morning, it's derelicts, and these weird spooky kids like they have recently arrived from outer space, but not to stay. The cloverleafs, they got a thing in them, it spins me off. There's little back roads and little towns sometimes I never heard of them. I start to expect the gas station attendants to know me when I arrive. I get excited that I've been there before. I want them to welcome me. I'm disappointed when they don't. Something that I don't want to be true starts lookin' like it's all that's true only I don't know what it is. No. No. I need my marriage. I come here to tell you. I got to stay married. I'm lost without her.

Jerker, or The Helping Hand
Robert Chesley

Premiere: Celebration Theatre, Los Angeles, California, 1986
Publisher: Grove Press (in *Out Front: Contemporary Gay and Lesbian Plays*)
Setting: San Francisco, 1985

Jerker, or The Helping Hand is subtitled "A Pornographic Elegy with Redeeming Social Value and A Hymn to the Queer Men of San Francisco in Twenty Telephone Calls, Many of Them Dirty." One night while in bed, Bert, a gay man in his thirties to fifties, or possibly older but youthful in appearance, is awakened by an anonymous call. The voice asks him if he's hard. Bert decides to go along with the call, and the two men have sex over the phone. J.R. and Bert have phone sex several nights, talking out their fantasies while jerking off. They met by the men's room at Badlands, a San Francisco bar, on Bert's birthday. Bert gave J.R. his phone number, but doesn't remember him.

Tonight Bert is in bed crying. He lets his answering machine pick up, then changes his mind and answers the phone. He does not want to have sex, but is very upset and wants to talk. J.R. wants to hear. Bert's friend has AIDS

and is in the hospital hooked up to a respirator. He has
gotten so thin, Bert didn't recognize him. It is clear his
friend is going to die.

NOTE: Robert Chesley writes that both men are "San
Francisco faggots," whom he describes as "beautiful, loving, sexy men. They have facial hair, fairly often in the
extravagant, fanciful styles of the Old West. Their eyes are
alive, and their voices are relaxed and gentle. Their beauty
transcends any considerations of age, race, body type or
traditional 'good looks.' "

BERT

Look . . . I want to tell you, okay? I want to tell you about
this guy, I mean: I mean the way he *was*, 'cause he was a
beautiful guy. Is that okay?

[J.R.

Sure. I'd like to hear. Tell me.]

BERT

He's . . . okay, well his name is David, and I guess all I
really have to say about him is . . . he's a *decent* guy. And
beautiful, too, you know—not because he was any movie-
idol type, not because he was a muscle builder or anything,
but . . . because it was like there was a light inside him
which made him strong, gentle . . . kind. *That* kind of
beauty, you know: sexy, sure—sexy as anything, but *more*,
too, and *all together*.

[J.R.

Yeah?]

BERT

Yeah, and . . . well, like I said: decent. *Nobody* deserves
what—what he's going through, I know, nobody. But . . . !
It just makes me *sick*, inside, because it's so fucking
unfair! He came to San Francisco—[you really want to
hear this?

J.R.

Sure. If you want to tell me.]

(*Pause.*)

BERT

I do. He] . . . well, like a *lot* of other guys, he left the Midwest. I know it's a joke, people put down the Castro for being Midwest, but it *isn't*, really: it *isn't* a *joke*. Okay, so David cuts hair, and I know that's a joke, too, a cliché—but he set himself up in business and he did well enough for himself, and that's not a joke either: he had to fight to have his own life the way he wanted it. That's how I knew him first, see, he cut my hair, and, well, sure . . . he *did* a *lot* of his customers, of course, right there in the barber's chair. He was a hot guy, and . . . lots of fun and . . . sweet, beautiful. And horny.

(Nearly in tears.)

And fuck it all, *there's nothing wrong with that!*

[J.R.

I didn't say there was.

BERT

Yeah, I know—no, you didn't.] But, you know, everyone's putting it down nowadays.

(Mimicking.)

"The party's over! The party's over!"

(Own voice.)

Well, fuck it all, *no! That wasn't just a party!* It was more: a *lot* more, at least to some of us, and it was *connected* to other parts of our lives, *deep* parts, *deep* connections. I'm not gonna deny that drugs were part of it, and I *know* for some guys it was—or it turned out to be—hell. But that's not the whole story. For me, for a *lot* of guys, it was . . . *living*; and it was *loving*. Yeah: *It was loving*, even if you didn't know whose cock it was in the dark, or whose asshole you were sucking. And *I don't regret a single moment of it: not one.*

Laughing Wild

Christopher Durang

Premiere: Playwrights Horizons, NYC, 1987
Publisher: Dramatists Play Service, Inc.
Setting: New York City

Laughing Wild is a play in three parts. In the first two, "Laughing Wild" and "Seeking Wild," characters identified only as a Woman and a Man address their monologues directly to the audience. In the third, "Dreaming Wild," they interact with each other in variations on a random attack at the tuna fish shelf of a New York supermarket and a Sally Jessy Raphael interview with the Infant of Prague.

"Seeking Wild" is a talk given by a man who is struggling to maintain his Personality Workshop–inspired optimism in the face of supermarket attacks and other modern crises, great and small. This is the opening of his nineteen-page monologue.

> (*The* MAN *is dressed well, maybe even a little trendy. He is dressed up to give a talk, to share his new thoughts. He carries with him a few file cards that he has made notes on. He smiles at the audience briefly, checks his first note card quickly before beginning, and then speaks with earnestness and purpose.*)

MAN

I used to be a very negative person. But then I took this personality workshop that totally turned my life around. Now when something bad or negative happens, I can see the positive. Now when I have a really bad day or when someone I thought was a really good friend betrays me, or maybe when I've been hit by one of those damn people riding bicycles the opposite way on a one-way street, so, of course, one hadn't looked in that direction and there they are bearing down on you, about to kill or maim you—

anyway, I look at any of these things and I say to myself:
this glass is not half full, it's half empty.

No—I said it backwards, force of habit. This glass is
not half empty, it is half *full*.

Of course, if they hit you with the stupid bicycle your
glass will not be half full or half empty, it will be shattered
to pieces, and you'll be dead or in the hospital.

But really I'm trying to be positive, that's what I'm
doing with my life these days.

(Reads from a note card.)

I was tired of not being joyful and happy, I was sick of
my personality, and I had to change it.

(Off the card; back to speaking extempora-
neously.)

Half full, *not* half empty. I had to say to myself: you
do not have cancer—at least not today. You are not blind.
You are not one of the starving children in India or China
or in Africa. Look at the sunset, look at the sunrise, why
don't you enjoy them, for God's sake? And now I do.

(Almost as a sidetrack to himself.)

Except if it's cloudy, of course, and you can't see the sun.
Or if it's cold. Or if it's too hot.

(Hearing his negativity above.)

I probably need to take a few more personality work-
shops to complete the process. It's still not quite within
my grasp, this being positive business.

(Reads from cards again.)

But I'm making great strides. My friends don't recognize me.

(Smiles.)
(Off the cards again.)

And it is hard for me to be positive because I'm very
sensitive to the vibrations of people around me, or maybe
I'm just paranoid. But in any case, I used to find it difficult
to go out of the house sometimes because of coming into
contact with other people.

You've probably experienced something similar—you

know, the tough on the subway who keeps staring at you and you're the only two people in the car and he keeps staring and after a while you think, does he want to kill me? Or just intimidate me? Which is annoying enough.

Or the people in movie theatres who talk endlessly during the opening credits so you can just *tell* they're going to talk through the entire movie and that it will be utterly useless to ask them not to talk.

And even if you do ask them not to talk and they ungraciously acquiesce, they're going to send out vibrations that they hate you all during the entire film, and then it will be impossible to concentrate.

You can move, but the person next to you in the new location will probably, you know, rattle candy wrappers endlessly all through the movie. Basically I don't go to the movies anymore. What's the point?

The Loman Family Picnic
Donald Margulies

Premiere: Manhattan Theatre Club, NYC, 1989
Publisher: Dramatists Play Service, Inc.
Setting: A high-rise apartment in Coney Island, Brooklyn, 1965

Herbie and Doris have just celebrated their eighteenth anniversary. At the start of the play, Doris is cutting her wedding gown in shreds with a pair of scissors, though she insists—before anyone asks—that she's not disenchanted with her marriage. Their thirteen-year-old son, Stewie, is having second thoughts about his impending bar mitzvah, and eleven-year-old Mitchell is writing the upbeat musical version of *Death of a Salesman* that gives the play its title.

Herbie is an ineffectual, stolid provider who comes home from a hard day at work and finds his whole family asleep. Doris tries to rouse the boys to show off for their father, but no one is interested. As Doris's restlessness increases to the point where she starts chatting with her long-dead free-spirit Aunt Marsha, Herbie retreats more and more into silence.

In this scene, Herbie's two sons watch him talk to himself as he gets dressed for work at six in the morning. This speech is addressed directly to the audience.

HERBIE
(To us.)

Maybe I don't have dreams anymore. I mean I must, but I don't remember. I don't remember a thing. My childhood? The war? Show me a picture of me taken someplace and I couldn't tell you where. I won't remember the name of the buddy I had my arm around. Ask me what year my kids were born, I couldn't tell you. Either of them. I know I was married eighteen years ago 'cause that's what Doris told me; the other night was our anniversary. I know how old I am; I'm forty years old. I was born in '25, but the exact date they're not sure, and the midwife who signed the birth certificate put my sex down as female. So I don't know; I don't know. I remember Dame May Whitty was in *The Lady Vanishes* . . . but I don't remember my father even shaking my hand.

[STEWIE
(To Mitchell.)

He's crazy. Let's face it. He's gone. Lost in action.]

HERBIE
(To us.)

Did *my* father throw *me* a bar mitzvah? I don't even remember *being* bar mitzvahed. If I *was* you can be sure nobody thought twice about it. They say we were very poor when I was young.

(Shrugs.)

I don't remember. Supposedly we were on relief. Six kids in three rooms. No doors. No privacy. Hand-me-downs from my brothers . . . Nothing ever started with me, it

ended with me. I didn't have much; that much I remember.
You stop *wanting*, so what you don't *have* doesn't matter.
This is the Depression I'm talking about. I got through
those years with my eyes shut tight and holding my breath
like when you're under water. Got the hell outta *there*,
straight to the Army. War was an improvement. Then I
met Doris, then I married her, got this job, kids. . . . And
I go through every day with my eyes shut tight and holding
my breath, till the day is over and I can come home. To
what? What kind of home is left to come home to by the
time I come home?

No Man's Land

Harold Pinter

Premiere: National Theatre, London, England, 1975
Publisher: Grove Press
Setting: A large room in a house in North West London

Two elderly men named Spooner and Hirst share a
drink and make mysterious and pungent conversation. They
may or may not be old acquaintances. Into this "no man's
land" come two rather sinister younger men. Foster claims
to be Hirst's son. The other man, Briggs, does not identify
himself, but appears to be Hirst's manservant, filling and
refilling his glass with liquor and finally handing him the
whole bottle.

The following morning, Spooner is still at his host's. He
appears to have slept fully clothed in his chair, and the
door is locked. Briggs opens it with a key and brings him
a champagne breakfast on a silver tray, making apologies
for someone named Jack. When Spooner asks, "Who's the
cook?" Briggs answers, "We share all burdens, Jack and
I." He pulls up a chair and watches as Spooner eats breakfast.

Briggs

We're old friends, Jack and myself. We met at a street corner. I should tell you he'll deny this account. His story will be different. I was standing at a street corner. A car drew up. It was him. He asked me the way to Bolsover street. I told him Bolsover street was in the middle of an intricate one-way system. It was a one-way system easy enough to get into. The only trouble was that, once in, you couldn't get out. I told him his best bet, if he really wanted to get to Bolsover street, was to take the first left, first right, second right, third on the left, keep his eye open for a hardware shop, go right round the square, keeping to the inside lane, take the second Mews on the right and then stop. He will find himself facing a very tall office block, with a crescent courtyard. He can take advantage of this office block. He can go round the crescent, come out the other way, follow the arrows, go past two sets of traffic lights and take the next left indicated by the first green filter he comes across. He's got the Post Office Tower in his vision the whole time. All he's got to do is to reverse into the underground car park, change gear, go straight on, and he'll find himself in Bolsover street with no trouble at all. I did warn him, though, that he'll still be faced with the problem, having found Bolsover street, of losing it. I told him I knew one or two people who'd been wandering up and down Bolsover street for years. They'd wasted their bloody youth there. The people who live there, their faces are grey, they're in a state of despair, but nobody pays any attention, you see. All people are worried about is their illgotten gains. I wrote to the *Times* about it. Life At A Dead End, I called it. Went for nothing. Anyway, I told him that probably the best thing he could do was to forget the whole idea of getting to Bolsover street. I remember saying to him: This trip you've got in mind, drop it, it could prove fatal. But he said he had to deliver a parcel. Anyway, I took all this trouble with him because he had a nice open face. He looked like a man who would always do good to others himself. Normally I wouldn't give a fuck. I should tell you he'll deny this account. His story will be different.

The Normal Heart
Larry Kramer

Premiere: New York Shakespeare Festival, NYC, 1985
Publisher: Samuel French, Inc.
Setting: Various locations in New York City, 1981–1984

The Normal Heart chronicles a time in the shockingly recent past when AIDS was a little-known and virtually unpublicized disease. (During the first seventeen months after the epidemic was officially declared in 1981, the *New York Times* wrote about it only seven times, though nearly a thousand cases had been reported. During the three months of the 1982 Tylenol scare, the *Times* wrote about it fifty-four times, though only seven cases were reported.) The play describes the efforts of gay activists and medical professionals to break press taboos and organize support services. It also shows the epidemic's devastating impact on its characters' personal lives.

Ned Weeks and Bruce Niles are the leaders of a new gay political organization dedicated to fighting AIDS. Ned is a hotheaded gadfly, where Bruce is smooth-tempered, likable, and gorgeous. A former Green Beret and a vice president of Citibank, Bruce's public persona is still in the closet. After his lover Craig died of AIDS, he started dating a Calvin Klein model named Albert. Soon Albert got sick. Though Bruce is still healthy, he is terrified that he infected his lovers.

Ned and Bruce fight constantly and vehemently over the direction their organization should take. Another staff member says they're all "a little bit yelled out. We've got a lot of different styles that don't quite mesh. We've got

ourselves a lot of bereavement overload." At the end of one
especially heated staff meeting, Bruce opens up to Ned.

BRUCE

Ned, Albert is dead.

[NED

Oh, no.

BRUCE

What's today?

NED

Wednesday.]

BRUCE

He's been dead a week.

[NED

I didn't know he was so close.

BRUCE

No one did.] He wouldn't tell anyone. Do you know why?
Because of me. Because he knows I'm so scared I'm some
sort of carrier. This makes three people I've been with who
are dead. I went to Emma and I begged her: please test
me somehow, please tell me if I'm giving this to people.
And she said she couldn't, there isn't any way they can find
out anything because they still don't know what they're
looking for. Albert, I think I loved him best of all, and he
went so fast. His mother wanted him back in Phoenix before
he died, this was last week when it was obvious, so I get
permission from Emma and bundle him all up and take
him to the plane in an ambulance. The pilot wouldn't take
off and I refused to leave the plane—you would have been
proud of me—so finally they get another pilot. Then, after
we take off, Albert loses his mind, not recognizing me, not
knowing where he is or that he's going home, and then,
right there, on the plane, he becomes . . . incontinent. He
starts doing it in his pants and all over the seat; shit, piss,
everything. I pulled down my suitcase and yanked out
whatever clothes were in there and I start mopping him
up as best I can, and all these people are staring at us and

moving away in droves and . . . I ram all these clothes back in the suitcase and I sit there holding his hand, saying, "Albert, please, no more, hold it in, man, I beg you, just for us, for Bruce and Albert." And when we got to Phoenix, there's a police van waiting for us and all the police are in complete protective rubber clothing, they looked like fucking astronauts, and by the time we got to the hospital where his mother had fixed up his room real nice, Albert was dead.

(NED *starts toward him.*)

Wait. It gets worse. The hospital doctors refused to examine him to put a cause of death on the death certificate, and without a death certificate the undertakers wouldn't take him away, and neither would the police. Finally, some orderly comes in and stuffs Albert in a heavy-duty Glad Bag and motions us with finger to follow and he puts him out in the back alley with the garbage. He says, "Hey, man. See what a big favor I've done for you, I got him out, I want fifty bucks." I paid him and then his mother and I carried the bag to her car and we finally found a black undertaker who cremated him for a thousand dollars, no questions asked.

(NED *crosses to* BRUCE *and embraces him;*

BRUCE *put his arms around* NED.)

Would you and Felix mind if I spent the night on your sofa? Just one night. I don't want to go home.

The Norman Conquests
Alan Ayckbourn

Premiere: Liberty Theatre, Scarborough, England, 1973
Publisher: Grove Press
Setting: An English home badly in need of redecoration, one weekend in July

The Norman Conquests is a trilogy of plays all taking place the same weekend, but each in a different part of the house. Norman Dewers, an assistant librarian, is a disheveled womanizer—"a gigolo trapped inside a haystack." He makes plans to go off for a romantic weekend with his sister-in-law, Annie, whose life revolves around caring for her invalid mother, as well as time spent with Tom, a dimwitted veterinarian. Their plans are disrupted by Sarah, the prudish, autocratic wife of Norman's brother-in-law. Norman and Sarah are constantly at odds. When she asks him if he likes her, he responds, "I—don't dislike you. You're like—mild athlete's foot. You make me irritable." He goes on to explain.

NOTE: This monologue takes place in the third play, *Round and Round the Garden*.

NORMAN

I'll tell you. When I was at my Primary school—mixed infants—we had a little girl just like you. She was very pretty, very smart and clean—beautifully dressed—always a nicely starched little frock on—nicely ironed bow in her hair . . . butter wouldn't melt anywhere. Let alone her mouth. And she ran that little school with more sheer ruthless efficiency than the head of the Mafia. She asked you to do something for her and you did it. You never argued. It was no good arguing with her. She was cleverer than you were. Precociously clever. She could reduce a nine-year-old thug to tears with her sarcasm. And it was no use trying to thump her either. She'd seduced all the best muscle in the place. She had a body guard five deep. Not that she ever needed it. For some reason, she took a real dislike to me. Maybe because she could see what I really thought of her. She made my life murder. I was terrified to go to school. I used to pretend to be sick—I used to hide—play truant—anything rather than go . . . And then one day, in the holidays, she came round with her mother to our house to see my mother. A sociable tea and chat.

And they sent us two out on our own to play together. And suddenly there we were, not in the school, not in the playground—which was definitely her territory—but on mine. My garden, my patch. And we stood there and we just looked at each other. And I thought what am I frightened of you for? A skinny little girl with knock knees and a front tooth missing—what on earth have I been frightened of you for, for heaven's sake? So I picked her up, like this under one arm and I carried her right down the bottom of the garden by the rubbish tip—she never made a sound during this, not a word, nothing—and I found the biggest patch of stinging nettles I could find and I pulled down her knickers and sat her right in the middle of them. I felt marvellous. It was a beautiful moment. Magic. And she sat there for a very long time—not moving, just looking at me—weighing me up, you know. Then she got up, pulled up her knickers, very quietly took hold of my hand, gave me a big kiss and we went in and had our tea. I've never been in love like that again.

The Piano Lesson
August Wilson

Premiere: Yale Repertory Theatre, New Haven, Connecticut, 1987
Publisher: Plume
Setting: Home of Doaker Charles and his niece, Berniece, Pittsburgh, 1936

Early one morning, Boy Willie shows up at the home of his uncle, Doaker, and sister, Berniece. Thirty years old, Boy Willie has "an infectious grin and a boyishness that is apt for his name. He is brash and impulsive, talkative and somewhat crude in speech and manner." He and his friend, Lymon, have driven for two days from Jackson, Mississippi, with a truckload of watermelons they plan to sell. Boy Willie plans to buy some land back home with the money he makes from the watermelons, and by convincing Berniece to sell the family piano.

Ornately hand-carved by their great-grandfather, the piano dominates the parlor. Its carvings tell their family history. Berniece has seen too much bloodshed over the piano, which caused their family to be split up as slaves, cost their father his life, and created tremendous pain for their mother. She will not sell it and wants Boy Willie, and all the trouble he brings, out of her house immediately.

In the first monologue, Doaker, their forty-seven-year-old uncle, tells his philosophy after working twenty-seven years on the railroad. While in his youth he lined track, he now works as a railroad cook. "A tall, thin man with severe features, he has for all intents and purposes withdrawn from the world."

In the second monologue, Boy Willie tells the difference between him and Berniece, and why he needs to sell the piano.

———— 1 ————

DOAKER

Twenty-seven years. Now, I'll tell you something about the railroad. What I done learned after twenty-seven years. See, you got North. You got West. You look over here you got South. Over there you got East. Now, you can start from anywhere. Don't care where you at. You got to go one of them four ways. And whichever way you decide to go they got a railroad that will take you there. Now, that's something simple. You think anybody would be able to understand that. But you'd be surprised how many people trying to go North get on a train going West. They think the train's supposed to go where they going rather than where it's going.

Now, why people going? Their sister's sick. They leaving before they kill somebody . . . and they sitting across from somebody who's leaving to keep from getting killed. They leaving 'cause they can't get satisfied. They going to meet someone. I wish I had a dollar for every time that someone wasn't at the station to meet them. I done seen that a lot. In between the time they sent the telegram and the time the person get there . . . they done forgot all about them.

They got so many trains out there they have a hard time keeping them from running into each other. Got trains going every whichaway. Got people on all of them. Somebody going where somebody just left. If everybody stay in one place I believe this would be a better world. Now what I done learned after twenty-seven years of railroading is this . . . if the train stays on the track . . . it's going to get where it's going. It might not be where you going. If it ain't, then all you got to do is sit and wait cause the train's coming back to get you. The train don't never stop. It'll come back every time.

———— 2 ————

BOY WILLIE

See now . . . I'll tell you something about me. I done strung along and strung along. Going this way and that. Whatever way would lead me to a moment of peace. That's all I want. To be as easy with everything. But I wasn't born to that. I was born to a time of fire.

The world ain't wanted no part of me. I could see that since I was about seven. The world say it's better off without me. See, Berniece accept that. She trying to come up to where she can prove something to the world. Hell, the world a better place 'cause of me. I don't see it like Berniece. I got a heart that beats here and it beats just as loud as the next fellow's. Don't care if he black or white. Sometime it beats louder. When it beats louder, then everybody can hear it. Some people get scared of that. Like Berniece.

Some people get scared to hear a nigger's heart beating. They think you ought to lay low with that heart. Make it beat quiet and go along with everything the way it is. But my mama ain't birthed me for nothing. So what I got to do? I got to mark my passing on the road. Just like you write on a tree, "Boy Willie was here."

That's all I'm trying to do with that piano. Trying to put my mark on the road. Like my daddy done. My heart say for me to sell that piano and get me some land so I can make a life for myself to live in my own way. Other than that I ain't thinking about nothing Berniece got to say.

The Promise

José Rivera

Premiere: Los Angeles Theatre Center, Los Angeles, California, 1988
Publisher: Broadway Play Publishing
Setting: The backyard of Guzman's home in Patchogue, Long Island

Guzman is "a tough, passionate, superstitious man whose true age is a mystery—maybe early forties. There isn't a gray hair on his head." This last is easy to explain—his eighteen-year-old daughter, Lilia, pulls out his gray hairs for him. Guzman is caught between two cultures—the magic and ritual of his native Marcario, Puerto Rico, and the mundane realities of suburban Long Island, where he now lives. He waters the stunted corn in his backyard with blood from his hand, waved in the sign of a cross, and holds conversations with his dead wife.

Guzman's son Milton broke his father's heart by running off to become the first Puerto Rican cowboy, and he has decided that his daughter will obey his wishes no matter what. He wants Lilia to marry a rich man named Hiberto

Munoz, even though she has given her soul to a tortured young man named Carmelo Alegria. On the day the wedding is scheduled, Guzman talks to his nervous, awkward future son-in-law.

GUZMAN

You marry her, my friend, and tonight you touch her. If that means tying her to the bed the way my great-grandparents did it, I'll lend you the rope myself.

(HIBERTO *starts to say something,* GUZMAN
cuts him off.)

I want six children. Like Elena and I had. Milton, Lilia, and four who died at birth—four souls killed by the jealous magic of Señor Alegria. They died so fast, some nights I still hear them cry with surprise!

(*Puts his arm around* HIBERTO.)

Just make sure you have at least one girl. That way you'll have one who *really* loves you: someone who doesn't go around laughing at you, calling you Stalin.

(*He looks at* HIBERTO *very pleased, and
gives him an affectionate hug as tears fill his
eyes.*)

You're my son now! That's why I'm giving you the most important thing I have. My book.

(*From the inside of the hollowed-out Virgin
Mary statue,* GUZMAN *produces an ancient,
yellowed manuscript.*)

Tales of Marcario. I wrote it for that ungrateful Milton, to teach him the beauty of our culture, and it's all the magic stories that happened in that poor, lost town.

(*Opening to the first page.*)

Page one: "Puerto Rico sits next to the huge U.S.A.—like a little star next to the sun. Poor little country! Getting wiped out by its huge neighbor!"

(*Kisses* HIBERTO.)

This book will come in handy when you liberate Puerto Rico for me—.

Sea Marks

Gardner McKay

Premiere: Players Theatre, NYC, 1981
Publisher: Samuel French, Inc.
Setting: Cliffhorn Heads, an island in the west of Ireland, and
Liverpool

Colm Primrose is a fisherman from a tiny, traditional
village on one of the western islands of Ireland. He is a
strong, simple man, a natural poet, and a self-described
"spinster-man." As the play opens, he stands at the window
of his stone cottage, looking out at the weather. McKay
describes the circumstances: "He talks to himself, including
the audience, summing up the terminal sameness of his
life, maybe composing a letter. It is his birthday and he is
on the verge of something new."

COLM

I live by the sea.

I have always lived by the sea.

I can't know what it would be like living anywhere else.

The house I live in is made of stone that the sea has
broken from these cliffs. It is a small house and stands close
to the edge of the full tide. I am watching the sea now. It
pushes up on the beach in front of the house. It is not a
pretty beach. It is made of gray stones which the sea turns
black by rising over them and falling away. The rain has
stopped now and the sea is gray. The sky is white and lines
of gray are being blown along further out at sea. There is
always a gale somewhere on a day like this.

Each morning by the way the sea looks, I know how
to feel. Its mood changes and so does mine. I can hear the
sea, too, always. And I've seen every kind of fit it's able to
throw against this shore. This shore. This shore is all the
sea I know. The sea is a continent, and all I know of it are
a few miles of this shore.

My house was built before I was born. And it was built

away from the sea wall and a mile from the fishing harbor. There is a room upstairs and a room downstairs. It is easy to heat from turf, or if there is wood, wood. I painted it white a few years back because no other house is white and I could better see it from off-shore when I went out to fish. I also painted it white because I felt like it.

I don't very often do things I feel like. Neither does anyone else around here. I know everyone around here and everyone knows me. We were all born on this island, and that's that. But because we began by the sea and have lived by the sea, there is no want to do anything apart from the sea. We could not be closer to the sea without drowning in it, which is what a few of us do every year.

Each spring when we tar the hulls and get ready for the mackerel, we sing some songs, the same songs. And when we're tired of working, we go the the Captain's and drink until wives start appearing at the door. But I have never married and find my way home alone.

I had a dog a few years back, I did, a black dog who went with me everywhere, even to fish. And when he died of fish poisoning, I missed him. Ah, he couldn't cook and he couldn't light the fire, and he was no good to talk to, but I missed him sitting there by the door. I suppose I still do. He cannot be replaced.

Some birds come around, sea birds, and they come up to me to feed. I give them bread or whatever scraps there is. The birds have wingspan, sure, but no sense, no feeling.

The wind blows off the sea. The only time I've ever seen it blow any other way was in the middle of storms when everything is confused and the wind backs around and seems to be coming from inside the cliffs.

I have a lot to remember and, I suppose, something to look forward to. Mainly I remember how lucky I've been, coming off the water at night. And the times I thought I might drown.

But I remember small things, too. There was a wedding where I met this girl from Liverpool, Maggie's cousin, visiting for a week. Pretty girl. Around here you don't see a girl like that.

Around here you don't court a girl unless you go to marry that girl. And I have never married. And so I have never courted. There was my teacher, Miss Minott, I think I loved her, but I was so young. You see, it's not a big place, the Heads, and I got to fishing, and that was what I did. I've been to Galway, but I've never paid to lay with a harridan. And so, I've never . . . courted.

I'm looking down at the sea and I have some feeling there from the sea.

(COLM *smiles, maybe laughs, and abruptly turns from the window.*)

Something like the start of love.

(*He takes a chamber pot from his wooden chest.*)

It was a pretty girl at the wedding. I talked with her. Would she remember? That was last winter. No, two winters ago.

Serious Bizness

Jennifer Allen, David Babcock, Winnie Holzman, Don Perman

Premiere: O'Neal's Cabaret Theatre, NYC, 1983
Publisher: Samuel French, Inc.
Setting: Cabaret stage

Serious Bizness is an evening of blackout sketches and songs for two men and two women. The following sketch is called "Where's the Spirit?"

(DAVE *stands* C. *stage holding a clipboard. His voice is tired and slightly hoarse. In the background we hear the faint sound of group cheers, a pep band, etc.*)

DAVE

Guys, ya wanna huddle in close here for a minute, my voice
is kind of . . .

(He pauses as the boys are obviously draw-
ing in.)

Okay, let's put that first half behind us now. Uh, we got
another sixteen minutes of basketball to play, and a lot of
other teams throughout history have overcome a deficit
of . . .

(Glancing at clipboard.)

Eighty-five points, so—

(Looking up.)

Huh?

(Re-checking the clipboard.)

All right, eighty-eight, eighty-five, it doesn't matter, Spitzbart. The point is it's still anybody's ballgame, and—

(Distracted again.)

Yeah, I agree it's most likely theirs, but as I always
say . . . Oh, jees, what do I always say? . . . Somebody
help me out here . . . No, it's a situation like this, I'm
talking to you guys, and—

(Getting help from Spitzbart.)

Quitting is not in the rulebook, thank you, Spitzbart. Now,
I have to admit that when I set up this exhibition game
with St. Mary's I had no idea they would be so tough. I
mean, who could've guessed that five nuns could play hoop
so well. But they're a spunky bunch of ladies and ya gotta
give 'em credit, they don't seem to be intimidated
by . . . those long dresses they're wearing.

Now, look, guys, ya know how I said before the game
that I wanted you to keep this one clean, because as I always
say, unsportsmanlike conduct . . .

(The boys are obviously finishing it for him.)

not . . . rulebook, right. Well, I'm gonna modify that and
ask you to, uh, soil the game up a bit.

(There is obviously some reaction to this.)

Well, yeah, I'm talking about elbows under the boards, a
stomp on the foot, a yank on those beads, I don't really
care. It's time to let 'em know we came to play. I mean,
fellas, eighty-five points is—

(Interrupted.)

Eighty-eight! All right, eighty-eight! Are ya happy, Spitzbart? All I know is we are not going to forfeit this game.
Why? Because *forfeiting is not in the rulebook.*

(Pulling a rulebook out of his back pocket.)

Believe me, I looked, it's just not there! We can't get out
of this one.

(Pausing, trying to hold back tears.)

All right, listen. One of the refs took me aside after the
first half and told me he thinks one of you guys has a sharp,
pointed object concealed in your sock. Is this true?

*(He waits for an answer and obviously gets
one.)*

Well, why the hell haven't you *used* it?! No, I'm just talking
about a little nick on the hand, she'll think it's a stigma,
have to come out of the game, and we'll be up a man. Come
on, use your heads.

*(He cries. Someone speaks to him. He looks
up, angry.)*

Crying is *too* in the rulebook, Spitzbart! . . . Oh, god, my
parents are here . . . this is awful . . .

*(There is a pause and then a buzzer is
heard.)*

All right, there's the buzzer. Get your hands in here.

(He holds his hand out in front of him.)

Okay, look, I want you to go out there and do it to 'em and
do it hard. But guys—be careful. I don't want *you* to get
hurt. So whatever you do, don't sass 'em back! All right,
here we go with our group prayer, come on.

(Collecting himself.)

Help us play this game fair, help us win it with ease. And
if you must, God, help us break a few knees.

(Pointing, desperate.)
Go get those gorillas!

Sex and Death
to the Age 14
Spalding Gray

Premiere: The performing Garage, NYC, 1979
Publisher: Vintage/Random House
Setting: Bare stage

Sex and Death to the Age 14, one of an ongoing series
of autobiographical story performances by Spalding Gray,
describes the writer's childhood brushes with sex and death
in post–World War II Barrington, Rhode Island. He has
just described the deaths and disappearances of several pet
dogs.

We gave up at last on dogs and switched to cats. Our first
cat's name was Kitzel. All I remember about Kitzel was
that she was a calico who lived a long time and liked to eat
corn-on-the-cob. After Kitzel grew up, I wanted a kitten,
so I got a kitten from the Griggses that I called Mittens. I
named her Mittens because she had little white markings
on her front paws. And I had this relationship with Mittens:
I would make a sound, kind of a half-blow, half-whistle (we
called it a *wumple*), and Mittens would come running. Then
one weekend she didn't come and I looked everywhere for
her. The only place I did not look was the cellar of our
barn. My brother Rocky told me that he had seen footprints
of the Blain brothers down there. The Blain brothers were
ten-foot-tall hairy men who roamed the Rhode Island countryside and were known to jump over eight-foot-high hur-
ricane fences with a deer under each arm, or a child,
because they were running out of deer in Rhode Island.

Rocky told me the brothers had last been seen at the Boy Scout camp, Camp Yiago, not too far from where we lived.

At the end of the weekend, my mother said that she had seen the trash truck pick up Mittens's little body on Friday by the side of Rumstick Road, and she hadn't had the heart to tell me. Mom cheered me up by telling me that I could get another kitten.

And I did. I got another kitten and I named it Mittens, Mittens the Second. That Mittens was killed on Rumstick Road by Mrs. Jessup driving a large black Chrysler at dusk. I saw it happen and began to run away, and Mrs. Jessup ran after me to try to apologize and comfort me, but I ran ahead of her because I didn't want to see her. I ran into my house and up to my bedroom. I couldn't catch my breath and felt like I was suffocating.

This reminded me of the time when I woke up in the middle of the night and saw my brother Rocky standing on his bed, blue in the face and gasping for air, crying out that he was dying. My mother and father were standing beside the bed trying to quiet him, and Mom said, "Calm down, dear, it's all in your mind." And after he calmed down, my father went back to bed, and my mother turned out the light and sat on the edge of Rocky's bed in the dark. The only illumination in the room was a cluster of fluorescent decals on the ceiling, of the Big Dipper, the Little Dipper, Saturn, and the Moon. We were all there very quiet, in the dark, and then Rocky would start in, "Mom, when I die, is it forever?" and Mom said, "Yes." And then Rocky said, "Mom, when I die is it forever and ever?" And she said, "Yes, dear." And then he said, "Mom, when I die is it forever and ever and ever?" And she said, "Uh-huh, dear." And he said, "Mom when I die is it forever and ever and ever and ever? . . . " I just went right off to this.

Split Second
Dennis McIntyre

Premiere: Theatre Four, NYC, 1984
Publisher: Samuel French, Inc.
Setting: New York City, July 4th weekend

A black policeman named Val Johnson apprehends William H. Willis, a white lowlife, in the act of breaking into a car. At first Willis tries to negotiate, but when it becomes clear that Val is going by the book, he lets loose such a virulent torrent of racist abuse that Val draws his revolver. Willis taunts him still further: "Just try it! Go on! See where it fucking gets you! You don't got the balls, do you? . . . What's the difference between a nigger cop and a pile of shit? No difference, man! Get it?" Val shoots him. Then he removes Willis's handcuffs and puts a knife into his hand, trying to make it look as if the white man attacked him physically as well as verbally.

Split Second is the story of Val's crisis of conscience. He knows what he's done is both morally wrong and illegal, but he stands by his falsified story, even though his supervisor is suspicious of the perfectly aimed, point-blank shot. The incident haunts Val. He goes to see his father, Rusty, a rigorously moral ex-cop who thinks his son "snapped" and ought to take responsibility for his actions: "You pulled the trigger! Not me! I didn't ask you to be a goddamn cop!" Val responds.

VAL
(Crosses US to RUSTY.)

I grew up with cops. The only people who ever came over to our house were cops. Cops and cops' wives. Cops and cops' kids. And once in a while, a real distinction—some goddamn prosecutor who should have been a cop! I mean, traffic cops, vice cops, street cops, homicide—Lloyd, Frank, Daryll, every partner you ever had!

[RUSTY

That's how I kept my job!

(Crosses DSR, sits on platform.)

VAL

The hell it was!] You loved it. Being a cop, that was special.
The world couldn't get along without cops. In fact, cops
ruled the world. That's how society functioned. I remember, Mom and me, we must have spent two thousand hours
waiting for you to change your goddamn uniform. And
where in the hell were you? Drinking your "Rolling Rock"
with the boys, that's where you were. Cleaning your gun,
loading it, unloading it—

[RUSTY

It came in handy, my gun!

VAL

(Crosses DS to Rusty.)

Sure it did.] But where were we, Mom and me? Out front,
waiting, watching the hookers get booked. Or the guy
who'd just carved up his wife with a screwdriver and then
blown off his six-year-old daughter's head with a shotgun.
Or the broad who'd just burned down her house, except
her husband and four kids just happened to be in it. What
are you talking about "you didn't ask me to be cop"?! I
started being a cop at five. The first Christmas I can remember, under the tree, a fingerprint kit. A goddamn fingerprint kit. And a black-and-white, made out of tin, with
your name painted on the hood, "Rusty," and the number
of your squad car, "183." I broke it Christmas Day, winding
it up, listening to the siren. My God, you had me in uniform
when I was ten. All those precinct blasts in "Oakland."
Fake ribbons. Fake medals. All the ribbons and medals I
was supposed to earn when I grew up. First in the army,
and then on the force. You got me a flasher for my bike. I
was eleven years old, and I was arresting every other kid
on the block!

The Tooth of Crime
Sam Shepard

Premiere: Open Space, London, England, 1972
Publisher: Bantam Books (in *Seven Plays* by Sam Shepard)
Setting: Bare stage with an evil-looking throne

The Tooth of Crime is set in a surreal future where rock 'n' roll "markers" duel to the death with hot cars, gleaming weapons, and language. Hoss is a star marker, "a killer's killer," on top of the charts. But he's restless, starting to feel as if he's losing his edge and toying with thoughts of suicide: "Pull the trigger! Drive it off the cliff! It's all an open highway. Long and clean and deadly beautiful. Deadly and lonesome as a jukebox." Fame has made Hoss feel over-insulated and impotent. He longs for a challenge. He gets it.

Crow is a Gypsy Killer, an upstart young blood driving a '58 Impala to challenge the star. Hoss is intrigued by Crow's style. His advisers recommend a quick kill, but Hoss disagrees.

Hoss

There's another code in focus here. An outside code. Once I knew this cat in High School who was a Creole. His name was Moose. He was real light skinned and big, curly blond hair, blue eyes. He could pass easy as a jock. Good musician. Tough in football but kinda dumb. Dumb in that way—that people put you down for in High School. Dumb in class. He passed as white until his sister started hangin' around with the black chicks. Then the white kids figured it out. He was black to them even though he looked white. He was a nigger, a coon, a jungle bunny. A Rock Town boy from that day on. We ran together, Moose and me and another cat from Canada who dressed and wore his hair like Elvis. They put him down too because he was too smart. His name was Cruise and he got straight A's without readin' none a' the books. Slept in a garage with his aunt.

Built himself a cot right over an old Studebaker. His mother was killed by his father who drove skidders for a lumber company up near Vancouver. Got drunk and busted her in the head with a tire iron. The three of us had a brotherhood, a trust. Something unspoken. Then one day it came to the test. I was sorta' ridin' between 'em. I'd shift my personality from one to the other but they dug me 'cause I'd go crazy drunk all the time. We all went out to Bob's Big Boy in Pasadena to cruise the chicks and this time we got spotted by some jocks from our High School. Our own High School. There were eight of 'em, all crew cut and hot for blood. This was the old days ya' know. So they started in on Cruise 'cause he was the skinniest. Smackin' him around and pushin' him into the car. We was right in the parking lot there. Moose told 'em to ease off but they kept it up. They were really out to choose Moose. He was their mark. They wanted him bad. Girls and dates started gathering around until we was right in the center of a huge crowd a' kids. Then I saw it. This was a class war. These were rich white kids from Arcadia who got T-birds and deuce coups for Xmas from Mommy and Daddy. All them cardigan sweaters and chicks with ponytails and pedal pushers and bubble hair-do's. Soon as I saw that I flipped out. I found my strength. I started kickin' shit, man. Hard and fast. Three of 'em went down screamin' and holdin' their balls. Moose and Cruise went right into action. It was like John Wayne, Robert Mitchum and Kirk Douglas all in one movie. Those chumps must a' swung on us three times and that was all she wrote. We had all eight of 'em bleedin' and cryin' for Ma right there in the parking lot at Bob's Big Boy. I'll never forget that. The courage we had. The look in all them rich kids' faces. The way they stepped aside just like they did for "Big John." The three of us had a silent pride. We just walked strong, straight into that fuckin' burger palace and ordered three cherry cokes with lemon and a order a fries.

Women and Shoes
Nina Shengold

Premiere: Manhattan Punch Line, NYC, 1984
Publisher: —
Setting: A blue-collar bar in a city near you

Two drinkers named Willis and Seb try to solve the eternal question: Why are women obsessed with shoes? This monologue opens the play.

(WILLIS *and* SEB *at a bar.*)

WILLIS

I got a question. You ready for this? It's a question. I wanna know how come it is—and I want you should think about this—there's not one single female woman on earth that can walk past a shoe store without looking in. Never happen. I ask myself. You're out there walking, this woman and you, you're out taking the air in a strolling along kind of walking kind of way, or not even. You could be *going* somewhere. You could be walking along with a purpose, some kind of intentional purpose, she's *still* gonna look at that shoe store. Now you could be talking about anything, right, with this woman you're with here, like *sex* you could be talking about and she's still gonna check out those shoes. The day that a woman walks right past a shoe store I tell you, Seb, hell will grow ice pops. Now what I'm intending to ask myself here is just how come this is. Who looks at their feet? *You* look at their feet? I never look at their feet. You ask what my wife stuck her feet in the last five days running, I have not a clue what my wife stuck her feet in. Shoes, all right? Shoes. But the same shoes? All different shoes? What do I know? She got forty-five pairs lined up under the bed. She got bags on the door with 'em. She got 'em in boxes. My wife she got shoes like if there was legs coming out of each pair and a girl coming out of each legs I'd be set up for life. And yet and in spite of all this and in spite of the fact that I don't give a rat butt what shoes she got stuck on her feet that I don't even notice, we walk by a shoe store, that's death. I mean we could be talking about *sports*. Go and figure it. Shoes.

[SEB

My wife likes 'em too.

WILLIS

I am not talking *like* them. I am talking the universe hangs on two pieces of leather.] Plus which also they're silly, the shoes women wear. Little strappy things. Heels look like screwdrivers. Colors. You ever seen a man wear red shoes and I'm not talking sneakers here nor am I talking a man of a sort that you catch my drift *might* wear red shoes but just regular shoes on a man they do not come in red. They do not *need* to come in red. Shoes are for keeping your feet clean. Off the street, out of the mud and out of the rain as I see it. This is how I see the function of shoes.

Yellow Fever
R. A. Shiomi

Premiere: Asian American Theater Company, San Francisco, 1982
Publisher: Playwrights Canada
Setting: Powell Street in Vancouver, British Columbia, Canada

Sam Shikaze, forty-five, is a second-generation Japanese-Canadian detective, a hard-boiled loner in the Sam Spade tradition. He appears in a spotlight. This monologue opens the play.

SAM

Monday, March 9th, 1973, I walked down to my office on Powell Street. It used to be our main strip. Used to be snack bars, general stores, boarding houses, gambling joints, we had it all . . . That was back in '41, when I was

a kid running groceries for Mrs. Sato. World War Two came
and the government moved us out, sent us packing into
the mountains, herded onto trains and dumped off in god-
forsaken ghost towns . . . After the war it was never the
same. They didn't let us back to the coast till '49, and by
then we were scattered east of the Rockies. A few of us
returned, not just to Vancouver, but to Powell Street . . .
Times have changed, now my nisei friends tell me I should
move downtown, forget the past and get a decent job. I
just tell them I like the local colour . . . Being a private
eye doesn't give you that nine-to-five respectability, but
you call your own shots and you don't have to smile for a
living . . . and that's the way I like it.

(SAM *exits through alleyway.*)

•

Columbus Avenue
David Mamet

Publisher: Grove Press, Inc.
Setting: A shop on Columbus Avenue, New York City

Mamet wrote this piece for *The Village Voice* in 1980.
It is presented here in its entirety.

I felt the cold steel of a gun against my head three times.

Twenty-six years we have been here. A tailor fourteen
years before that here. Fifty-one years.

And he's an Orthodox Jew, and his father said (when
he was managing: when first we settled on a price; and,
you know, we *negotiated* . . . but when we were done he
told me): "I will never throw you out."

The boy, he said, "Before I do a thing we'll talk." Today
I get his letter in the mail. And I go there. I say, "You said
that we were going to talk." He said, "I thought instead of
talking I'd send you a letter."

So what am I going to do? Where am I going to go?

My customers are going to follow me? Can I ask them
to walk for twenty blocks?

If even he gave me a *ten*-year lease, at least then I could
sell the business.

So I said *double* the rent. *Triple* the rent, I told
him.

He has got a *guy* is going to pay two thousand a month,
he says. *And* he's going to put in fifty-thousand dollars
restoration.

I told him, "How is he going to make the *rent*?"

He said, "He'll break his back. He'll break his back the
first year," (he didn't say "back") "and, after that, he *fails*,

I've got his fifty thousand he put in my building, and I rent
the place again."

It's like that the whole street: Things you don't want at
what you can't afford, and nothing that you need.

No services.

Where am I going to go?

If I was twenty, if I was even ten years *younger* . . .

Where am I going to go? I got to move the *press*, I got
to move the *racks*; by the time I put *in* I put in all my
savings to the *business* to go somewhere else and I have
nothing. And I have to start again. Twenty-six years.

I told him, "I hate to remind you what your *father*
said." He shrugged.

My *wife* went. I was getting sick. He said he'd give us
an extension for six months.

It's the same all the neighborhood.

Let the depression come, and see who pays the rent.

Twenty-six years I've been here, and there are no more
services on this street anymore.

What will people do I don't know what he thinks.

I don't know.

I don't know what I can say.

Joe Turner's Come and Gone
August Wilson

Premiere: Yale Repertory Theatre, New Haven, Connecticut,
1986
Publisher: Plume
Setting: Boarding house of Seth and Bertha Holly

Joe Turner's Come and Gone is the story of the black
residents of a Pittsburg boarding house in 1911. One of the
residents, Bynum, is a conjure man or root worker in his
early sixties. Unflappable, he "gives the impression of al-

ways being in control of everything. He seems to be lost in a world of his own making" and to accept any challenge life brings. Here he tells how he came by his name.

BYNUM

This fellow don't have no name. I call him John 'cause it was up around Johnstown where I seen him. I ain't even so sure he's one special fellow. That shine could pass on to anybody. He could be anybody shining.

[SELIG

Well, what's he look like beside being shiny. There's lots of shiny nigras.]

BYNUM

He's just a man I seen out on the road. He ain't had no special look. Just a man walking toward me on the road. He come up and asked me which way the road went. I told him everything I knew about the road, where it went and all, and he asked me did I have anything to eat 'cause he was hungry. Say he ain't had nothing to eat in three days. Well, I never be out there on the road without a piece of dried meat. Or an orange or an apple. So I give this fellow an orange. He take and eat that orange and told me to come and go along the road a little ways with him, that he had something he wanted to show me. He had a look about him made me wanna go with him, see what he gonna show me.

We walked on a bit and it's getting kind of far from where I met him when it come up on me all of a sudden, we wasn't going the way he had come from, we was going back my way. Since he said he ain't knew nothing about the road, I asked him about this. He say he had a voice inside him telling him which way to go and if I come and go along with him he was gonna show me the Secret of Life. Quite naturally I followed him. A fellow that's gonna show you the Secret of Life ain't to be taken lightly. We get near this bend in the road . . .

[(SETH *enters with an assortment of pots,*
crosses to SELIG.)

SETH

I got six here, Selig.

SELIG

Wait a minute, Seth. Bynum's telling me about the secret of life. Go ahead Bynum, I wanna hear this.]

BYNUM

We get near this bend in the road and he told me to hold out my hands. Then he rubbed them together with his and I look down and see they had blood on them . . . I look down and see they had blood on them. Told me to take and rub it all over me, say that was a way of cleaning myself. Then we went around the bend in that road. Got around that bend and it seem like all of a sudden we ain't in the same place. Turn around that bend and everything look like it was twice as big as it was. The trees and everything bigger than life. Sparrows big as eagles. I turned around to look at this fellow and he had this light coming out of him. I had to cover up my eyes to keep from being blinded. He shining like new money with that light seemed like it seeped out of him and then he was gone and I was by myself in this strange place where everything was bigger than life.

I wandered around there looking for that road, trying to find my way back from this big place, and I looked over and seen my daddy standing there. He was the same size he always was, except for his hands and his mouth. He had a great big old mouth that looked like it took up his whole face and his hands were as big as hams. Look like they was too big to carry around. My daddy called me to him. Said he had been thinking about me and it grieved him to see me in the world carrying other people's songs and not having one of my own. Told me he was gonna show me how to find my song. Then he carried me further into this big place until we come to this ocean. Then he showed me something I ain't got words to tell you. If you stand to witness it, you done seen something there. I stayed in that place awhile and my daddy taught me the meaning of this thing that I had seen and showed me how to find my song. I asked him about the shiny man and he tole me he was the One Who Goes Before and Shows the Way. Say there was lot of shiny men and if I ever saw one again before I died that I would know that my song had been accepted and worked its full power in the world and I could lay down and die a happy man. A man who done left his mark on life. On the way people cling to each other out of the truth they find in themselves. The he showed me how to get back to the road. I came out to where everything was its own size and I had my song. I had the Binding Song. I choose that song because that's what I seen most when I was traveling . . . people walking away and leaving one another. So I takes the power of my song and binds them together.

Been binding people ever since. That's why they call me Bynum. Just like glue I sticks people together.

Largo Desolato
Václav Havel

English Version by Tom Stoppard

Premiere: US: New York Shakespeare Festival, NYC
Publisher: Grove Press
Setting: An Eastern European intellectual's living room

Professor Leopold Nettles is a philosopher whose most recent book contains a paragraph that lays him open to charges of "disturbing the intellectual peace." The government presses him for a statement recanting what he wrote. Two paper mill workers press him to "take the initiative" and become a populist leader. Leopold is afraid to leave the house and suffers from "a touch of vertigo, suggestion of an upset stomach, tingling in the joints, loss of appetite, and even the possibility of constipation."

Leopold's wife comes and goes. A concerned friend pays a visit, which only adds to the pressure. And Leopold's lover Lucy comes to sleep with him, but she too makes demands: she insists that he "admit to yourself that you love me." Leopold tries to convince her "You deserve some-one better. I'm just worthless."

NOTE: Václav Havel's plays were banned in his native Czechoslovakia from 1969 to 1989, and he was frequently jailed for his human rights activities. After the "velvet rev-olution" of 1989, Havel was elected President of Czecho-slovakia.

LEOPOLD

It's true, Lucy. I can't get rid of the awful feeling that lately something has begun to collapse inside me—as if some axis which was holding me together has broken, the ground collapsing under my feet, as if I'd gone lame inside—I sometimes have the feeling that I'm acting the part of myself instead of being myself. I'm lacking a fixed point out of which I can grow and develop. I'm erratic—I'm letting myself be tossed about by chance currents—I'm sinking deeper and deeper into a void and I can no longer get a grip on things. In truth I'm just waiting for this thing that's going to happen and am no longer the self-aware subject of my own life but becoming merely its passive object—I have a feeling sometimes that all I am doing is listening helplessly to the passing of the time. What happened to my perspective on things? My humour? My industry and persistence? The pointedness of my observations? My irony and self-irony? My capacity for enthusiasm, for emotional involvement, for commitment, even for sacrifice? The op-pressive atmosphere in which I have been forced to live for so long is bound to have left its mark! Outwardly I go on acting my role as if nothing has happened but inside I'm no longer the person you all take me for. It's hard to admit it to myself, but if *I* can all the more reason for you to! It's a touching and beautiful thing that you don't lose hope of making me into someone better than I am but—don't be angry—it's an illusion. I've fallen apart, I'm paralysed, I won't change and it would be best if they came for me and took me where I would no longer be the cause of unhappiness and disillusion—

> (LUCY *gets up, upset, goes quickly to the balcony door. She opens it and goes out on to the balcony and stands looking out into the night with her back to the room. Soon it becomes clear that she is crying.* LEOPOLD *looks at her perplexed and after a while speaks to her.*)

Lucy—

> (LUCY *doesn't react. Pause.*)

There, there, Lucy, what's the matter?

> (LUCY *doesn't react. Pause.* LEOPOLD *gets up and approaches her slowly, still wrapped up in a blanket.*)

Are you crying, Lucy?

> (*Pause.*)

Why are you crying?

> (*Pause.*)

Don't cry!

> (*Pause.*)

I didn't want to upset you—I didn't realize—

My Children! My Africa!
Athol Fugard

Premiere: Market Theatre, Johannesburg, South Africa, 1989
Publisher: Theatre Communications Group
Setting: A small Eastern Cape Karoo town, 1984

Anela Myalatya ("Mr. M" to his students) is a dedicated
teacher in a Black South African township school called
Zolile High School. Trying to instill in his students his
passionate belief in the spoken word, he instigates a formal
debate between his own students and a debate team from
a white girls' prep school. It is a smashing success, and Mr.
M realizes "They shouldn't be fighting each other. They
should be fighting together!" He approaches Isabel Dyson,
the captain of the white girls' team, about joining his pro-
tégé Thami Mbikwana as a team in the upcoming inter-
school English literature quiz. The idealistic Isabel leaps
at the chance. But Thami is not so sure. He is a brilliant
student, but as a contemporary Black South African, he
feels Mr. M's approach is "old-fashioned," that the times
demand radical action, not symbolic tokenism. It is *this*
debate that fuels *My Children! My Africa!*, coming to a
violent boil as the township lurches toward rioting—and a
school boycott.

Mr. M has just signed Isabel onto his interracial debate
team. He talks directly to the audience.

Mr. M

"I am a man who in the eager pursuit of knowledge forgets
his food and in the joy of its attainment forgets his sorrows,
and who does not perceive that old age is coming on."
(He shakes his head.)
No. As I'm sure you have already guessed, that is not
me. My pursuit of knowledge is eager, but I do perceive,
and only too clearly, that old age is coming on, and at the
best of times I do a bad job of forgetting my sorrows. Those
wonderful words come from the finest teacher I have ever
had, that most wise of all the ancient philoso-
phers . . . Confucius! Yes. I am a Confucian. A black Confucian! There are not many of us. In fact I think there's a
good chance that the only one in the country is talking to
you at this moment.

I claim him as my teacher because I have read very

carefully, and many times, and I will read it many times more, a little book I have about him, his life, his thoughts and utterances. Truly, they *are* wonderful words my friends, wonderful, wonderful words! My classroom motto comes from its pages: "Learning undigested by thought is labor lost. Thought unassisted by learning is perilous!" But the words that challenge me most these days, is something he said towards the end of his life. At the age of seventy he turned to his pupils one day and said that he could do whatever his heart prompted, without transgressing what was right.

What do you say to that?

Think about it. *Anything* his heart prompted, *anything* that rose up as a spontaneous urge in his soul, *without* transgressing what was right!

What a heart my friends! Aren't you envious of old Confucius? Wouldn't it be marvelous to have a heart you could trust like that? Imagine being able to wake up in the morning in your little room, yawn and stretch, scratch a few fleabites and then jump out of your bed and eat your bowl of *mealie-pap* and sour milk with a happy heart because you know that when you walk out into the world you will be free to obey and act out, with a clear conscience, all the promptings of your heart. No matter what you see out there on the battle grounds of location streets, and believe me, there are days now when my eyesight feels more like a curse than a blessing, no matter what stories of hardship and suffering you hear, or how bad the news you read in the newspaper, knowing that the whole truth, which can't be printed, is even worse . . . in spite of all that, you need have no fear of your spontaneous urges, because in obeying them you will not transgress what is right.

(Another shake of his head, another rueful smile.)

No yet again. Not in this life, and most certainly not in this world where I find myself, will those wonderful

words of Confucius ever be mine. Not even if I lived to be
one hundred and seventy will I end up a calm, gentle
Chinese heart like his. I wish I could. Believe me, I really
wish I could. Because I am frightened of the one I've got.
I don't get gentle promptings from it my friends. I get heart
attacks. When I walk out into those streets, and I see what
is happening to my people, it jumps out and savages me
like a wild beast.

    (Thumping his chest with a clenched fist.)

I've got a whole zoo in here, a mad zoo of hungry animals . . . and the keeper is frightened! All of them. Mad
and savage!

    Look at me! I'm sweating today. I've been sweating for
a week. Why? Because one of those animals, the one called
Hope, has broken loose and is looking for food. Don't be
fooled by its gentle name. It is as dangerous as Hate and
Despair would be if they ever managed to break out. You
think I'm exaggerating? Pushing my metaphor a little too
far? Then I'd like to put you inside a black skin and ask
you to keep Hope alive, find food for it on these streets
where our children, our loved and precious children go
hungry and die of malnutrition. No, believe me, it is a
dangerous animal for a black man to have prowling around
in his heart. So how do I manage to keep mine alive, you
ask. Friends, I am going to let you in on a terrible secret.
That is why I am a teacher.

    It is all part of a secret plan to keep alive this savage
Hope of mine. The truth is that I am worse than Nero
feeding Christians to the lions. I feed young people to my
Hope. Every young body behind a school desk keeps it
alive.

    So you've been warned! If you see a hungry gleam in
my eyes when I look at your children . . . you know what
it means. That is the monster that stands here before you.
Full name: Anela Myalatya. Age: fifty-seven. Marital status:
bachelor. Occupation: teacher. Address: the back room of
the Reverend Mbopa's house next to the Anglican Church

of St. Mark. It's a little on the small side. You know those big kitchen-size boxes of matches they sell these days . . . well if you imagine one of those as Number One Classroom at Zolile High, then the little matchbox you put in your pocket is my room at the Reverend Mbopa's. But I'm not complaining. It has got all I need . . . a table and chair where I correct homework and prepare lessons, a comfortable bed for a good night's insomnia and a reserved space for my chair in front of the television set in the Reverend Mbopa's lounge.

So there you have it. What I call my life rattles around in these two matchboxes . . . the classroom and the back room. If you see me hurrying along the streets you can be reasonably certain that one of those two is my urgent destination. The people tease me. "Faster Mr. M" they shout to me from their front doors. "You'll be late." They think it's a funny joke. They don't know how close they are to a terrible truth . . .

Yes! The clocks are ticking my friends. History has got a strict timetable. If we're not careful we might be remembered as the country where everybody arrived too late.

Split Decision
Kevin Heelan

Publisher: Samuel French, Inc.
Setting: A locker room below Madison Square Garden

Bernie is a boxing manager who has devoted his life to a talented Jamaican fighter named Willie Barnes. Willie is past his prime, and the "comeback" fight he has just surrendered will probably be his last. But Bernie's not willing to give up. Seven years ago, he became the laughing stock of the boxing world when he jumped into the ring of a championship fight in Buenos Aires, costing Willie the title.

Bernie has lived with the shame ever since, but tonight he tells his partner Sal what really happened.

BERNIE

Ready? Ready? We were never more ready!

[SAL

Bullshit.]

BERNIE

It was textbook preparation. For six weeks. Textbook! Oh, I was scared at first, I'll give ya that. Christ, who wouldn't be? Outdoor stadium. Sixty-seven thousand people. Who wouldn't be nervous? Down in that locker room all you could hear was thousands of feet smashin on the roof above us. Keepin time while they chanted, "Lu-is! Lu-is!" When that guy stuck his head in and said, "It's time," I got all cramped up, I'm not ashamed to tell ya. But it wasn't from fear. It was cause I had to puke up every miserable hour I spent in the gym with lousy fighters. All the times I listened to slugs, who never accomplished anything, tell me I couldn't handle a championship fighter. I had to puke but I couldn't. And then I realized I didn't want to. I wanted to wait and spew it all over the sixty-seven thousand people in the seats when Willie sent Palermo crawlin for his life. "Let's go!" the guy yells. And I threw Willie's robe over his shoulders and put his hood over his head. You couldn't hear him breathe . . . just quiet black inside that hood. And I put my face in there and I said, "Willie, I love you. It's us against the maniacs up there. Now, when you get in that ring and look across at Luis Palermo, you just see the chart, Willie. You just hit the chart hard and fast and we go home kings." And he winked. Winked! He was ready. He knows what he's gonna do and so do I. The first few rounds were a nightmare. It was like bein on a roller coaster that wouldn't stop. Palermo was jabbin and scootin. He looked like he weighed a hundred and twenty pounds . . . ting, ting, jab and scoot, jab and scoot. He was circlin, always circlin. But so smooth you never saw his steps. He got from one place to another by magic. Willie couldn't find him. He was fightin the wind and the ringsiders were laughin and lickin their chops. But he kept comin. Palermo was pilin up the points. Pop and goodbye. Pop and goodbye. And now he's gettin leverage, too. He's plantin his feet more. He's still the ghost but now he's got glass in his gloves. Willie's eyebrow starts to swell up, his bones are sheerin off little slivers of flesh. Willie's blinkin like a bird, tryin to keep the blood from his eyeball, tryin to keep half his world from going black. Palermo stops scootin. He sees that eye and he decides to stand and rip. He's throwin eight punches at a time, tryin to turn Willie's socket to soup. But Willie keeps comin. He keeps goin to Palermo's body. Into the mush, into the mush! Palermo throws everything he has into the middle rounds but Willie gets through em. And now Palermo can't stay on his toes anymore, he's runnin down. And Willie is plantin shot after shot into his gut and his side and his chest. Palermo is wincin now. His stomach is weltin up on him, his mouth is open and grabbin for air. He's flat-footed and slumped. His body is screamin at his brain to stop and all of a sudden it's the fourteenth round! It's the fourteenth round and the son of a bitch has had it! He can hardly stand! It's only greatness keepin him up 'cause everything else is gone! Willie is snortin with every punch. He's leavin his feet every time he digs one into Palermo's ribs. They're right above me. I can hear Palermo whimperin like a pup with every shot. Willie is suckin the whole stadium, the whole universe, into his arms and legs. All the hours in the gym, all the work was payin off. And all of a sudden, it was there. The space, the opening! And Willie hits Palermo with a punch that came from the center of the earth! The whole stadium heaves forward with their mouths open but no sound comin out. Sixty-seven thousand people all chokin at the same time. Palermo's head drops to one side like he'd been shotgunned. His mouthpiece drops out red and his eyes go back into his brain. He tries to get away but his heart won't help

him. He's trapped. Right above me. I can see him tryin to
keep his arms up . . . but it's no use. His mind is shuttin
down, his body wants rest. And then, them long, beautiful shiney arms just fall down to his sides. Willie's hips
pivot, his muscles pop up like snakes under his skin.
There isn't a single sound in that stadium as Willie brings
his right hand back. And I know when he throws it the
world finds out who the fuck we are. Let it go, Willie.
Throw it, baby . . . Willie!? Throw it, Willie!! Throw it!
THROOOWWW IIIIITTTTTT!!!

(Pause.)

But Willie don't throw it. His eyes go off . . . away . . . He
looks at the ref but the ref don't move. He motions Willie
to go on in . . . but Willie hesitates. The championship of
the planet and he hesitates. I came off the floor. I jumped
onto the ropes. The ref saw me and stopped the fight to
tell me to get down. He took his sweet time doin it,
too . . . So the damage was done. Palermo had already
recovered. He got back his senses. The next round he was
poppin and scootin but he was scared, real scared. So he
mostly just ran. And ran. There isn't no fighter on earth
can run like him. We were in Buenos Aires so . . . so Luis
Palermo won a split decision. And our lives turned to garbage.

(Pause.)

He promised to give Willie a rematch but he didn't want
to get hurt like that again. Nobody else did either. We
couldn't get a good fight for a long time. Not till Willie got
a little older and a little slower. And I became the laughing
stock of the boxing world. The manager who cost his fighter
the championship. All these years I let them say that to
me. I never told nobody what really happened. I told everybody I thought I heard a bell. I let 'em laugh at me 'cause
I didn't want nobody sayin nothin bad about Willie. Nobody
was gonna make a fool outta him. So, I let 'em make a fool
outta me.

The Value of Names
Jeffrey Sweet

Premiere: Actors Theatre of Louisville, Louisville, Kentucky, 1982
Publisher: Dramatists Play Service, Inc.
Setting: A patio high up in the Hollywood Hills

Benny Silverman is a successful comic actor, famous for his long-running role as the crazy neighbor on a sitcom called "Rich But Happy." His career began with an idealistic political theater group called The New Labor Players, and came to a jolting halt during the McCarthy era, when his director friend Leo Greshen named Benny's name to the House Un-American Activities Committee in order to save his own skin.

Now Benny's daughter Norma, an aspiring actress, has been cast in a role that could give her career a big boost. She is staying with her father, who disapproves of the script's call for nudity—and Norma's decision to change her name for the stage. One week into the rehearsal period, the director has a stroke. The producers decide to replace him with Leo Greshen.

Benny is outraged. Norma has to weigh her loyalties to her father, her own sense of guilt, and her personal ambition. The issue comes to a head when Leo invites himself onto Benny's patio. He hopes to talk to Norma about the job, but beyond that, he hopes for some kind of resolution with Benny.

LEO

I was given an honorary degree, you know. Last spring.

[BENNY

In what—communications?]

LEO

A doctor of letters, actually. Avery College, New Hampshire. For my body of work. That's how they phrased it.

Sounds cadaverous, doesn't it? "Here lies Leo Greshen's body of work." I had to laugh when I was told. But I said sure. Sure, I'd be honored to be honored. And, generous fellow that I am, I say I'll throw in a seminar on directing or some damn thing. They couldn't be happier. I'm met at the airport. I have dinner with a bunch of deans and professors and nice faculty wives, faculty husbands, whatever. Some nice stroking. Springtime in New Hampshire. Who could object to that? So I'm scheduled to speak to this media studies class. The guy who runs the class introduces me. My pictures, the plays I've directed, blah, blah, blah, and would you please welcome. Applause. All very nice. He asks me questions. I answer. I make jokes. He tosses in a quip or two like a regular Dick Cavett. Everything's bopping along well. About forty-five minutes of this, he says he's going to open the floor to questions. Four or five hands shoot up. I see this one intent kid off to the side, near the window. Skinny kid with eyes like lasers. I look at him and I know he's going to ask it. I just know it. But my friend, the would-be Dick Cavett, calls on some girl who asks me how it was to work with so-and-so, and I tell an amusing story and everybody laughs in the right place except for the kid with the laser eyes. I've barely finished my amusing story when his hand shoots up again. The professor again chooses another hand. Bearded kid wants to know if I storyboard when I'm in pre-production. I tell another amusing story. Soon as I'm finished with that one, again that kid's hand shoots up. Again my host chooses another hand, but I interrupt him. I say, "Wait a second. There's a young man over there by the window seems to have something urgent to ask. Yes, son, what is it?" Yes, son, I'm thinking, go ahead and prove how brave and liberal you are. Nail me in front of all your nice classmates and your nice teacher on this nice, nice campus in New Hampshire. "Yes, son," I say, "what's your question?" He doesn't disappoint. No sooner has he said the magic words "House Committee on Un-American Activities" than my friend the professor interrupts, says that we are not here to discuss that. "We are here to discuss Mr. Greshen's art, Mr. Greshen's craft. We are here to learn what we can from Mr. Greshen's years of experience in the theater and film. Politics has nothing to do with it." And he asks if there are any other questions. I answer two more, and my friend the professor wraps it up by thanking me on behalf of the class for my generosity and candor. Applause. My host and I go to the faculty lounge. He buys me a drink and tells me that he's sorry about the boy's rudeness. Apparently that boy has a habit of stirring things up. Doesn't accept the fact that the sixties were over years ago. And that was why my friend hadn't wanted to call on him. He was trying to protect me. Seems like this kid has circulated a petition calling on the college to rescind the honorary degree. That it would not redound to the school's credit to honor a stoolie. This was not quite how my friend put it, but that was the jist of it. So there was a ceremony, I got my degree, shook a lot of nice hands and went home. And all through this I was thinking of how I should have answered the little bastard.

[BENNY

And what would you have said?]

LEO

That he hadn't earned the right to ask me that question. He hadn't earned the right to brandish his moral indignation in my face.

Yankee Dawg You Die
Philip Kan Gotanda

Premiere: Berkeley Repertory Theatre, Berkeley, California, 1988
Publisher: Dramatists Play Service, Inc.
Setting: Various locations in and around Hollywood

Two Asian-American actors meet at a party in the Hollywood Hills, at an audition, and again in an acting class. It's a spiky relationship. Vincent Chang, "a youthful, silver-maned late sixties," began his career as a hoofer on the "Chop Suey Circuit" and later broke into movies, playing a variety of Oriental villains, inscrutable servants, and other clichés. He is gay, but has spent a lifetime in the closet out of fear for his career. Bradley Yamashita is an ambitious young theater actor with one independent film credit and a chip on his shoulder about Asian-American consciousness. At one point in the play, Bradley attacks Vincent for playing "a Chinese Stepin Fetchit"; at another, he tells him he grew up watching Vincent on TV ("You were sort of my hero"). Vincent responds that *his* hero was Fred Astaire. A dance fan, Bradley asks Vincent to show him some dance moves.

VINCENT

Well. All right.
          (*He gets up.*)
A little soft-shoe routine . . .
          (VINCENT *does a small sampling of some
          dance moves ending with a small flourish.*)
          [BRADLEY
          (*Applauds.*)
Great! That was great!]
          VINCENT
Back then you did everything. Tell jokes, juggle, sing—The Kanazawa Trio, great jugglers. Oh, and Jade Wing, a wonderful, wonderful, dancer. The Wongettes—like the Andrews Sisters. On and on, all great performers. We all worked the Chop Suey Circuit.
          [BRADLEY
Chop Suey Circuit?]

VINCENT

In San Francisco you had of course, Forbidden City, Kubla Kan, New York's China Doll—some of the greatest oriental acts ever to go down. That's my theater background.

(VINCENT *tries to catch his breath.*)

See, there was this one routine that Jade—Jade Wing, she was my partner—and I did that was special. We had developed it ourselves and at the end we did this spectacular move where I pull her up on my shoulders, she falls back, and as she's falling I reach under, grab her hands and pull her through my legs thrusting her into the air . . . And I catch her! Tadah! We were rather famous for it. This one night we performed it—we were in town here, I forget the name of the club—and as the audience began to clap, these two people at one of the front tables stood up, applauding enthusiastically. Everyone followed. It was an amazing feeling to have the whole house on their feet. And then we saw the two people leading the standing ovation. We couldn't believe our eyes—Anna Mae Wong, the "Chinese Flapper" herself, and Sessue Hayakawa. The two most famous oriental stars of the day. They invited us to their table, Hayakawa with his fancy Japanese cigarettes and his thick accent. It was a good thing that I spoke Japanese.

[BRADLEY

You speak Japanese?]

VINCENT

A little, I speak a little. But Anna Mae Wong spoke impeccable English. In fact, she had an English accent, can you believe that? "Vincent, you danced like you were floating on air." We nearly died then and there. Jade and I sitting at the same table with Anna Mae and Sessue.

MONOLOGUES FOR MEN PLAYING WOMEN

•

Psycho Beach Party
Charles Busch

Premiere: Limbo Lounge, NYC, 1986
Publisher: Samuel French, Inc.
Setting: On and around a beach in Malibu, 1962

Psycho Beach Party is a spoof—a cross between a 1960s beach party movie, like *Gidget*, and a psychological melodrama, like *The Three Faces of Eve* or *Marnie*.

Marvel Ann, a "gorgeous blonde high school vamp," goes to the beach with her two friends on a manhunt. She flirts with Star Cat, a "hunk of a California he-man," who once longed to be a psychiatrist, until he realized his dream was childish, and now wants to be a surf bum.

The next day, Marvel Ann tells him she was up all night thinking of the two of them married. He nervously tries to dissuade her, insisting he rejects materialism, and that she deserves better than a good-for-nothing beach bum.

NOTE: In the introduction to the play, Charles Busch writes that while the role of Marvel Ann was originally played by a man, it can also be performed by a woman.

MARVEL ANN
(Petulant but still pleasant.)
You don't know what you want. I think it's a horrid shame that you're throwing away a great future as a psychiatrist. All your wonderful compassion going to waste.
(STAR CAT tries to interject.)
Oh, I know what you're going to say, "I just want a little shack by the water." Well, you can't expect me to live like

that. Imagine me serving my friends Steak Diane Flambé in a lean-to.

(STAR CAT *tries to interject.*)

Don't say a word, I know what you're thinking, "Marvel Ann is such a lovely person, in time she'd grow used to such a life."

(*With growing emotion and intensity.*)

Well, I'd be humiliated. Oh, I can read you like the funny papers.

(*With growing fury.*)

You think I'm so head over heels in love with you, I'll accept whatever crumbs you have to offer. Well, no siree Bob, I am hardly a desperate female. Ohhh, look at that awful expression in your eyes. I bet you think you don't even have to marry me, that I'd shack up with you like a common whore. Now you've really done it. I am livid. How could you think of such filth! You are a selfish, egocentric creep and my advice to you is to straighten up, buckle down and apply youself like any other decent, normal Presbyterian!!

(*She stalks off in a fury.*)

Secret Lives of the Sexists
Charles Ludlam

Premiere: Ridiculous Theatrical Company, NYC, 1982
Publisher: Harper/Collins (in *The Complete Plays of Charles Ludlam*)
Setting: Basement flat on the Lower East Side, Swan Beauty Salon, Rally of Women Against Stenography, and other locations

Secret Lives of the Sexists is subtitled "The Farce of Modern Life." Fanny and her husband, Izzy, have been married a year, but have never had sex. As she states, "All I'm getting out of this marriage is bed and bored." She desperately wants to have sex with Izzy, and has tried everything, including the manual *The Art of Heterosexual Love*, which lists over six-thousand positions for intercourse. Unfortunately, he is turned off by her eagerness and only wishes she would play hard to get. The situation is complicated by the fact that Fanny stands to inherit two hundred thousand dollars from her father when she has her first child.

Fanny is best friends with her sister-in-law, Nadine. Nadine mistakenly believes her husband, Buddy, is having an affair with Zeena, who, in fact, is Nadine's long lost mother. Nadine and Buddy have a huge fight, and she runs off to attend a rally of the radical feminist group, Women Against Stenography. She insists Fanny join her. Nadine makes a speech calling for the abolishment of the two sexes and believes women should legally be declared men. "Some men would have mammary glands and vaginas and some men would carry the seed. This tiny degree of specialization, however, would not be regarded as sufficiently significant to warrant two completely different sexes with different roles and legal status." Nadine, "Mr. Husband," then introduces Fanny.

FANNY

Thank you Mr. Husband. This afternoon I would like to call all of your attention to the subject of men—a burden to society. Mr. Husband, although I cannot help but admire the development of your theme, and I feel the deepest sympathy with your sense of injustice, I cannot agree to your solution to the problem. Why should we women aspire to be the equals of men, a distinctly inferior subspecies? Biologically speaking, men are a necessary evil. Darwin, a man, tried cleverly to cover up this fact with his theory of evolution when he said that man descended from the apes. I think this theory maligns the ape. A far more likely theory is that the apes evolved from man and the male sex. These hairy seed-bearers are living proof of this fact. The hairy growth on their arms, legs, chests, and buttocks points the way to the brutality for which they must inevitably be held responsible. Whether it be a gymnast swinging by his arms from a jungle gym or a pack of them chasing a ball around a field, it always leads back to the same thing—a beckoning beastliness. And what is the alternative? I say it is selective breeding. And this is how it would be accomplished: First we would cull all the males for those that were the least hairy. These would be kept on reservations and cared for as breeders. The rest would be put to death. Historically all evolution has not been toward a higher form of life. The early Neanderthal was more advanced than the late Neanderthal. Unless something is done at once to stop our interbreeding with these hairy lower forms of humanity our species will degenerate in stages; first to overall hairiness; then to a semierect; and finally to a form of man that is never erect again. Thank you.

INDEX OF PLAYWRIGHTS

INDEX OF SUBJECTS

INDEX OF TITLES